Early Praise for *Seven Web Frameworks in Seven Weeks*

The title implies a breadth-first analysis of some fairly disparate technologies, but there is a surprising amount of depth here, more than enough to emphasize the essential qualities of each one. If you're a polyglot, or aspire to be, this book is a very large ball of awesome.

➤ Jim Crossley
    Immutant core team member; principal software engineer, Red Hat

Objective and clear. More than an introduction, it's a head start! Just as wide and as deep as any modern developer would like. I definitely recommend it.

➤ Pablo Aguiar
    Software engineering consultant

This book is great fun. The authors guide you quickly through each framework, in each case giving you a fast but clear, coherent, and surprisingly detailed taste that includes major features, design philosophy, implementation, and testing, plus hints for further investigation. Two JavaScript frameworks, one Ruby, one Haskell, two Clojure, and one Erlang. If you like web programming, you're going to enjoy this book.

➤ Giles Bowkett
    Experienced developer and well-known blogger

I thoroughly enjoyed reading the book. In fact, the Yesod chapter even gave me fresh ideas on how to expose non-Haskellers to the strengths of a strong type system.

➤ Michael Snoyman
    Creator of Yesod; lead software engineer, FP Complete

Seven Web Frameworks in Seven Weeks
Adventures in Better Web Apps

Jack Moffitt
Fred Daoud

The Pragmatic Bookshelf

Dallas, Texas • Raleigh, North Carolina

Many of the designations used by manufacturers and sellers to distinguish their products are claimed as trademarks. Where those designations appear in this book, and The Pragmatic Programmers, LLC was aware of a trademark claim, the designations have been printed in initial capital letters or in all capitals. The Pragmatic Starter Kit, The Pragmatic Programmer, Pragmatic Programming, Pragmatic Bookshelf, PragProg and the linking *g* device are trademarks of The Pragmatic Programmers, LLC.

Every precaution was taken in the preparation of this book. However, the publisher assumes no responsibility for errors or omissions, or for damages that may result from the use of information (including program listings) contained herein.

Our Pragmatic courses, workshops, and other products can help you and your team create better software and have more fun. For more information, as well as the latest Pragmatic titles, please visit us at *http://pragprog.com.*

The team that produced this book includes:

Bruce A. Tate (series editor)
Jacquelyn Carter (editor)
Potomac Indexing, LLC (indexer)
Molly McBeath (copyeditor)
David J Kelly (typesetter)
Janet Furlow (producer)
Juliet Benda (rights)
Ellie Callahan (support)

Printed in the United States of America.
ISBN-13: 978-1-93778-563-5
Printed on acid-free paper.
Book version: P1.0—January 2014

Contents

Foreword

In 2003, I took my family to Durango, Colorado, where we rode on the Durango & Silverton train. The narrow gauges of the railroad once served well against the narrow red sandstone cliffs, where every inch of space was at a premium. These days, the train is a relic of the past, rendered obsolete by cars and planes that are safer and more efficient. Time marches on.

Today, too, we witness revolution. Single-core computers are dead or dying. True, their multicore descendants are technical marvels. They also represent a tremendous technical challenge. The languages we used to depend on do not work as well as they once did. As a result, we are seeing a new generation of languages emerge. So far, no one has been kind enough to declare a winner.

Against this backdrop in 2010, I wrote *Seven Languages in Seven Weeks*. In truth, I didn't expect it to sell many copies. After all, it was a book about languages in a Java world; a book about programming paradigms in a time where everything was object oriented. Still, programmers sensed the danger of our stagnating skills and embraced the concept that learning programming languages *for the sake of learning them* can make you smarter and better able to cope with change. The book was a resounding success.

Three years later, there's still no clear leader, though functional programming is starting to gain traction. We're finding that the multicore wafer tossed into our virtual pond years ago has created waves that are increasing in size and velocity. We need more than inheritance to organize our code. We need robust frameworks on the client to handle the robust development that is happening there. And we need true concurrent frameworks to take full advantage of their concurrent languages.

It's just not enough to lay wider tracks over the narrow tracks we used last year.

In this book, Fred and Jack will show you the leading edge of people who are reinventing the way web development should be done. You'll see a traditional object-oriented framework called Sinatra. You'll move on to the client side, where exciting things are happening with JavaScript. You'll take a tour of CanJS and AngularJS to see how to do full, rich client-side development. Next, you'll swing back to the server side to see what's happening in functional languages. You'll encounter two Clojure frameworks in the minimalist Ring and the robust Immutant. You'll see a state machine–based design in Erlang called WebMachine. If those aren't enough to blow your mind, you'll find the incredibly powerful Haskell framework called Yesod.

The "Seven in Seven" books are designed to expand your mind. I am extremely proud to bring you this next installment, *Seven Web Frameworks in Seven Weeks*. It's my sincerest hope that this book will take you beyond whatever tracks are holding you back.

Best regards,

Bruce Tate
CTO, icanmakeitbetter.com

Acknowledgments

We would like to thank the team at the Pragmatic Bookshelf for making this book possible. Thanks especially to Jackie Carter, our editor, for all of her expertise and tireless efforts to make this book better and for bringing it to the finish line. Thanks also to Bruce Tate—we are both fans of his book, and we are honored to follow in his footsteps. Thank you, Andy Hunt and Dave Thomas, for creating such a great environment in which to write about the technical subjects that we all find fascinating.

Thanks to the technical reviewers who contributed their expert advice on each framework: Konstantin Haase (Sinatra), David Luecke (CanJS), Miško Hevery (AngularJS), James Reeves (Ring), Justin Sheehy (Webmachine), Michael Snoyman (Yesod), Jim Crossley and Toby Crawley (Immutant) and to the reviewers who offered their comments and suggestions for various chapters of the book: Kimberly Hagen, Kevin Wiley, Pablo Aguiar, Mick Thompson, Christopher Zorn, Nathaniel Schutta, and Aaron Bedra.

We would not have such innovative frameworks to write about were it not for their creators: Blake Mizerany, Justin Meyer, Miško Hevery, Adam Abrons, Justin Sheehy, Andy Gross, Mark McGranaghan, James Reeves, Jim Crossley, Toby Crawley, Michael Snoyman, and their respective teams and contributors.

Thanks also to the readers who contributed to the beta-book process on the errata page; you have helped make this book better.

From Jack: I'd like to thank my wife, Kim, for encouraging me to write another book, being a sounding board for my ideas, and spending time reviewing the book. Thanks also to my two children—Beatrix and Jasper—who provided many happy distractions. I'd also like to thank Sean Johnson, who introduced me to Bruce, which got the whole project started.

From Fred: Thanks to my wife, Nadia, for being such a beautiful person in every way. Life is everything with you. Thanks to Lily and Ruby for adding so much fun and excitement to our family!

I shall be telling this with a sigh
Somewhere ages and ages hence:
Two roads diverged in a wood, and I—
I took the one less traveled by,
And that has made all the difference.

　≫　*Robert Frost*

Preface

It is usually not long after we start writing web apps that we wonder if it can be done differently or if there is a better way to get the job done. While no framework is perfect, exploring the landscape of ideas that are collected in other frameworks is both satisfying in its own right and extremely helpful in finding new ways to solve problems with our current tools.

This book documents some of our own explorations in a quest to find new ideas and better ways of building apps. We hope that you will enjoy this tour of the modern, and still mostly unexplored, world of web programming.

Why Seven Web Frameworks?

You likely already have a framework that you use for your job or that you work with as a hobby. You might love or hate it, but chances are that you've wondered if there isn't something better out there. Even if you aren't looking to switch frameworks or learn a new language, we think that exposure to the great ideas of other developers can only positively affect your own work and thinking.

We are lifelong learners with a passion for new ideas and adventurous programming. With so many web frameworks and languages available these days, it's easy to have a lot of fun and learn interesting, new things, and it's difficult to get bored. We've experimented with many frameworks during our careers. Some of these became our new favorites, others just inspired us, and a few gave us good ideas that we put into practice in more familiar territory.

This book aims to give you a taste of seven very different web frameworks, both to expose you to their key ideas but also to tickle your own curiosity and sense of adventure. Each framework we explore has something unique to teach us. Compared to mainstream frameworks, they are roads less traveled, full of wonder and surprise, adventure and reward.

About This Book

This book follows in the footsteps of the Pragmatic Bookshelf's "Seven in Seven" series, including *Seven Languages in Seven Weeks [Tat10]* and *Seven Databases in Seven Weeks [RW12]*. Each chapter in this book covers a different web framework, often in a different language, with the goal of providing you with a broad overview of the ideas, styles, and techniques used to develop modern web apps.

Each chapter is self-contained and organized around three days in which we'll introduce the framework and show off its unique features in a practical setting. While there is a loose ordering of the frameworks covered, you do not need to consume the chapters in order and should feel free to jump into any framework you find interesting.

Each framework was chosen for its unique features, and not necessarily for its mainstream popularity. There are bound to be both languages and frameworks that you've never heard of, but sometimes that is where the best ideas are hiding.

We start off in Chapter 1, *Sinatra*, on page 1, with one of the simplest frameworks the Ruby world has produced. While we explore this small, elegant framework, we'll build and test a bookmarking application.

In Chapter 2, *CanJS*, on page 35, we look at one of the newest trends in web apps: client-side frameworks. Using JavaScript and the Sinatra back end, we'll reimplement the bookmarking application and show off the power of dynamic models that can observe and react.

Chapter 3, *AngularJS*, on page 73, tours another client-side JavaScript framework with a completely different style. AngularJS is declarative and integrates directly into your HTML. You tell it what you want, but not how to do it.

Lispers have a saying that "code is data," and in Chapter 4, *Ring*, on page 115, you'll see that web applications are data too. Ring apps build on top of a sophisticated but simple abstraction, and they leverage functional programming techniques.

Your view of how web apps work is sure to be challenged in Chapter 5, *Webmachine*, on page 155. This Erlang-based framework models HTTP as a state machine and allows you to harness the full power of the protocol—power that most frameworks hide from you.

Chapter 6, *Yesod*, on page 197, puts Haskell's strong, static type system to work, preventing many common web app errors. Your application won't pass through the compiler if you have broken links or fail to properly sanitize user-generated content.

Finally, Chapter 7, *Immutant*, on page 233, reinvents the enterprise Java web framework by wrapping the JBoss system in Clojure and removing all the ceremony and cruft. The result is a combination of enterprise class features that you'll enjoy using.

What This Book Is Not

It's difficult to do justice to so many ideas in a single book, and so we've had to trim features that you might expect to find in books dedicated to a single language or framework.

Not a Web Programming Tutorial

We assume you have some familiarity with web applications already. We provide no explanations of HTML, CSS, or the basics around how web applications work. Hopefully you've built one or two web applications already, but if not, the level of knowledge assumed is fairly basic.

Not a Language Tutorial

We cover seven web frameworks across five different programming languages. Some of these languages are probably familiar to you, like Ruby and Java-Script, and some are quite strange. We don't have enough room in the book to include language introductions, but we have tried to accommodate readers who are seeing these languages for the first time. Even if you don't know one of the languages, you should still be able to grasp the key ideas presented in each framework. Many of these ideas are applicable in any language.

Not an Installation or Deployment Guide

Installing languages and web frameworks is getting easier every day, but in order to keep chapters focused on essentials, we do not go into much detail about installation or deployment. In most cases, package managers and build tools take care of the hard work, but if you run into problems, you can turn to online tutorials for help with each language that you can find via your favorite search engine.

Code Examples and Conventions

We aspire to cover as much as possible about each framework within a single chapter, but in some cases we have omitted code from the text that is not relevant to our explanation but is still required for the apps to run. In some cases this code is generated by scaffolding applications that we demonstrate how to use, but in other cases you'll have to get the code from the downloadable code package. You'll find the complete source code for every application in the book there. Feel free to work directly from the downloadable code instead of typing everything in by hand.

For each language in the book, we have tried to stick to the popular conventions and tooling used by the language's community at the time of writing.

Online Resources

The apps and examples shown in this book can be found at the Pragmatic Programmer's website for this book.[1] You'll also find the community forum and the errata submission form, which is where you can report problems with the text or make suggestions for future versions.

We hope you enjoy your adventure through these seven unique frameworks, and let the many good ideas they contain inspire you.

Jack Moffitt and Fred Daoud
December 2013

---

1.   http://pragprog.com/book/7web/seven-web-frameworks-in-seven-weeks

CHAPTER 1

Sinatra

The Tower of Hanoi is a puzzle game where you have three rods and a number of disks of different sizes. The game starts with the disks on the first rod, and the goal is to move all the disks to the third rod without ever putting a larger disk on top of a smaller disk. It's not particularly difficult to solve the puzzle, but the real challenge is to find the simplest solution—completing the task in the least possible number of moves.

Web frameworks solve the problem of writing web applications. Sinatra takes on the additional challenge of being a particularly simple and lightweight framework, allowing you to write a web application with the least possible amount of code.[1] Case in point, "Hello, world" in Sinatra is strikingly minimal:

sinatra/hello/app.rb
```ruby
require "sinatra"
get "/hello" do
  "Hello, Sinatra"
end
```

We have the request method (get), the URI (/hello), and the result. That's it. When a GET request to /hello comes in, the response will be "Hello, Sinatra."

A Simple Domain-Specific Language

Sinatra takes advantage of Ruby's elegant syntax to define a simple domain-specific language (DSL) for implementing web applications. Method calls like get, put, and post correspond to the HTTP method of the request. When the method and the URI match, the code block handles the request and returns the result as an HTTP response. This DSL provides an expressive and natural way of developing a web application. Sinatra is particularly well suited to build a server that provides a RESTful API to its clients.

---

1.   http://sinatrarb.com

Sinatra is a very lightweight framework with few dependencies. Getting started and developing an application are effortless. Our example will be a bookmarking application: users can save and view their bookmarks, tag them, and search by tags.

Sinatra really shines when it comes to creating RESTful applications, helping you create a server that provides an HTTP API. You can then write a front end with a JavaScript framework. In fact, we'll be doing that in the CanJS and AngularJS chapters. However, using a JavaScript framework is not a requirement. Sinatra can also provide the front end.

We'll starting building our example application on Day 1 by creating a model for bookmarks, providing database persistence, and defining a RESTful API. During Day 2 we'll create HTML views with different templating engines. On Day 3, we'll add validation and tag support to the application using Sinatra's block parameters, filters, and regular expression route matching.

Day 1: Building a Bookmarking Application

In our first day of learning Sinatra, we'll begin by setting up a "Hello, world" example to make sure our environment is working properly. We'll also see how we can write automated tests that exercise the code we wrote. Without any further ado, we'll jump into creating a sample application that we'll grow throughout the chapter as we discover more of Sinatra's features.

Let's start by saying hello to Sinatra.

Hello, Sinatra

From your command line, make sure you have Ruby and RubyGems installed:

```
$ ruby -v
ruby 2.0.0

$ gem -v
2.0.2
```

We're using Ruby 2.0, but Sinatra works just as well with Ruby 1.9. If these commands do not work, visit the Ruby download page to install Ruby for your operating system.[2] If your system comes with Ruby 1.8.7, please note that while Sinatra works well with it, the book's sample code requires Ruby 1.9 or above.

Now, install the Sinatra gem:

```
$ gem install sinatra
```

---

2.   http://www.ruby-lang.org/en/downloads

That's all you need to get started with Sinatra. We'll install more gems throughout the chapter as we need them. You'll also find more detailed configuration settings in the Sinatra documentation.[3]

We'll start with a file named app.rb:

```
sinatra/hello/app.rb
require "sinatra"
get "/hello" do
  "Hello, Sinatra"
end
```

Then, we'll run it:

```
$ ruby app.rb
== Sinatra/1.4.3 has taken the stage on 4567
```

The output tells us that the application is running on port 4567. So go ahead and open http://localhost:4567/hello in your browser. You should see the greeting "Hello, Sinatra."

It's certainly satisfying to see the result of our work in the browser. Manually testing a web application, however, can quickly get tiresome and error-prone. Let's see how we can address this situation.

Testing with RSpec

Writing code that tests the features of our application is very appealing, because it automates the process of making sure our application works. We can run all the tests again and again to make sure that the changes we make have not caused any breakage somewhere else in the application.

A web application that serves up a RESTful API, such as the bookmarking application that we will create in this chapter, is particularly well suited for automated tests. This type of application returns data rather than visual pages, making it straightforward to write robust tests.

RSpec is a testing tool that we can use to write automated tests for our web application.[4] After installing the rspec and rack-test gems, we're ready to go.

```
$ gem install rspec rack-test
```

Let's write a simple test for confirming that a GET request to /hello returns a success response code and the greeting we want, "Hello, Sinatra."

---

3.   http://www.sinatrarb.com/configuration.html
4.   http://rspec.info

sinatra/hello/app_test.rb
```ruby
require_relative "app"
require "rspec"
require "rack/test"

describe "Hello application" do
  include Rack::Test::Methods

  def app
    Sinatra::Application
  end

  it "says hello" do
    get "/hello"
    last_response.should be_ok
    last_response.body.should == "Hello, Sinatra"
  end
end
```

After setting up our application for testing, we have a describe block. These blocks organize RSpec test cases into groups with a description that we specify as a string. Within the describe block, we define test cases with it blocks, again with a string description. The idea is to write code that reads like plain English: *Describe the Hello application. It says hello.* The code within the it block performs actions and verifies expectations with calls to should.

The rspec command runs the test:

```
$ rspec app_test.rb
.

Finished in 0.02436 seconds
1 example, 0 failures
```

A dot in the output indicates a test that was successful. The message at the bottom of the output shows that there were no failures. Now, if we had a failing test, such as expecting "Hello, Sinatra!" with an exclamation mark, we'll get an output like so:

```
$ rspec app_test.rb
F

Failures:

  1) Hello application says hello
     Failure/Error: last_response.body.should == "Hello, Sinatra!"
     expected: "Hello, Sinatra!"
          got: "Hello, Sinatra" (using ==)
     # ./app_test.rb:15:in `block (2 levels) in <top (required)>'
```

```
Finished in 0.01612 seconds
1 example, 1 failure

Failed examples:

rspec ./app_test.rb:12 # Hello application says hello
```

Notice the F in place of the dot, indicating a failure. The output provides many useful details about the failed test: the description from the strings that we provided when calling the describe and it blocks, the line of code where the failure occurred, and the expected and actual values so that we can readily compare them.

Writing automated tests is a great way to confirm that the code we have written works as expected. Sinatra and RSpec make writing test code quite convenient. Throughout the rest of this chapter, we'll occasionally use tests to exercise our bookmarking application.

A RESTful API

We'll now get started on implementing a simple bookmarking application. Users can save their bookmarks, give them tags, and retrieve them as a list. Unlike saving bookmarks directly in a browser, the motivation for having them in an online application is to provide users with access to their bookmarks from anywhere. It also gives users a central place to store all their bookmarks.

The server that we will build provides the following RESTful API:

```
GET    /bookmarks    - get a list of all bookmarks
GET    /bookmarks/ID - get the details of bookmark ID
POST   /bookmarks    - create a new bookmark
PUT    /bookmarks/ID - update an existing bookmark
DELETE /bookmarks/ID - delete a bookmark
```

Our first iteration of the bookmarking application will be to implement CRUD for bookmarks: create, read, update, and delete. To achieve this task, we'll start with some data persistence.

Data Persistence

We need a place to store the bookmarks. Let's use the SQLite database,[5] and for object relational mapping (ORM), let's use DataMapper.[6] Both are as lightweight and easy to use as Sinatra, and they work well together.

---

5. http://www.sqlite.org
6. http://www.datamapper.org

We'll install the necessary gems:

```
$ gem install sqlite3 data_mapper dm-sqlite-adapter
```

SQLite and DataMapper are ready to use. DataMapper takes Ruby classes and turns them into DataMapper *resources*, which makes them map to a database table. We set up DataMapper to point to an SQLite database, and we define our model classes. DataMapper then takes care of creating tables, saving data from models to the database, and retrieving data back into the models.

We'll start with a simple Bookmark model class:

sinatra/crud/bookmark.rb
```ruby
require "data_mapper"

class Bookmark
  include DataMapper::Resource

  property :id, Serial
  property :url, String
  property :title, String
end
```

DataMapper makes creating a resource straightforward. We've declared the Bookmark class as a DataMapper resource, and we've defined three properties. DataMapper maps these properties to columns in the corresponding database table.

In our Sinatra application, setting up DataMapper involves importing the DataMapper gem and our Bookmark class. Then we use DataMapper::setup to point to our SQLite database and DataMapper.finalize.auto_upgrade! to set up the database tables:

sinatra/crud/app.rb
```ruby
require "sinatra"
require "data_mapper"
require_relative "bookmark"

DataMapper::setup(:default, "sqlite3://#{Dir.pwd}/bookmarks.db")
DataMapper.finalize.auto_upgrade!
```

We've set up DataMapper to create an SQLite database in the current directory using the bookmarks.db file.

The call to auto_upgrade! creates the database table for the Bookmark class but keeps the table if it already exists. It also updates the table by creating new columns if we've added new fields to the model class. That makes auto_upgrade!

keep our previous data between restarts of the application. The other option for finalize is auto_migrate!, which wipes out and re-creates the database structure every time. We'd use auto_migrate! if we wanted to start with empty data at every application restart, such as for testing purposes.

Creating and Reading Bookmarks

We're ready to write Sinatra methods for serving up bookmarks. Let's start with a simple GET request to /bookmarks that returns all bookmarks in JSON format. To convert DataMapper classes to JSON, we can use the dm-serializer gem:

```
$ gem install dm-serializer
```

sinatra/crud/app.rb
```
require "dm-serializer"

def get_all_bookmarks
  Bookmark.all(:order => :title)
end
get "/bookmarks" do
  content_type :json
  get_all_bookmarks.to_json
end
```

After setting the HTTP response content type to JSON, we return all bookmarks by using DataMapper's all method and then converting the result to JSON.

Our bookmark list method is ready, but it won't return much unless we create some bookmarks and save them to the database. To create a bookmark, we'll accept a POST request to /bookmarks and use DataMapper's create method:

sinatra/crud/app.rb
```
post "/bookmarks" do
  input = params.slice "url", "title"
  bookmark = Bookmark.create input
  # Created
  [201, "/bookmarks/#{bookmark['id']}"]
end
```

After creating the bookmark, we return the 201 status code, Created, along with the URI to the newly created bookmark with its ID. This tells the client how to access the bookmark.

If you return an array with two elements, Sinatra automatically uses the first element as the HTTP status code and the second element as the response body. You can also return an array with three elements: the HTTP status code, a hash of the response headers, and the response body.

You can also return just the status code or just the response body, for which Sinatra will use a 200 status code. However, returning a 201 status code is more specific, indicating that a resource has been created. The World Wide Web Consortium (W3C) discusses the preferred response status codes for each HTTP method in its documentation.[7] The W3C also defines status codes in more detail.[8]

When creating the bookmark from the request input, notice that we used the slice method to filter out everything from the request parameters except for the values that we need, the URL, and the title. This prevents polluting the model with unwanted data and also acts as a security feature that prevents malicious users from binding values directly into the model without our knowing about it.

The slice method is not built in, but we can add it to the Hash class:

sinatra/crud/app.rb
```
class Hash
  def slice(*whitelist)
    whitelist.inject({}) {|result, key| result.merge(key => self[key])}
  end
end
```

We're producing a hash that only includes the keys provided in the whitelist.

To retrieve a single bookmark, we handle a GET request with the bookmark ID:

sinatra/crud/app.rb
```
get "/bookmarks/:id" do
  id = params[:id]
  bookmark = Bookmark.get(id)
  content_type :json
  bookmark.to_json
end
```

We're off to a fine start for our bookmarking application.

Writing Automated Tests

Let's write an RSpec test to confirm that creating a bookmark works. Our strategy is to get the list of bookmarks and keep track of the list's size. Then, after creating a bookmark, we get the list again and expect the new size to be one more than the previous size. We also check the response of the POST request:

---

7. http://www.w3.org/Protocols/rfc2616/rfc2616-sec9.html
8. http://www.w3.org/Protocols/rfc2616/rfc2616-sec10.html

sinatra/crud/app_test.rb

```
it "creates a new bookmark" do
  get "/bookmarks"
  bookmarks = JSON.parse(last_response.body)
① last_size = bookmarks.size

  post "/bookmarks",
    {:url => "http://www.test.com", :title => "Test"}

  last_response.status.should == 201
② last_response.body.should match(/\/bookmarks\/\d+/)

  get "/bookmarks"
  bookmarks = JSON.parse(last_response.body)
③ expect(bookmarks.size).to eq(last_size + 1)

end
```

❶ We've kept track of the last bookmark list size.

❷ After creating a bookmark, the response body should contain a link to the newly created bookmark.

❸ To confirm that a new bookmark was created, we're expecting the current bookmark list size to be the previous size plus one.

Running the test with rspec app_test.rb confirms that our handler for creating a bookmark works properly.

Updating and Deleting Bookmarks

Updating an existing bookmark is equally straightforward. When a PUT request arrives with the bookmark ID, we retrieve the bookmark from the database, update it with the request input, and return a status code:

sinatra/crud/app.rb

```
put "/bookmarks/:id" do
  id = params[:id]
  bookmark = Bookmark.get(id)
  input = params.slice "url", "title"
  bookmark.update input
  204 # No Content
end
```

We're returning the 204 status code, No Content, because this is the appropriate response to a PUT request when the server has no additional information to give back to the client.

Let's write an RSpec test for that too.

sinatra/crud/app_test.rb

```
it "updates a bookmark" do
  post "/bookmarks",
    {:url => "http://www.test.com", :title => "Test"}
  bookmark_uri = last_response.body
❶ id = bookmark_uri.split("/").last

❷ put "/bookmarks/#{id}", {:title => "Success"}
  last_response.status.should == 204

  get "/bookmarks/#{id}"
  retrieved_bookmark = JSON.parse(last_response.body)
❸ expect(retrieved_bookmark["title"]).to eq("Success")
end
```

❶ We start by creating a new bookmark and using the response to get its ID.

❷ We can now use the ID to issue a PUT request to update the bookmark with a different title.

❸ Getting the bookmark by its ID, we confirm that the title has indeed been updated.

Our final task for CRUD support is to delete a bookmark. DataMapper provides a destroy method for deleting an object from the database:

sinatra/crud/app.rb

```
delete "/bookmarks/:id" do
  id = params[:id]
  bookmark = Bookmark.get(id)
  bookmark.destroy
  200 # OK
end
```

We now have a basic implementation of a RESTful server API to create, read, update, and delete bookmarks, and it was all very straightforward. You can see why Sinatra has a sweet spot for this type of application.

What We Learned on Day 1

Today, we got started with Sinatra with an example of a "Hello, World" greeting. From there we went into building a RESTful API for managing bookmarks. We hooked up Sinatra to DataMapper and SQLite to back our bookmarks with a database. We also looked at how we can write automated tests with RSpec. This was a very productive first day, as we put several pieces in place that give us a clean and powerful way of developing web applications.

Day 1 Self-Study

Find:

- The Sinatra reference documentation
- The documentation and examples for DataMapper

Do:

- Write an automated test for confirming that deleting a bookmark works correctly.
- Add a property to the bookmark resource for the creation date.
- Create a handler for getting the bookmark list in order of creation date.

Day 2: Creating Views

We've completed a Sinatra web application that provides a basic RESTful API for managing bookmarks. This is a terrific achievement, but it would be even better with a user interface.

Although Sinatra works great for creating a RESTful API, it is not limited in that respect. You can also produce HTML pages quite easily, and that is what we'll do today. You can choose among many libraries for templating HTML and use them from within Sinatra. We'll look at three of them: ERB, Mustache, and Slim.

ERB comes with Sinatra and is easy to use. Mustache is an interesting choice if you prefer to have less syntax and no logic in your view templates. Slim is even more concise because it generates HTML tags for you. With these three engines, we'll explore different approaches to templating and see how easy it is to switch libraries when working with Sinatra.

Let's start with ERB.

ERB

ERB (embedded Ruby) is a templating system that uses Ruby for the dynamic parts of the output. ERB is included in the Ruby standard library, and Sinatra supports it out-of-the box, so you don't need to install anything to use it.

When creating an ERB template, you combine Ruby code with regular HTML, enclosing the Ruby code within either <% %> or <%= %>. The former is for executing a statement, while the latter is for outputting the result of an expression.

To render an ERB template, call the erb method with a keyword indicating the name of the template file:

```
sinatra/erb/app.rb
get "/" do
  @bookmarks = get_all_bookmarks
➤ erb :bookmark_list
end
```

Sinatra finds the template in the views directory, using the keyword as the file name and adding the .erb extension:

```
views/bookmark_list.erb
```

To communicate data from the handler to the template, we use instance variables. Having loaded the bookmark list into @bookmarks, we can render it in the view:

```
sinatra/erb/views/bookmark_list.erb
<a href="/bookmark/new">Add New Bookmark</a>
<h2>List of Bookmarks (ERB)</h2>
<ul>
  <% @bookmarks.each do |bookmark| %>
    <li>
      <a href="/bookmarks/<%= bookmark.id %>">Edit</a>
      <form action="/bookmarks/<%= bookmark.id %>" method="post">
        <input type="hidden" name="_method" value="delete">
        <input type="submit" value="Delete">
      </form>
      |
      <a href="<%= bookmark.url %>"><%=h bookmark.title %></a>
      ( <a href="<%= bookmark.url %>"><%= bookmark.url %></a> )
    </li>
  <% end %>
</ul>
```

❶ We're executing a statement by enclosing Ruby code within <% %>. The code loops through @bookmarks, executing a block for each bookmark. HTML within the block will be rendered as many times as there are bookmarks in the list.

❷ By enclosing Ruby code within <%= %>, we are rendering the result of the expression: the bookmark ID. This allows us to dynamically create a link to edit the corresponding bookmark.

❸ To delete a bookmark, we need to issue a DELETE request. Since we cannot do that directly with a link, we're using a form that sends a POST request with a hidden _method parameter that has the value delete. Sinatra automatically converts such a request into a DELETE request.

❹ When rendering the bookmark title, we want to escape the HTML in case the user has included any code when entering the title. To escape the HTML, we're calling the h method. This is a method that we provide. To keep templates simple, such methods are not defined in templates but rather as *helpers*.

Sinatra has a helpers method to add code that view templates can call. Within a code block, we add the h method to escape HTML:

sinatra/erb/app.rb
```
helpers do
  def h(text)
    Rack::Utils.escape_html(text)
  end
end
```

We can now use <%=h expr %> from a view template whenever we want to escape the HTML resulting from expr.

Handling JSON and HTML Requests

We added a handler with the "/" URI that returns the bookmark list. That is handy for an HTML client, such as users navigating with their browsers, because they can access our application with the default path.

We also have another handler for GET requests to "/bookmarks" that returns the bookmark list in JSON format. It would be nice to be able to reuse the handler for serving the bookmark list in HTML as well. To determine which format to return, we can read the value of the HTTP request's Accept header.

Even better, instead of sprinkling our code with if statements to return JSON or HTML depending on the Accept header, we can use a Sinatra plugin called RespondWith, which comes with the sinatra-contrib package. First, we'll install the gem:

```
$ gem install sinatra-contrib
```

Next, we'll use the respond_with method:

sinatra/erb/app.rb
```
require "sinatra/respond_with"

get "/bookmarks" do
  @bookmarks = get_all_bookmarks
  respond_with :bookmark_list, @bookmarks
end
```

This returns a JSON result if the header contains Accept: application/json and an HTML view for the Accept: text/html header. Using the first parameter as the template name, the RespondWith plugin automatically renders the view using the templating engine for which it finds a template in the views directory. Since we passed :bookmark_list and have a views/bookmark_list.erb file in our project, the plugin uses ERB.

Using Partials

Partials are templates that are meant to be pulled into other templates to form a complete page. Partials are handy for reusing chunks of view code in multiple pages, or even just to break up a page into separate templates. We'll use a partial for the form inputs of the bookmark form.

At the top of our bookmark list template, we added a link to /bookmark/new to add a new bookmark. Let's add a handler that renders the view template for the bookmark form:

```
sinatra/erb/app.rb
get "/bookmark/new" do
  erb :bookmark_form_new
end
```

Next, we'll create the template itself. The bookmark form for adding a new bookmark is very similar to the one for editing an existing bookmark. First let's look at the template for creating a new bookmark:

```
sinatra/erb/views/bookmark_form_new.erb
<h2>New Bookmark</h2>
<form action="/bookmarks" method="post">
  <%= erb :bookmark_form_inputs %>
</form>
```

Pretty simple—the form issues a POST request to /bookmarks and includes the form inputs from another template: bookmark_form_inputs.erb. Notice how we can call erb from a template, just as we did from a handler method. Having the form inputs in a separate template makes it easy to reuse them for the template that edits an existing bookmark:

```
sinatra/erb/views/bookmark_form_edit.erb
<h2>Edit Bookmark</h2>
<form action="/bookmarks/<%= @bookmark.id %>" method="post">
  <input type="hidden" name="_method" value="put">
  <%= erb :bookmark_form_inputs %>
</form>
```

Besides the heading, the difference here is that the form is configured to send a PUT request to /bookmarks/<id>. Having method="put" on a <form> tag does not work, so the workaround is to add a hidden input with name="_method" and the value set to the HTTP method that we want. Sinatra makes the conversion automatically.

The form inputs are the same for creating and updating a bookmark. The difference between the two are the form actions: POST to /bookmarks versus PUT to /bookmarks/<id>. We can render the form inputs in a partial template:

```
sinatra/erb/views/bookmark_form_inputs.erb
<label>
  URL:
  <input type="text" name="url" value="<%= @bookmark && @bookmark.url %>">
</label>
<label>
  Title:
  <input type="text" name="title" value="<%= @bookmark && @bookmark.title %>">
</label>
<input type="submit" name="save" value="Save">
<a href="/">Cancel</a>
```

We're reusing the partial in the bookmark_form_new.erb and bookmark_form_edit.erb templates.

Speaking of reuse, we'll round out our ERB implementation by adding a layout that will be reused for every page of our application:

```
sinatra/erb/views/layout.erb
<html lang="en">
  <head>
    <meta charset="utf-8">
    <title>Bookmarking App</title>
    <link href="/css/bootstrap.min.css" rel="stylesheet">
    <link href="/css/app.css" rel="stylesheet">
  </head>
  <body>
    <div class="container">
      <h1>Bookmarking App</h1>
      <hr>
      <div>
        <%= yield %>
      </div>
    </div>
  </body>
</html>
```

When we call the erb method, Sinatra automatically uses the layout because it is located in the views/layout.erb file. Notice the call to yield: that is where each page's content will be placed.

We also have references to two CSS files. For Sinatra to find these and other static files (.js files, images, and so on), we need to either place them under the public/ directory of our application or specify a different location by configuring the :public_folder option:

```
set :public_folder, settings.root + '/my_static_file_folder'
```

Let's continue our discussion of views with another templating engine: Mustache.

Mustache

Mustache is a specification for templates with just a few simple syntax rules.[9] Mustache is worth looking into as an alternative to ERB because you usually end up with less code in the templates. No if statements, else clauses, or for loops are allowed.

We'll need two gems to use Mustache, mustache and sinatra-mustache:

```
$ gem install mustache sinatra-mustache
```

Then, in our Ruby code, we add a require statement, and we're ready to use Mustache:

sinatra/mustache/app.rb
```
require "sinatra/mustache"
```

Much like ERB, a simple call to mustache with the template name as a keyword renders the corresponding .mustache file from the views directory.

sinatra/mustache/app.rb
```
get "/" do
  @bookmarks = get_all_bookmarks
  mustache :bookmark_list # renders views/bookmark_list.mustache
end
```

Again, similar to ERB, Mustache templates are regular HTML with a special syntax for the dynamic parts. Unlike ERB, however, there is no arbitrary code to be executed. Mustache templates are script-free and devoid of logic on purpose, to keep things simple.

The syntax is also very simple:

- {{x}} outputs the value of a property x, escaping any HTML code.
- {{{x}}} does the same as {{x}}, but it does not escape HTML.
- {{#x}} and {{/x}} loop through the items in x.
- {{> x}} renders x as a partial template, which is equivalent to <%= erb :x %> in ERB. The template is found in views/x.mustache.

---

9.   http://mustache.github.io

That's it for our needs. You can find more details on the syntax rules in the Mustache documentation.[10]

To use Mustache with Sinatra, we just need to assign data to instance variables to make them available to the template. In ERB, we referred to those variables with the same syntax as in Ruby, such as @bookmarks. In Mustache, we refer to the variable without the @. To loop through bookmarks, we use {{#bookmarks}} and {{/bookmarks}}. Within the loop, we can refer to each bookmark's property with {{x}}. Here, then, is the template for rendering the list of bookmarks:

```
sinatra/mustache/views/bookmark_list.mustache
<a href="/bookmark/new">Add New Bookmark</a>
<h2>List of Bookmarks (Mustache)</h2>
<ul>
  {{#bookmarks}}
    <li>
        <a href="/bookmarks/{{id}}">Edit</a>
        <form action="/bookmarks/{{id}}" method="post">
            <input type="hidden" name="_method" value="delete">
            <input type="submit" value="Delete">
        </form>
        |
        <a href="{{url}}">{{title}}</a>
      ( <a href="{{url}}">{{url}}</a> )
    </li>
  {{/bookmarks}}
</ul>
```

As you can see, Mustache templates are very straightforward. With Mustache, we can create partial templates that we can reuse, just as we did with ERB. Here is the partial template for the bookmark form inputs:

```
sinatra/mustache/views/bookmark_form_inputs.mustache
<label>
  URL:
  <input type="text" name="url" value="{{bookmark.url}}">
</label>
<label>
  Title:
  <input type="text" name="title" value="{{bookmark.title}}">
</label>
<input type="submit" name="save" value="Save">
<a href="/">Cancel</a>
```

The Mustache syntax for loading a partial template is {{> template_name}}, where the template name does not include the .mustache extension. For example, here is how we load our partial in the view for creating a new bookmark:

---

10. http://mustache.github.io/mustache.5.html

```
sinatra/mustache/views/bookmark_form_new.mustache
<h2>New Bookmark</h2>
<form action="/bookmarks" method="post">
  {{> bookmark_form_inputs}}
</form>
```

For a common layout, all we need to do is create a template located in the views/layout.mustache file. To indicate where to render the output of each specific page, we call yield. Since we don't want to escape the HTML of the output, we use a set of three braces, {{{yield}}}:

```
sinatra/mustache/views/layout.mustache
<!doctype html>
<html lang="en">
  <head>
    <meta charset="utf-8">
    <title>Bookmarking App</title>
    <link href="/css/bootstrap.min.css" rel="stylesheet">
    <link href="/css/app.css" rel="stylesheet">
  </head>
  <body>
    <div class="container">
      <h1>Bookmarking App</h1>
      <hr>
      <div>
        {{{yield}}}
      </div>
    </div>
  </body>
</html>
```

That's it for Mustache. We'll use it again with CanJS and Webmachine. We'll also use a similar {{ }} syntax in AngularJS. Now let's finish the day with one last templating framework with another different syntax, Slim. (We're looking at different templating styles to give you a taste of what's available. There are as many options as there are personal tastes for syntax, so you're sure to find something that is to your liking.)

Slim

Slim aims to make markup more concise (see http://slim-lang.com/). Slim takes a different approach to templating by taking over the whole rendering process instead of using regular HTML with a special syntax just for the dynamic parts.

To use Slim, we need to install this gem:

```
$ gem install slim
```

To render a template, we need to require the gem and call the slim method with a keyword for the template. Sinatra finds the corresponding template file in the views/ directory with the .slim file extension.

sinatra/slim/app.rb
```
require "slim"
get "/" do
  @bookmarks = get_all_bookmarks
  slim :bookmark_list # renders views/bookmark_list.slim
end
```

The syntax for Slim templates is quite different from what we've seen so far with ERB and Mustache. With Slim, you use the syntax for the whole template, including all HTML tags. The syntax is designed to be more concise than regular HTML tags. For example, consider this HTML page:

sinatra/slim/views/example.html
```
<html>
  <head>
    <link href="/css/bootstrap.min.css" rel="stylesheet" />
  </head>
  <body>
    <div class="container">
      <h1>Bookmarking App</h1>
    </div>
    <div id="footer">
      <small>Footer goes here</small>
    </div>
  </body>
</html>
```

To generate that HTML output, you would write this Slim template:

sinatra/slim/views/example.slim
```
html
  head
    link href="/css/bootstrap.min.css" rel="stylesheet"
  body
    .container
      h1 Bookmarking App
    #footer
      small Footer goes here
```

You can see how the Slim template is more concise than regular HTML. Let's discuss the syntax in more detail.

Instead of angle brackets, HTML tags are created from the first token on each line and without a closing tag. This is part of Slim's conciseness: the indentation determines the tag structure, and Slim takes care of closing tags for you. A tag's attributes and content follow the tag, as in a href="http://pragprog.com" The

Pragmatic Programmers. The tags that are one level of indentation deeper automatically become the children of the current tag.

To keep templates even more brief, Slim generates a <div> tag by default if you do not specify a tag. Furthermore, because id= and class= attributes are so commonly used, you can imitate the CSS syntax for those. You can see that in the example, where .container generates <div class="container"> and #footer produces <div id="footer">.

Let's look at the template for our bookmark list to see how you add dynamic content to Slim templates:

```
sinatra/slim/views/bookmark_list.slim
a href="/bookmark/new" Add New Bookmark
h2 List of Bookmarks (Slim)
ul
  - for bookmark in @bookmarks do
    li
      a> href="/bookmarks/#{bookmark.id}" Edit
      form> action="/bookmarks/#{bookmark.id}" method="post"
        input type="hidden" name="_method" value="delete"
        input type="submit" value="Delete"
      | |
      a<> href="bookmark.url" = bookmark.title
      | (
      a<> href="bookmark.url" == bookmark.url
      | )
```

We have some new Slim syntax. First, the hyphen, -, evaluates Ruby code. We're using that to iterate over @bookmarks and render each bookmark. Again, we don't have to worry about closing the block, because indentation determines where the block ends. Slim takes care of wrapping things up for us.

Next, we have the bookmark ID in the link to edit a bookmark. The syntax there is the same as in Ruby strings, with the dynamic content within #{ }. We're also using that for the form that posts a DELETE request.

Also note that the <, >, or <> following a tag indicates to add a leading or a trailing whitespace or both. When we want text without a tag, we use a pipe (|) character.

Finally, we use = to output dynamic content within a tag, and == to output without HTML escaping. That's how we're rendering the bookmark title and URL.

Again, we'll create a partial template for the form inputs that we can reuse for creating and updating bookmarks:

sinatra/slim/views/bookmark_form_inputs.slim

```
label
  | URL:
  input< type="text" name="url" value="#{@bookmark && @bookmark.url}"
label
  | Title:
  input< type="text" name="title" value="#{@bookmark && @bookmark.title}"
input> type="submit" name="save" value="Save"
a href="/" Cancel
```

To render the partial, we call = slim :bookmark_form_inputs, which is the same Ruby method that we would call to render the template from Sinatra:

sinatra/slim/views/bookmark_form_new.slim

```
h2 New Bookmark
form action="/bookmarks" method="post"
  == slim :bookmark_form_inputs
```

We can reuse the partial in the template for editing a bookmark:

sinatra/slim/views/bookmark_form_edit.slim

```
h2 Edit Bookmark
form action="/bookmarks/#{@bookmark.id}" method="post"
  input type="hidden" name="_method" value="put"
  input type="hidden" name="format" value="html"
  == slim :bookmark_form_inputs
```

Finally, Slim supports specifying the doctype with doctype. For HTML 5, we can just use doctype html. For more details on other doctypes, and on the Slim syntax for that matter, see the Slim reference documentation.[11]

sinatra/slim/views/layout.slim

```
doctype html
html lang="en"
  head
    meta charset="utf-8"
    title Bookmarking App
    link href="/css/bootstrap.min.css" rel="stylesheet"
    link href="/css/app.css" rel="stylesheet"
  body
    .container
      h1 Bookmarking App
      hr
      div
        == yield
```

That is our page layout. Notice the call to yield to indicate where to put the content of the current page.

---

11. http://rdoc.info/gems/slim/frames

Slim is an altogether different creature than ERB or Mustache. One thing is for sure, you have no shortage of options when it comes to HTML templating engines to use with Sinatra.

What We Learned on Day 2

Our second day of Sinatra was all about rendering HTML views with different templating engines. This gave us the capability of developing a web application complete with user interface.

Day 2 Self-Study

Find:

- Additional ERB, Mustache, and Slim tutorials and examples
- More templating alternatives and their support in Sinatra

Do:

- Use one of the templating engines that you found to re-create the views of the bookmarking application.

- Write tests to confirm the behavior of the views that you created.

- Determine if respond_with works with Slim and Mustache as it does with ERB to respond with HTML or JSON, depending on the request headers.

Day 3: Adding Features

Today, we dig a little deeper into Sinatra and use what we learn to add some features to our bookmarking application. We'll make the application more robust with some validation, use block parameters and filters to refactor and improve our code, and end the day by implementing a new feature: adding tags to bookmarks.

Let's begin by making the application more resistant to invalid input by providing validation.

Validation

We can create and update bookmarks, but we're not validating anything. Let's address that now. We want all bookmarks to have a title and a URL, and we want the URL's format to be valid. DataMapper makes it easy to add these constraints to the Bookmark model:

```
sinatra/validation/bookmark.rb
class Bookmark
  include DataMapper::Resource
```

```
    property :id, Serial
➤   property :url, String, :required => true, :format => :url
➤   property :title, String, :required => true
  end
```

With that in place, calls to bookmark.save and bookmark.update will return false if the input is not valid. What we want to do in that case is return an HTTP error code: 400, Bad Request. Let's write the RSpec test first:

sinatra/validation/app_test.rb
```
it "sends an error code for an invalid create request" do
  post "/bookmarks", {:url => "test", :title => "Test"}
  last_response.status.should == 400
end
```

At this point, we run the test and make sure that it fails. This is what we expect, since we haven't written the application code yet. In this approach, called test-driven development (TDD), you write the test code for a feature *before* you write the code that implements the feature. This can be very effective at making sure that you have tests for all of your features. You also have to think about how you're going to implement a feature and about what situations you need to consider before you write the code.

We're sending a POST request to create a bookmark, but the URL is not valid. We're expecting the response status code to be 400. Now, to implement this in the application, we need to check whether bookmark.save returns true. If not, we return the 400 code:

sinatra/validation/app.rb
```
post "/bookmarks" do
  input = params.slice "url", "title"
  bookmark = Bookmark.new input
➤ if bookmark.save
    # Created
    [201, "/bookmarks/#{bookmark['id']}"]
  else
➤   400 # Bad Request
  end
end
```

Now that we've written the application code to implement the feature that we're adding, we can run the test again and make sure that it passes.

We are now preventing bookmarks from being created with missing URLs or titles or with invalid URLs. This takes care of bookmark creation, but we must do the same for updating a bookmark. Even if a bookmark was previously valid, it could possibly become invalid if an update request is made with a missing title or a missing or invalid URL. Just like bookmark.save, the call to

bookmark.update returns a boolean value indicating whether the update was
valid. Again, we'll return the 400 code for an invalid request:

sinatra/validation/app.rb
```ruby
put "/bookmarks/:id" do
  id = params[:id]
  bookmark = Bookmark.get(id)

  if bookmark
    input = params.slice "url", "title"
    if bookmark.update input
      204 # No Content
    else
      400 # Bad Request
    end
  else
    [404, "bookmark #{id} not found"]
  end
end
```

When editing an existing bookmark, we need to make sure that the bookmark
ID that was received in the URI does indeed exist in our database. We're validating that with if bookmark. If that returns false, our else block returns a 404
status code, Not Found.

We'll add an RSpec test to make sure that an invalid PUT request returns the
400 code:

sinatra/validation/app_test.rb
```ruby
it "sends an error code for an invalid update request" do
  get "/bookmarks"
  bookmarks = JSON.parse(last_response.body)
  id = bookmarks.first['id']

  put "/bookmarks/#{id}", {:url => "Invalid"}
  last_response.status.should == 400
end
```

By running rspec app_test.rb, we can verify that the tests pass.

We'll now look at two Sinatra features that we can use to refactor and improve
our code: block parameters and filters.

Block Parameters

When we call a Sinatra method for handling a request, such as get, put, and
so on, we pass a URI that may contain parameters, denoted by the : prefix,
as in /bookmarks/:id. To retrieve the id parameter, we've been using params[:id].

That's simple enough, but there's another way that is even more concise: a block parameter (whereas before we used params):

sinatra/validation/app.rb
```
get "/bookmarks/:id" do
  id = params[:id]
  bookmark = Bookmark.get(id)
```

We can use a block parameter instead, like this:

sinatra/blockparameters/app.rb
```
get "/bookmarks/:id" do |id|
  bookmark = Bookmark.get(id)
```

Using a block parameter has saved us a line of code. We'd save even more with multiple parameters.

It's worth noting that when pulling out parameters from the params hash, the key names correspond to the names that we gave to the parameters in the URI. For block parameters, however, the variable names do *not* pull out values from the corresponding names in the URI. Instead, parameters are bound to variables in *order*. For example, we could write this:

sinatra/blockparameters/app.rb
```
get "/test/:one/:two" do |creature, sound|
  "a #{creature} says #{sound}"
end
```

The following RSpec test confirms that a request to /test/duck/quack returns a duck says quack:

sinatra/blockparameters/app_test.rb
```
it "binds block parameters by order, not by name" do
  get "/test/duck/quack"
  last_response.body.should == "a duck says quack"
end
```

Of course, using variable names that correspond to the names in the URI is a good idea, for clarity's sake.

Filters

Each call to methods that correspond to HTTP verbs, such as get, post, and so on, sets up a handler for a request. We can also set up handlers for *every* request that get called *before* or *after* the request handler. These handlers are known as *filters*. Filters are a great way to refactor out and reuse common code.

To create a filter with Sinatra, we call the before or after method with the URI
to intercept (or with no URI to intercept *all* requests) and the code block to
execute. The code looks a lot like what we've been writing with get, post, and
so on. In fact, we can even use block parameters with before and after.

For example, all handlers called on /bookmarks/:id should ensure that the id
corresponds to an existing bookmark, and if not, should return a 404, Not
Found. Moreover, we'll hold on to the existing bookmark in an instance variable to use it later without repeating the database lookup. We can do all of
that in a before filter:

sinatra/filter/app.rb

```ruby
before "/bookmarks/:id" do |id|
  @bookmark = Bookmark.get(id)
  if !@bookmark
    halt 404, "bookmark #{id} not found"
  end
end
```

With that in place, we can simplify our code. For example, this was our put
handler previously:

sinatra/blockparameters/app.rb

```ruby
put "/bookmarks/:id" do |id|
  bookmark = Bookmark.get(id)
  if bookmark
    input = params.slice "url", "title"
    if bookmark.update input
      204 # No Content
    else
      400 # Bad Request
    end
  else
    [404, "bookmark #{id} not found"]
  end
end
```

With our before filter creating the @bookmark instance variable and validating
the id, our put handler can focus on updating the bookmark:

sinatra/filter/app.rb

```ruby
put "/bookmarks/:id" do
  input = params.slice "url", "title"

  if @bookmark.update input
    204 # No Content
  else
    400 # Bad Request
  end
end
```

Similarly, other methods that handle requests to /bookmarks/:id can be simplified to use @bookmark, knowing that the filter loads the bookmark from the ID and returns a 404 status code if the bookmark was not found.

Tagging Bookmarks

Our bookmarks are looking good, but we need a way to organize them. Let's add *tagging* to our app: a way for the user to add any number of tags to bookmarks. Then you can browse or search by these tags. Such a system is easy to use—you can make tags up as you go and give multiple tags to a bookmark. This is less restrictive than, say, folders, where a bookmark belongs to only one folder at a time.

Because a bookmark can have many tags and the same tag can be associated with multiple bookmarks, the bookmark-tag model relationship is a many-to-many association. For this to work, we need something between a bookmark and a tag, something that says, "This bookmark and this tag are linked." In database terms, this is a *join table*. For the bookmarking application, we'll call this a *tagging*.

In our model, then, we'll want a bookmark to have many taggings, a tag to have many taggings, and a tagging to belong to a bookmark and a tag. Even better, we'll want to say that a bookmark has many tags and a tag has many bookmarks. Because the tagging serves as a bridge, we say that bookmarks have many tags *through* taggings, and tags also have many bookmarks *through* taggings.

Each tagging links *one* bookmark to *one* tag. But because each bookmark can have *many* taggings, and each *tag* can have many taggings, you can see the end result: a bookmark can have *many* tags, and more than one bookmark can have the *same* tag. In Figure 1, *Model for bookmark tags*, on page 28, Bookmark 1 and Bookmark 2 each have two tags, and they both have Tag 2.

Enough talk—let's code this. First, we'll create the Tagging class:

sinatra/tagging/tagging.rb

```
require "data_mapper"

class Tagging
  include DataMapper::Resource

  belongs_to :tag, :key => true
  belongs_to :bookmark, :key => true
end
```

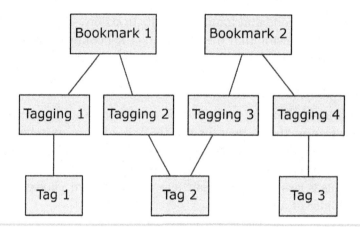

Figure 1—Model for bookmark tags

This is a DataMapper resource. As we've discussed, we're defining the Tagging class as belonging to a bookmark and a tag. Because the relationships make up the keys of the Tagging model, we're telling DataMapper to include them as primary keys with the :key => true option.

Next, we'll add the Tag class:

```
sinatra/tagging/tag.rb
require "data_mapper"

class Tag
  include DataMapper::Resource

  property :id, Serial
  property :label, String, :required => true

  has n, :taggings
  has n, :bookmarks, :through => :taggings, :order => [:title.asc]
end
```

DataMapper makes it easy to add a relationship with has n. We've indicated that a tag *has n* taggings and *has n* bookmarks *through* taggings. We can now use tag.bookmarks to get a tag's bookmarks without having to manually go through the tagging part of the model.

We'll now enhance our Bookmark class to establish the relationships with tag-gings and tags. While we're at it, we'll also add a convenience method, tagList, for getting a list of tags as *strings*, instead of a list of tag *objects* from which we'd have to pull out the labels:

```
sinatra/tagging/bookmark.rb
require "data_mapper"
class Bookmark
  include DataMapper::Resource
  property :id, Serial
  property :url, String, :required => true, :format => :url
  property :title, String, :required => true
  # Add tag support
  has n, :taggings, :constraint => :destroy
  has n, :tags, :through => :taggings, :order => [:label.asc]
  def tagList
    tags.collect do |tag|
      tag.label
    end
  end
end
```

Our model is ready to support tagging.

Adding Tag Support to the API

In our Sinatra application, we want to support specifying tags as a single string, with the tags separated by commas. This makes it easy for the user to indicate an arbitrary number of tags for a bookmark. We'll call this parameter tagsAsString.

To handle the tagsAsString value, we'll create an add_tags helper method. Let's start by splitting the string on commas and stripping out blanks:

```
sinatra/tagging/app.rb
helpers do
  def add_tags(bookmark)
    labels = (params["tagsAsString"] || "").split(",").map(&:strip)
    # more code to come
  end
end
```

Next, by iterating over the bookmark's previously existing tags, we compare with the new list of tags. We'll keep track of matching tags and delete those that previously existed but were not sent in the current request.

```
sinatra/tagging/app.rb
existing_labels = []
bookmark.taggings.each do |tagging|
  if labels.include? tagging.tag.label
    existing_labels.push tagging.tag.label
  else
    tagging.destroy
  end
end
```

Finally, we'll go though the list of tags that we sent and create any tags that are not in the list of already existing tags. We need to create a tagging to link the bookmark to the tag and create or reuse the tag depending on whether it had already been created for another bookmark.

```
sinatra/tagging/app.rb
(labels - existing_labels).each do |label|
  tag = {:label => label}
  existing = Tag.first tag
  if !existing
    existing = Tag.create tag
  end
  Tagging.create :tag => existing, :bookmark => bookmark
end
```

Now when creating a bookmark, we can just call add_tags to take care of tagging:

```
sinatra/tagging/app.rb
post "/bookmarks" do
  input = params.slice "url", "title"
  bookmark = Bookmark.new input
  if bookmark.save
➤   add_tags(bookmark)

    # Created
    [201, "/bookmarks/#{bookmark['id']}"]
  else
    400 # Bad Request
  end
end
```

We've successfully added functionality for putting tags on bookmarks. To use this feature, let's allow for searching bookmarks by tag. Even better, we'll support multiple tags and return just the bookmarks that have all the specified tags. We'll do this by accepting GET requests to URIs such as /bookmarks/tag1, /bookmarks/tag1/tag2, and so on, with the desired tags separated by a forward slash in the URI.

Sinatra handles an arbitrary number of parameters in the URI with the asterisk, *, also known as the *splat*. In fact, the parameter name for retrieving the values from the URI is called :splat. Since you can have multiple splats in the URI, such as /one/*/two/*, params[:splat] returns an array of values. We only have one, so we can retrieve its value with params[:splat].first. That contains the string with the tags separated by slashes, such as tag1/tag2. We can retrieve the array of tags by splitting the string using the slash as the separator. Putting it all together, here's what we have:

```
sinatra/tagging/app.rb
get "/bookmarks/*" do
  tags = params[:splat].first.split "/"
  bookmarks = Bookmark.all
  tags.each do |tag|
    bookmarks = bookmarks.all({:taggings => {:tag => {:label => tag}}})
  end
  bookmarks.to_json with_tagList
end
```

After retrieving the list of tags by which to filter the bookmarks, we start with the complete bookmark list. Then we successively filter the list by each tag, using the all method on the bookmark list to keep reducing the list as each filter by tag is applied. Finally, we return the final list as JSON.

You noticed the with_tagList parameter in the call to bookmarks.to_json. Let's look at the code for with_tagList first:

```
sinatra/tagging/app.rb
with_tagList = {:methods => [:tagList]}
```

By default, to_json does not include associations when serializing objects. A hash with :methods and a list of keywords indicates the associations that we want to include—:tagList in this case. That way, we have each bookmark's tags in the results that we return.

Matching Routes with Regular Expressions

We now have a route for filtering bookmarks by tags. But we have a problem—it conflicts with another one of our routes: GET /bookmarks/<id> for retrieving a bookmark by its ID.

We can resolve this dilemma by taking advantage of two of Sinatra's features: (1) routes can be matched using regular expressions, and (2) routes are matched in the order that they are defined.

When getting a bookmark, the ID that we specify in the URI must be a numerical value. We can restrict the URI with a regular expression that matches only digits after bookmarks/:

```
sinatra/tagging/app.rb
get %r{/bookmarks/\d+} do
  content_type :json

  @bookmark.to_json with_tagList
end
```

By placing the handler for filtering bookmarks by tags *after* the one for retrieving a bookmark by its ID, we've resolved the conflict.

We'll use the same regular expression for the routes that match our *before* filter, as well as the handlers for updating and deleting a bookmark:

```
sinatra/tagging/app.rb
before %r{/bookmarks/(\d+)} do |id|
  # ...
end
put %r{/bookmarks/\d+} do
  # ...
end
delete %r{/bookmarks/\d+} do
  # ...
end
```

We now have an enhanced version of our bookmarking API. Clients can issue requests to create bookmarks with tags and obtain bookmark lists that are filtered by one or more tags.

What We Learned on Day 3

Today was action-packed with more Sinatra and DataMapper features. We added validation to bookmarks. We used block parameters and regular expressions to vary how we implement handlers for URIs. We spent the rest of the day implementing a new feature, bookmark tagging, and covered all the layers: the database, model, and web application.

Day 3 Self-Study

Find:

- The documentation for creating a custom route matcher
- Examples of real-world web applications that use Sinatra

Do:

- Use curl to issue requests that create bookmarks with tags and to retrieve bookmarks filtered by tags.

- Write automated tests to verify the results of updating bookmarks with tags.

- Add tag support to the view templates of your choice.

Wrapping Up

Sinatra is a Ruby framework that provides a simple and natural DSL for developing web applications. Why should things be complicated when they can be simple? With Sinatra, you can get started quickly and without the complexity of a large framework.

Because Sinatra is so nimble, it offers a compelling solution to turn your existing Ruby applications into web applications. As we saw in this chapter, Sinatra is also very easy to unit test, whether with RSpec or with another testing framework of your choice.

Sinatra's Strengths

Developing a RESTful API is particularly sweet in Sinatra. Handling routes, clean URIs with parameters, using regular expressions, and so on, is effortless, as is returning HTTP status codes, messages, and JSON responses.

Sinatra tightly focuses on doing a few things and doing them well. Learning the framework is not an overwhelming task, and you can become productive very quickly.

We also saw how easy it is to use the templating solution of your choice with Sinatra. We looked at three examples, but Sinatra supports many other templating engines as well. You are free to pick your preferred templating style.

The same goes for a persistence library. We used DataMapper, and combining it with Sinatra was effortless. You could just as easily use other ORMs such as MongoMapper, Sequel, or ActiveRecord, to name a few.

Sinatra's Weaknesses

Sinatra's simplicity and narrow scope are virtues, but they can also be considered weaknesses. When building a large application for which you need various web development features, you'll have to turn elsewhere to fill your needs, adding libraries as you go.

Another shortcoming comes not from Sinatra specifically, but from its host language. Ruby is designed to be easy to use. One of the design decisions is to punt on the complexity of running code in parallel and instead stick to single-threaded code. While servers like Thin, Unicorn, and Puma relieve this concern somewhat, there is no doubt that with Ruby and other object-oriented languages, you'll likely struggle with true multithreaded applications.

Final Thoughts

Sinatra makes good use of Ruby's simple and expressive syntax to provide an elegant and easy-to-use web framework. Sinatra is particularly well suited for RESTful applications and also integrates seamlessly with templating engines to produce HTML pages. By focusing only on being a web framework, Sinatra is lightweight and gives you the freedom of completing your application stack with the libraries of your choice.

CHAPTER 2

CanJS

Bejeweled is a game of colored gems where the player swaps adjacent gems to form sequences of identical gems that are then removed from the board. The game becomes even more exciting when chain reactions happen as falling gems appear to replace the previous sequence and in turn form more sequences. The skilled player can plan ahead for these chain reactions but only has to swap a single pair of gems to set things off. The game engine manages the chain reactions.

Likewise, CanJS is a JavaScript framework that lets you write code that makes *one* change and then takes care of the chain reaction of updates that need to happen.[1] You no longer have to manually write code to refresh views, change the state of UI widgets, and send an update to the server. You just make a change to the model, and CanJS, with the judicious use of the observer pattern combined with live binding, makes it all happen automatically.

What Makes CanJS Unique?

CanJS helps you organize your web application following model-view-controller architecture. This is hardly an original approach; most JavaScript frameworks follow the MVC pattern (or some close variant). What makes CanJS shine is its unique balance of features and straightforward, easy-to-understand methodology. With CanJS, your code stays modular, with a clean separation of concerns.

When using CanJS, you use objects that notify listeners when attributes change. This helps keep components separate, because they communicate with events rather than with direct references to each other. CanJS also renders dynamic views from templates and *automatically* updates them when

---

1.   http://canjs.com

models change. You also have models that take care of issuing Ajax requests and handling responses to keep things synchronized between client and server. You can easily organize your application with controllers that handle user interface events while remaining modular and neatly decoupled from each other. As we'll discover, CanJS also provides routing, partial views, filtered data, and more!

CanJS provides all of this while remaining relatively small in size. It does require one of the following libraries: jQuery,[2] Zepto,[3] Dojo,[4] Mootools,[5] or YUI.[6] We'll be using jQuery in the code examples.

Several core components make up the core of CanJS. The following figure shows how they all fit together. can.Construct creates objects with static and prototype properties that can be inherited and overridden. Most of the other parts of CanJS extend can.Construct, so we'll spend a bit of time learning and understanding how it works.

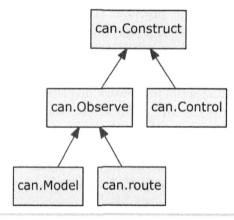

Figure 2—The core CanJS stack

can.Observe creates objects that others can observe and be notified about when attributes change. As mentioned earlier, using events to communicate between components avoids having to tie them together. In fact, observable objects are very much the *essence* of CanJS.

2.   http://jquery.com
3.   http://zeptojs.com
4.   http://dojotoolkit.org
5.   http://www.mootools.net
6.   http://yuilibrary.com/

can.Model augments can.Observe to synchronize changes between client and server. This saves you from manually having to issue Ajax requests and handle server responses.

can.view loads and renders templates with Mustache or EJS.[7] This not only keeps your templates simple and easy to follow, but it also provides *live binding*. You can focus on updating models and let CanJS refresh the views for you.

can.Control builds widgets that combine model and view. As we'll discover, controls provide a convenient way of listening for view events while remaining neatly encapsulated in its own part of the page without risking interference with other components.

can.route provides routing by managing the browser's hash. This makes single-page CanJS applications bookmarkable and navigable with the browser's Back and Forward buttons.

On Day 1, we'll work with can.Construct, can.Observe, can.Model, and can.view. Day 2 will be dedicated to can.Control, combining models with views and handling UI events. We'll spend Day 3 digging deeper into models and wrap up the chapter by learning how to use can.route.

We have many exciting features to learn, so let's get started!

Day 1: Building Objects and Synchronizing Changes

In the first day of our CanJS journey, we'll learn how can.Construct helps with creating hierarchies with inheritance. This is useful in itself but is also important to know because the other parts of CanJS build on can.Construct.

Next, we'll discover can.Observe, an extremely useful part of CanJS that triggers events when changes occur. This helps with keeping components independent. We'll also see how can.Model makes it easy to keep data synchronized between client and server. Finally, we'll discuss view rendering and how using can.Observe objects in views is particularly useful because of live binding.

Let's begin by setting up the CanJS library and its supporting cast.

Hello, CanJS!

The first thing we'll do is look at a minimal setup for loading and using CanJS with jQuery. By running the following "Hello, World"–type of program on your

---

7. http://mustache.github.com/ and http://embeddedjs.com, respectively.

own computer, you'll confirm that you've got things working properly and you'll be able to modify the files to experiment with your own code.

If you look at the book's sample code, under the canjs/public folder, you'll find that jQuery and CanJS are set up in the lib directory as follows:

```
+lib
 |+canjs.com-1.1.8
 |  `-can.jquery.js
 |  `-(other can.*.js files)
 `+jquery
    `-jquery-1.10.2.js
```

Now, look at the canjs/public/index-basic.html file. This is a regular HTML page that loads jQuery and CanJS using the standard <script> tags:

```
canjs/public/index-basic.html
<!doctype html>
<html lang="en">
  <head>
    <meta charset="utf-8">
    <title>CanJS Basic</title>
  </head>
  <body>
    <div id="result"></div>
  </body>
  <script src="lib/jquery/jquery-1.10.2.js"></script>
  <script src="lib/canjs.com-1.1.8/can.jquery.js"></script>
  <script src="index-basic.js"></script>
</html>
```

The last file, index-basic.js, is the place for you to write your code to experiment with CanJS. If you open the file in your favorite code editor, you'll see that it currently contains some simple code just to confirm that jQuery and CanJS are properly loaded:

```
canjs/public/index-basic.js
$(document).ready(function() {
  // Use can for CanJS
  var $result = $("#result");
  can.each(["One", "Two", "Three"], function(it) {
    $result.append(it).append(", ");
  });
  $result.append("Go CanJS!");
});
```

Open the index-basic.html file in your browser. If you see the result One, Two, Three, Go CanJS!, you know that both jQuery (from the use of $ in the preceding code) and CanJS (from the call to can.each) are working. That's all there is to it.

Congratulations, you're ready to start exploring CanJS! You can edit index-basic.html and index-basic.js to experiment with your own code.

Now let's start exploring the different moving parts of CanJS, beginning with the foundational building block, can.Construct.

Constructing and Extending Objects

As you can see in Figure 2, *The core CanJS stack*, on page 36, many parts of CanJS inherit from can.Construct. Let's have a closer look.

JavaScript is a *class-free* language. It uses prototypal inheritance instead of classical inheritance. The nuances involved can be a challenge, especially if you are used to more conventional object-oriented languages. can.Construct removes the complexity by providing a factory that makes it painless to quickly build objects with common properties. can.Construct is essentially a function that you call to create hierarchies with single-parent inheritance. You can call parent functions and even override them in the children.

To use can.Construct, call its extend function with an object containing properties, and you get back a constructor function. Use new to create objects with those properties. Here's an example:

```
canjs/public/concepts/concepts-test.js
var Example = can.Construct.extend({
  count: 1,
  increment: function() {
    this.count++;
  }
});

var example = new Example();
example.increment(); // example.count is now 2
```

To pass parameters when creating new objects, define an init function:

```
canjs/public/concepts/concepts-test.js
var Example = can.Construct.extend({
  init: function(count) {
    this.count = count;
  }
});
var example = new Example(42); // example.count is 42
```

Here's the kicker: for inheritance, define a child by calling the parent's constructor function (without new), passing the child's properties. The child inherits from the parent; it can add new properties and override the parent's properties. A child can even call its parent's functions with _super:

canjs/public/concepts/concepts-test.js
```js
var Parent = can.Construct.extend({
  init: function(count) {
    this.count = count;
  },
  increase: function() {
    this.count++;
  },
  read: function(prefix) {
    return prefix + " " + String(this.count);
  }
});

var Child = Parent({
  // Child inherits the init function

  // Override increase
  increase: function() {
    this.count += 10;
  },
  // Add new function: decrease
  decrease: function() {
    this.count--;
  },
  // Override read, but call parent's version
  read: function() {
    return this._super("Count is") + "!";
  }
});

var child = new Child(2); // calls Parent's init
child.increase(); // calls Child's increase
child.decrease(); // calls Child's decrease
child.count; // returns 11
child.read(); // returns "Count is 11!"
```

Finally, when you call can.Construct with *two* parameters, the first parameter defines the static properties. The second parameter is the prototype (or instance) properties we've been using so far. Here's an example of that:

canjs/public/concepts/concepts-test.js
```js
var Example = can.Construct.extend({
  staticCount: 0,
}, {
  protoCount: 0
});

var example1 = new Example();
var example2 = new Example();
```

```
example1.constructor.staticCount = 2;
example1.protoCount = 2;

Example.staticCount; // returns 2
example2.constructor.staticCount; // returns 2
example2.protoCount; // returns 0
```

Notice how static properties are accessed from an instance via its constructor property or are accessed directly from the constructor function itself, as in Example.staticCount.

Remember that if you pass only one parameter to can.Construct, you define *prototype* properties. If you need a constructor function with *only static* properties, be sure to pass *two* parameters, with an empty object as the second, like so:

canjs/public/concepts/concepts-test.js
```
var ExampleStatic = can.Construct.extend({
  staticCount: 4
}, {
});
```

Knowing how to define a construct with just static properties is useful because that's often all you need when creating models, as we'll soon see when we talk about can.Model.

Other core parts of CanJS, such as can.Observe, can.Model, and can.Control, build on can.Construct. Let's continue our CanJS tour with can.Observe.

Observing Attribute Changes

The core, the heart, the *soul* of a CanJS application is the observable object, or simply the "observe."

can.Observe provides the ability to observe attribute changes on an object. This is extremely important because it provides a great way to keep an application's components cleanly decoupled. As you build your application, blocks of code remain independent of each other and communicate via observable objects. You never end up with a tangled mess of unmaintainable code!

Imagine an online bookstore. You could have several user interface components on a page: a list of books, quantities remaining in the inventory, and the books in your cart with the total cost. When you add a book to your cart, each component needs to be refreshed to reflect recalculated values. As you can see in the following figure, if the "Add to cart" component refreshes the other components, you end up with direct references between components.

This is bad because components are tied to other components instead of being independent.

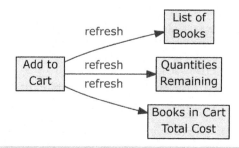

Figure 3—Direct references from one component to others

When using observes, the "Add to cart" component just needs to update an observe. The other components on the page *bind* to the observe, meaning that they listen for changes and update themselves to reflect the latest data. As shown in the next diagram, the "Add to cart" component is no longer tied to any other component. It just updates the observe, and components that listen for changes will be notified. "Add to cart" remains independent and doesn't need to know about the other components on the page.

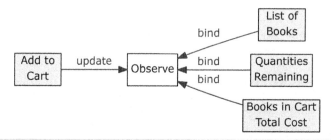

Figure 4—An observe keeps components decoupled

Here's how we create an observe and listen for changes on its attributes:

```
canjs/public/concepts/concepts-test.js
// Create an observe
var observe = new can.Observe({});

// Listen for changes on the "title" attribute
observe.bind("title", function(evt, newTitle, oldTitle) {
  console.log("title: newTitle=", newTitle, "oldTitle=", oldTitle);
});

// Set a value for the "title" attribute
observe.attr("title", "First");
```

```
// the console logs:
// title: newTitle= First oldTitle= undefined

// Set another value for the "title" attribute
observe.attr("title", "Second");
// the console logs:
// title: newTitle= Second oldTitle= First
```

As you can see, attributes are set with the attr method, with the attribute name and value as parameters. Supply only the attribute name to *read* the value, as in observe.attr("title").

You can also listen for changes on *any* attribute by binding to change:

canjs/public/concepts/concepts-test.js
```
observe.bind("change", function(evt, attr, how, newValue, oldValue) {
  console.log("change: attr=", attr, "how=", how,
    "newValue=", newValue, "oldValue=", oldValue);
});
observe.attr("title", "Third");
// change: attr= title how= set newValue= Third oldValue= Second
observe.removeAttr("title");
// change: attr= title how= remove newValue= undefined oldValue= Third
```

Note that if you actually have an attribute called change, you can also listen for changes with bind("change", ...). However, your function gets called for *all* changes, so you would check attr to see if change is the attribute that was changed.

Finally, observe *lists* are similar to observes but are for lists of values. In this case, we can listen for values being added to or removed from the list:

canjs/public/concepts/concepts-test.js
```
var observe = new can.Observe.List([42, 44, 46]);
observe.bind("add", function(evt, newValues, index) {
  console.log("add: newValues=", newValues, "index=", index);
});
observe.bind("remove", function(evt, oldValues, index) {
  console.log("remove: oldValues=", oldValues, "index=", index);
});

observe.push(48);
// add: newValues= [48] index= 3
observe.splice(1, 2);
// remove: oldValues= [44, 46] index= 1
```

We'll see more of how we can make observes work for us throughout the rest of the chapter.

Building a CanJS Bookmarking Application Front End

For the rest of the chapter, we're going to build a single-page JavaScript front end for the bookmark server application that we created in Chapter 1, *Sinatra*, on page 1. We had created a rudimentary user interface with Mustache templates, but now we'll build something snazzier that dynamically refreshes without doing full-page reloads. CanJS is a client-side-only framework that works best with a REST and JSON interface (although a REST/JSON server is not required). As such, it's a perfect match for our Sinatra server. The following screenshot shows what our application will look like when we finish.

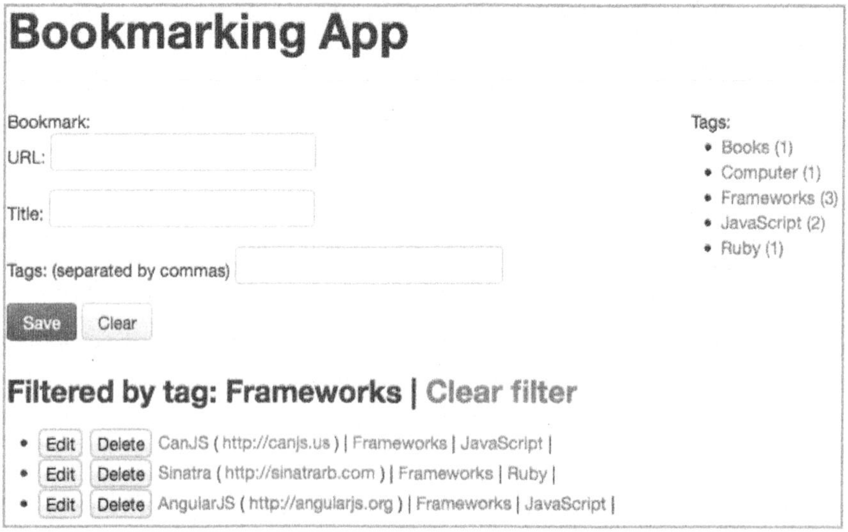

Figure 5—The complete CanJS bookmarking application

We'll begin building the application by creating a model for bookmarks that talks to our server.

Connecting Models to the Server

The first thing we'd like to do is retrieve the list of bookmarks from the server. We also want to think about keeping that data synchronized with the server. We could hook up listeners that send Ajax requests when attributes change and handle server responses to update attributes.

Or we could just use can.Model.

can.Model builds on can.Observe and adds a way to specify how you want your data to be retrieved from and sent to your server. Here is a Bookmark model that talks to our Sinatra bookmark server:

canjs/public/app/base/app.js
```
var Bookmark = can.Model.extend({
  findAll: "GET /bookmarks",
  create: "POST /bookmarks",
  update: "PUT /bookmarks/{id}",
  destroy: "DELETE /bookmarks/{id}",
}, {
});
```

We've defined the API that our server provides for creating, reading, updating, and deleting bookmarks. CanJS automatically converts the findAll, create, update, and destroy properties into functions that issue Ajax requests and handle responses using the strings that we've associated with those properties. The first part of the string is the request method (GET, POST, PUT, DELETE). The second part is the request URI. Any part between {} in the URI is replaced by the object's corresponding attribute. For example, to update an existing Bookmark object, CanJS first calls bookmark.attr("id"), places the value at the {id} part of the URI, and finally issues a PUT request.

Models also handle server responses. For GET requests, CanJS parses the response as JSON and creates model objects with the same attributes. For PUT and POST requests, the model object's attributes are sent to the server in the request body. Any attributes that the server returns are updated on the model object. In particular, in response to a POST request, the server should return the id of the newly created object and any other new or changed attributes. It does not need to return attributes that have not changed. For a DELETE request, the model just checks that the server returned a success response code.

There is one more REST method that CanJS automatically handles in a can.Model object. We haven't defined it here because we won't need it for our bookmarking application. Can you guess what it is?

If you answered findOne, reward yourself with a trip to the refrigerator! Indeed, that method is for getting a *single* model object from the server according to its ID. For our bookmark model, that would be findOne: "GET /bookmarks/{id}".

To use these methods, we can call findAll and findOne as functions on the Bookmark object and receive the bookmarks or single bookmark via a callback function:

canjs/public/app/base/app.js
```
Bookmark.findAll({}, function(bookmarks) {
});

Bookmark.findOne({id:42}, function(bookmark) {
});
```

Notice the first argument to findAll and findOne is an object with any parameters to be sent along with the request. For findOne, we specified the id parameter.

For create and update, a call to save() on a model instance automatically issues a POST or PUT request. The absence of an id attribute on the model instance makes it a *new* object, the presence of an id makes it an *existing* object, and CanJS calls create or update, respectively. Finally, calling destroy() on a model instance issues the DELETE request with the object's id.

For lists of models, can.Model.List is the same as can.Observe.List with one additional feature: can.Model.List automatically removes an object from the list after you call the destroy() function.

We're able to retrieve bookmarks from the server. How do we display them?

Rendering Views

CanJS renders views with Mustache or EJS. We'll be using Mustache. Remember that we looked at the Mustache syntax in *Mustache*, on page 16.

Here is a Mustache template that renders the list of bookmarks, each with an Edit and a Delete button:

```
canjs/public/app/base/bookmark_list.mustache
<ul>
  {{#bookmarks}}
    <li>
      <button class="edit">Edit</button>
      <button class="delete">Delete</button>
       <a href="{{url}}">{{title}}</a>
      ( <a href="{{url}}">{{url}}</a> )
    </li>
  {{/bookmarks}}
</ul>
```

To render the template, call the can.view function with the URI of the template file without the .mustache extension. Notice that the file is located at public/app/base/bookmark_list.mustache. Remember that Sinatra serves files from the public directory. The URI to use for the template is /app/base/bookmark_list.

The other parameter to pass to can.view is the model to use in the template. Putting it all together, we have this:

```
canjs/public/app/base/app-test.js
// a list of bookmarks, as we would receive from the server
var bookmarks = [
  {url:"http://one.com", title:"One"},
  {url:"http://two.com", title:"Two"}
];
```

```
var viewModel = {bookmarks:bookmarks};
var element = $("#target");

// Render view by calling can.view
element.html(can.view("/app/base/bookmark_list", viewModel));

// can.view is implicitly called
element.html("/app/base/bookmark_list", viewModel);
```

Notice that we called can.view and added the result to the page element with jQuery's html function. You can also just call the html function directly with the path to the template and the view model. CanJS implicitly calls can.view for you. This also works for other jQuery methods, such as append, prepend, after, and so on.

Live Binding

When the objects that are passed to the view are observes, CanJS automatically does *live binding* so that an attribute change on the observe updates the view. This also works for *lists* of observes; add or remove an object, and the list view is automatically refreshed. Let's see an example:

canjs/public/app/base/app-test.js
```
// 'bookmarks' is now a list of observes
var bookmarks = new can.Observe.List([
  {url:"http://one.com", title:"One"},
  {url:"http://two.com", title:"Two"}
]);
var viewModel = {bookmarks:bookmarks};
$("#target").html("/app/base/bookmark_list", viewModel);

// The view automatically refreshes to display these changes
bookmarks[0].attr("title", "Uno");
bookmarks.push({url:"http://three.com", title:"Three"});
```

With live binding, you can focus on working with *models* and let CanJS take care of keeping views up-to-date. Because can.Model extends can.Observe, the objects you get back from Ajax calls such as findAll are observes. You can use them directly as view models for your templates and benefit from live binding.

What We Learned on Day 1

Today we looked at some of the key parts of CanJS: can.Construct, can.Observe, can.Model, and can.view. We learned how to create object hierarchies and use inheritance. We discovered that using observes keeps different parts of an application independent from one another. We saw how to create models that synchronize with the server and how to display them with views. One more essential component of CanJS is can.Control, which we'll tackle tomorrow.

We discussed the core tenets of CanJS: keep components separate, and use observes to propagate changes between components and models to synchronize data with the server. Finally, we learned how to take advantage of live binding by using observes in views so that we don't have to do manual refreshes.

Day 1 Self-Study

Find:

- The main CanJS forum (Hint: CanJS is a child of JavaScriptMVC.)
- The CanJS API documentation
- The CanJS implementation of TodoMVC

Do:

- Set up a simple CanJS page with an observe. Change the observe in your browser's JavaScript console and see the view update itself automatically.
- Experiment with CanJS on jsFiddle with the CanJS jQuery Template.[8]

Day 2: Creating Controllers

We now have models and views. When models change, views automatically update. Now how about combining them into components? Also, when the user presses the Edit or Delete button in the list of bookmarks, we want to edit or delete the corresponding bookmark. We need a place for that event-handling code. This is where controllers, or just *controls* as they are called in CanJS, come into the picture. Today we discuss four vital aspects of can.Control:

1. Attaching a control to an element on the page
2. Listening to UI events
3. Using the data() function to retrieve a model from the page
4. Using an observe to communicate between controllers

In doing so, we'll create two controls: one for the bookmark list and one for the form that creates and edits bookmarks. By the end of the day, we'll have a base version of our bookmarking application.

Attaching a Control to an Element on the Page

When creating a control, you pass two parameters to the init function: an element to which the control will attach and an options object containing any additional parameters that you need. Here's an example:

---

8.   http://jsfiddle.net/donejs/qYdwR/

canjs/public/concepts/concepts-test.js

```
var MyControl = can.Control.extend({
  init: function(element, options) {
    var view = "/concepts/bookmarks";

    element.html(view, {bookmarks:options.bookmarks});
  }
});

var bookmarks = []; // this would normally be the real list of bookmarks
var options = {bookmarks:bookmarks};
new MyControl("#bookmark_container", options);
```

Notice that the element is a jQuery selector. In the preceding example, the control attaches to the element on the page that has id="bookmark_container". Even though the parameter is a string, CanJS automatically converts it to the matching jQuery element so that you can call functions on the element in the control's init function, as we are doing here in calling element.html(...).

You can also pass an actual jQuery element instead of a string:

```
var element = $("#bookmark_container");
new MyControl(element, ...);
```

As illustrated in the following figure, the control attaches to the element on the page:

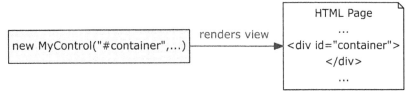

The control renders the view into the element and is *scoped* to that element, which means it only listens to UI events within that element.

In the init function, you typically use the model passed via the options object to render the view into the control's element. In other parts of the control, you can access the element and options using this.element and this.options; CanJS automatically sets these for you.

Listening to UI Events

After creating a control that uses a model to render a view into an element on the page, the next step is to handle UI events: the user pressing a button, clicking on a link, and so on. To do so, define a string property in the control with a function:

```
"selector eventType": function(el, evt) {
  // el is the element on which the event occurred
  // evt is the event object
}
```

This sets up a listener on the elements matched by the jQuery selector for the given event type, like this:

canjs/public/concepts/concepts-test.js
```
var MyControl = can.Control.extend({
  // Listen for click events on buttons
  "button click": function(el, evt) {
    // ...
  },
  // Listen for change events on checkboxes under elements with class="item"
  ".item :checkbox change": function(el, evt) {
    // ...
  }
});
```

Selectors only match *within the control's element*, so you don't have to worry about inadvertently picking up events from elements on other parts of the page.

Using the data() Function to Retrieve a Model from the Page

When listening for a UI event, the handler function receives the element and the event object. For example, the user presses the Edit or Delete button next to a bookmark. What we really need is the bookmark model object. Let's see how we retrieve it.

First, associate the model object with an element on the view using the data Mustache helper, {{data "name"}}. Pick the name that you want, something meaningful concerning the model object. In the bookmark list view, the bookmark model object is associated with the <li> element:

canjs/public/app/base/bookmark_list.mustache
```
<ul>
  {{#bookmarks}}
    <li {{data "bookmark"}}>
      <button class="edit">Edit</button>
      <button class="delete">Delete</button>
      <a href="{{url}}">{{title}}</a>
      ( <a href="{{url}}">{{url}}</a> )
    </li>
  {{/bookmarks}}
</ul>
```

To retrieve the model object, call element.data("name") in the control. The element must be the one that has {{data "name"}}. In the bookmark list, the user clicks on a button, so the element in the event-handling function is actually the <button> element. We can get the parent <li> element using jQuery's closest function, element.closest("li"). Finally, we get the bookmark object with data("bookmark"):

canjs/public/app/base/app.js
```
// retrieve the bookmark object from the <li> parent element
getBookmark: function(el) {
  return el.closest("li").data("bookmark");
},

// handle the click on the delete button, destroy the bookmark
".delete click": function(el, evt) {
  this.getBookmark(el).destroy();
},
```

Using data is a simple and straightforward way of retrieving model objects from the view layer.

Using an Observe to Communicate Between Controllers

To exchange events between controls while keeping them neatly decoupled, use an observe. This is often called a *state* or an *event hub*. As we saw in Figure 4, *An observe keeps components decoupled*, on page 42, the observe acts as the communication bridge between controls so that they need no direct reference to each other.

To trigger an event on the observe, call can.trigger(eventHub, "eventType", data). Let's put this and everything else we've learned into the control for the bookmark list:

canjs/public/app/base/app.js
```
var BookmarkListControl = can.Control.extend({
  view: "/app/base/bookmark_list",

  init: function(element, options) {
    // save a reference to the eventHub observe
    this.eventHub = options.eventHub;
    // render the view on the element with the bookmarks as the model
    var view = options.view || this.view;
    element.html(view, this.getViewModel(options));
  },

  getViewModel: function(options) {
    return {bookmarks:options.bookmarks};
  },
```

```
  // retrieve the bookmark object from the <li> parent element
  getBookmark: function(el) {
    return el.closest("li").data("bookmark");
  },

  // handle the click on the delete button, destroy the bookmark
  ".delete click": function(el, evt) {
    this.getBookmark(el).destroy();
  },

  // handle the click on the edit button, trigger an editBookmark event
  ".edit click": function(el, evt) {
    can.trigger(this.eventHub, "editBookmark", this.getBookmark(el));
  }
});
```

As you can see, we handle the Edit button by triggering an editBookmark event on the event hub object. The bookmark list does not need to know which components are involved in editing a bookmark. Moreover, the components listening to the editBookmark event do not need to know which parts of the application trigger the event.

To use the BookmarkListControl that we've created, we need to pass it the page element on which we want to attach and an options object with the event hub observe and the list of bookmarks:

canjs/public/app/base/app.js
```
var App_base = can.Construct.extend({
  init: function() {
    // Retrieve the bookmarks from the server
    Bookmark.findAll({}, function(bookmarks) {
      // Create the event hub observe
      var eventHub = new can.Observe({});
      // Create the options object with the event hub and the bookmarks
      var options = {eventHub:eventHub, bookmarks:bookmarks};

      // Create the control, attaching it to the element on the page
      // that has id="bookmark_list_container"
      new BookmarkListControl("#bookmark_list_container", options);

      // Create the bookmark form control (which we build in the
      // next section.)
      new BookmarkFormControl("#bookmark_form_container", options);
    });
  }
});
```

We've constructed the app with the bookmark list control. Notice that the code also includes the bookmark form control. We'll discuss how to create the form control in the next section, but for now, use the book's sample code bundle to run the app and try it out. To start the app, we can just call new App_base(). Let's do that within the main HTML page, where we have elements to which the controls attach:

```
canjs/views/index.mustache
<!doctype html>
<html lang="en">
  <head>
    <meta charset="utf-8">
    <title>Bookmarking App</title>
  </head>

  <body>
    <h1>Bookmarking App</h1>
    <hr>
➤   <div id="bookmark_form_container"></div>
➤   <div id="bookmark_list_container"></div>
  </body>

  <script src="/lib/jquery/jquery-1.10.2.js"></script>
  <script src="/lib/canjs.com-1.1.8/can.jquery.js"></script>
  <script src="/lib/canjs.com-1.1.8/can.construct.super.js"></script>
  <script src="/lib/canjs.com-1.1.8/can.observe.validations.js"></script>
  <script src="/lib/canjs.com-1.1.8/can.observe.list.js"></script>
  <script src="/lib/canjs.com-1.1.8/can.view.modifiers.js"></script>
  <script src="/lib/canjs.com-1.1.8/can.mustache.js"></script>
  <script src="/app/base/app.js"></script>
➤ <script>new App_base();</script>
</html>
```

You can run the app by starting the Sinatra server from the canjs directory of the sample code bundle:

```
$ ruby app.rb
```

Open http://localhost:4567 in your browser. The app should look like Figure 6, *A base version of the bookmarking application*, on page 54. Try creating, updating, and deleting bookmarks, and see how the bookmark list automatically refreshes.

Let's continue by having a closer look at how to build the bookmark form control.

Creating a Form Control

To create and update bookmarks, we're using a form with text inputs for the URL and the title. The view template for creating the form is straightforward:

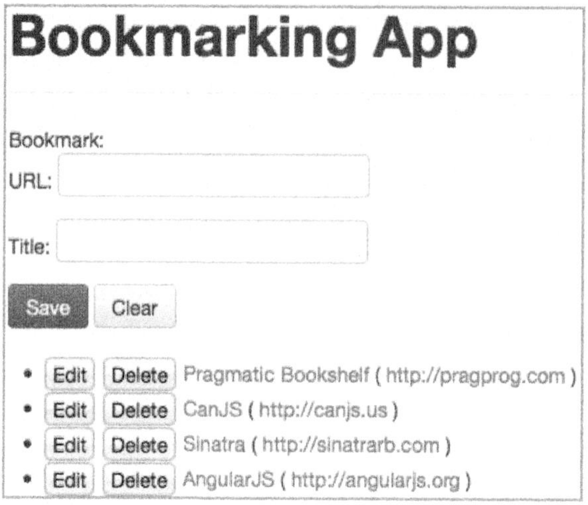

Bookmarking App

Bookmark:

URL:

Title:

Save   Clear

- Edit Delete Pragmatic Bookshelf (http://pragprog.com)
- Edit Delete CanJS (http://canjs.us)
- Edit Delete Sinatra (http://sinatrarb.com)
- Edit Delete AngularJS (http://angularjs.org)

Figure 6—A base version of the bookmarking application

```
canjs/public/app/base/bookmark_form.mustache
Bookmark:
<form action="/bookmarks" method="post">
  <label>
    URL:
❶   <input type="text" name="url" value="{{url}}">
  </label>
  <label>
    Title:
    <input type="text" name="title" value="{{title}}">
  </label>
❷ <button class="save btn btn-primary" {{data "bookmark"}}>Save</button>
  <button class="clear btn">Clear</button>
</form>
```

❶ The form uses a bookmark as its model. The url and title inputs use the bookmark's fields as values, effectively prepopulating the form when editing a bookmark.

❷ The bookmark is associated with the Save button using the data helper. We can readily retrieve the bookmark when we handle the Save button click event.

Let's build the bookmark form control, starting with a blank control that we'll fill out with properties:

```
canjs/public/app/base/app.js
var BookmarkFormControl = can.Control.extend({
  // Add properties here.
});
```

First, we'll use a property to define `Bookmark` as the bookmark model to use so that we can change it in the children of `BookmarkFormControl`. Similarly, we'll have a `view` property for the view template:

canjs/public/app/base/app.js
```
BookmarkModel: Bookmark,
view: "/app/base/bookmark_form",
```

Next, let's add functions to initialize the control and edit a bookmark:

canjs/public/app/base/app.js
```
init: function(element, options) {
  this.BookmarkModel.bind("created", function(evt, bookmark) {
    options.bookmarks.push(bookmark);
  });
  this.clearForm();
},
editBookmark: function(bookmark) {
  var view = this.options.view || this.view;
  this.element.html(view, bookmark);

  bookmark.bind("destroyed", this.clearForm.bind(this));
},
clearForm: function() {
  this.editBookmark(new this.BookmarkModel());
},
"{eventHub} editBookmark": function(eventHub, evt, bookmark) {
  this.editBookmark(bookmark);
},
```

❶ By binding to the `Bookmark` model's "created" event, we get notified when a bookmark is created by the form, at which point we add the bookmark to the bookmark list.

❷ We associate a bookmark object to the form by rendering the view with the bookmark as a model. Then we listen for the bookmark being destroyed, in which case we clear the form. This handles the case where a user edits a bookmark but then decides to delete it instead.

❸ To clear the form, we associate a new, blank bookmark object to the form.

❹ Remember how we triggered an "editBookmark" event from the bookmark list control? This is how we listen for that event in the form control. The {eventHub} syntax listens for events on the `options.eventHub` object. The function receives the object on which the event occurred, the event object, and any data that was sent along with the event. In our case, that data is the bookmark to be edited. We simply use our `editBookmark` function to associate the bookmark with the form.

We'll also add handlers to save the bookmark:

```
canjs/public/app/base/app.js
".save click": function(el, evt) {
  evt.preventDefault();
  var bookmark = el.data("bookmark");
  bookmark.attr(can.deparam(el.closest("form").serialize()));
  this.saveBookmark(bookmark);
},
saveBookmark: function(bookmark) {
  bookmark.save(this.clearForm.bind(this), this.signalError);
},
signalError: function() {
  alert("The input is not valid.");
},
```

❶ When saving the bookmark, we retrieve the bookmark model with the data function. We need to set the attributes from the values that the user entered in the form. We can do that without manually going over every input field on the form by calling serialize on the form object and using can.deparam. This creates an object that we can pass to attr to set the attributes of the model from the form's input values. This works because the name on each input matches the bookmark's attribute.

❷ To save the bookmark, we call the save function with two parameters: a callback for success and another in case of failure. On success, we clear the form, readying it for the next bookmark. On failure, we alert the user.

Finally, handling the clear button simply clears the form:

```
canjs/public/app/base/app.js
".clear click": function(el, evt) {
  evt.preventDefault();
  this.clearForm();
}
```

Adding the bookmark form control to the app works the same way as the bookmark list control—create an element on the page and instantiate the control, passing the element and the same options object:

```
canjs/views/index.mustache
<div id="bookmark_form_container"></div>
```

```
canjs/public/app/base/app.js
new BookmarkFormControl("#bookmark_form_container", options);
```

Congratulations. This completes our first iteration of the bookmark application. Go ahead and experiment with it!

What We Learned on Day 2

Today was all about CanJS controls. We learned how to combine model and view into a control that attaches to a page element. Controls handle UI events in listener functions, which easily retrieve model objects. We can build components that change model attributes and trigger events on observes, keeping with the core principle of building modules that are cleanly independent of each other.

We also built a first iteration of a front end for our bookmarking application. We have a form for creating and editing bookmarks, a model that synchronizes with the server, and a list that updates automatically. Tomorrow we'll learn more ways of working with models by adding features such as validation, tags, and filtering.

Day 2 Self-Study

Find:

- Documentation for *templated event handlers*, which is another way to listen for events in CanJS controls
- An example of using the on() function on can.Control.prototype to rebind event handlers to another model object

Do:

- Experiment with the base application from the book's source code.
- Explain why we need bind(this) in bookmark.bind("destroyed", this.clearForm.bind(this)); in the editBookmark
- function. What happens if we just write bookmark.bind("destroyed", this.clearForm); instead?

Change the rendering of the bookmark list view. For example, use icons for Edit and Delete. How does that change the event handling in the bookmark list control?

Day 3: Working with Models

In our third and final day of learning CanJS, we'll discover more ways of working with observes and models. Remember that they are two of the focal points of a CanJS application. Drive the model and let views update themselves. Trigger events on observes and handle them in controls.

Let's unravel how we can mold models to different requirements by creating filtered lists and by adding helper functions. We'll start with some validation on the bookmark model.

Adding Validation

In our Sinatra web application, each bookmark must have a title and a URL. We also check the URL's format. Server-side validation is nice—and essential—but client-side validation gives the user more immediate feedback and saves unnecessary client-server traffic.

We can add validation to the Bookmark model by calling the validate methods from the init function:

```
canjs/public/app/validation/app.js
// Extend the base Bookmark model
var ValidatingBookmark = Bookmark.extend({
  init: function() {
    var urlPattern = new RegExp(
      "(http|https):\\/\\/(\\w+:{0,1}\\w*@)?(\\S+)(:[0-9]+)?" +
      "(\\/|\\/([\\w#!:.?+=&%@!\\-\\/]))?");
    // Add validations
    this.validatePresenceOf(["url", "title"]);
    this.validateFormatOf("url", urlPattern);
  }
}, {
});
```

This requires the URL and the title using validatePresenceOf. The URL's format is verified with validateFormatOf and a regular expression. Other validate methods include the following:

- validateInclusionOf: Constrains an attribute to an array of valid values

- validateLengthOf: Sets a minimum and/or maximum length of an attribute

- validateRangeOf: Sets a minimum and/or maximum numeric value of an attribute

- validate: Sets a custom validation—you provide a function that accepts the value and attribute name to validate. Then you make the function return null if the value is valid, or an error message otherwise.

With that in place, we can run the validations on a model instance. Calling errors() obtains a key-value object where the key is the attribute name and the value is the error message. Using errors(attrName) instead gets a list of error messages specifically for attrName. In both cases, we'll get nothing if the object is valid.

For the bookmark form control with validation, we'll start by extending the previous control:

```
canjs/public/app/validation/app.js
// Extend the base bookmark form control
var ValidatingBookmarkFormControl = BookmarkFormControl.extend({
  // Add properties here.
});
```

The first thing we'll do is override the bookmark model to use the one with validation:

```
canjs/public/app/validation/app.js
BookmarkModel: ValidatingBookmark,
```

Next, we'll override the editBookmark function:

```
canjs/public/app/validation/app.js
editBookmark: function(bookmark) {
  this._super(bookmark);
  var self = this;
  bookmark.bind("change", function() {
    var errorMessage = bookmark.errors() ?
      can.map(bookmark.errors(), function(message, attrName) {
        return attrName + " " + message + ". ";
      }).join("")
      : "";
    self.element.find(".text-error").html(errorMessage);
  });
},
```

After calling editBookmark on the parent, we listen for attribute changes with the bind function. When a change occurs, we call errors() and build an error message or have it be blank if no errors are found. Then we display the error message on the page in the .text-error element. Finally, we override the saveBookmark function to first check for errors before saving the bookmark:

```
canjs/public/app/validation/app.js
saveBookmark: function(bookmark) {
  if (!bookmark.errors()) {
    this._super(bookmark);
  }
}
```

In the bookmark form template, we add the .text-error element after the last input in the form:

```
canjs/public/app/base/bookmark_form.mustache
<label>
  Title:
  <input type="text" name="title" value="{{title}}">
</label>
➤ <div class="text-error"></div>
```

Now when the URL or title is not valid, an error message appears as shown here:

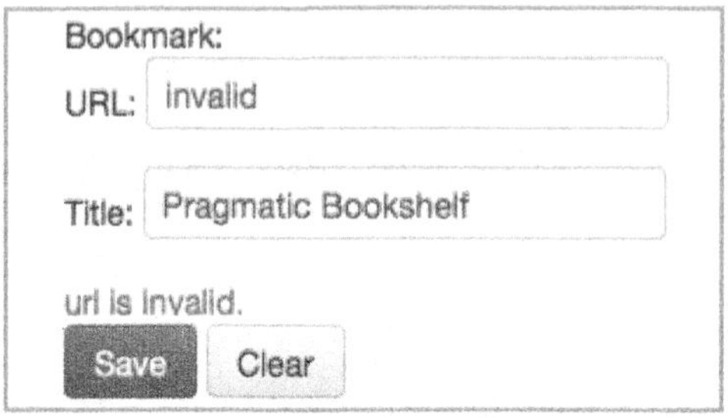

```
Bookmark:
URL:   invalid

Title:  Pragmatic Bookshelf

url is invalid.
  Save     Clear
```

Figure 7—Showing a validation error message

We now have a nicely validated form. Let's continue improving the application. Our Sinatra server handles the association of tags to bookmarks. We'll add an input field for entering tags in the bookmark form.

Implementing Tag Handling

The server returns a tagList attribute on each bookmark with the list of tags. For entering tags, however, a user can just enter tags into a single text box separated by commas. We can create a tagsAsString attribute on the bookmark model and handle the conversion to and from tagList as follows:

```
canjs/public/app/tagfilter/app.js
// Extend the validation bookmark model
var TaggedBookmark = ValidatingBookmark.extend({
  init: function() {
    // Initialize tagsAsString from tagList
    var tagList = this.attr("tagList");
    this.attr("tagsAsString", tagList.join(", "));

    // Listen for changes on tagsAsString and set tagList
    this.bind("tagsAsString", this.onTagsAsStringChange);
  },
  onTagsAsStringChange: function(evt, tagsAsString) {
    // Split the string by comma and trim whitespace
    var trimmed = can.map(tagsAsString.split(","), can.trim);

    // Ignore empty tags, for example if the user entered a,,,b
    var byNotEmpty = function(tag) {
      return tag.length > 0;
    };
    var notEmpty = can.filter(trimmed, byNotEmpty);
    var tagList = this.attr("tagList");
```

```
    // Update the tag list to match the ones entered by the user
    tagList.attr(notEmpty.sort(), true);
  }
});
```

We've added a new attribute to the bookmark model, tagsAsString. It is initialized at instantiation time from the value of tagList. By binding an event handler, we set the value of tagList when tagsAsString changes.

Now we can add a text input to our bookmark form template and bind the input to the tagsAsString attribute:

canjs/public/app/tagfilter/bookmark_form.mustache
```
<label>
  Title:
  <input type="text" name="title" value="{{title}}">
</label>
<label>
  Tags: (separated by commas)
  <input type="text" name="tagsAsString" value="{{tagsAsString}}">
</label>
```

Because our bookmark form control binds all form inputs to corresponding model attributes, we don't have to do anything else to save the tags. Remember that we used attr, can.deparam, and serialize to perform the binding of values from the form to the bookmark:

```
bookmark.attr(can.deparam(el.closest("form").serialize()));
```

Displaying the tags in the bookmark list is easy too:

canjs/public/app/tagfilter/bookmark_list.mustache
```
<ul>
  {{#bookmarks}}
    <li {{data "bookmark"}}>
      <button class="edit">Edit</button>
      <button class="delete">Delete</button>
      <a href="{{url}}">{{title}}</a>
      ( <a href="{{url}}">{{url}}</a> ) |
    {{#tagList}}
      <a class="tag" href="#" {{data "tag"}}>{{this}}</a> |
    {{/tagList}}
    </li>
  {{/bookmarks}}
</ul>
```

Next to each bookmark, a simple iteration shows a list of tags. All these tags are clickable, and the links have a reference to the associated tag with {{data "tag"}}. A nice feature would be to filter the bookmark list when a user clicks on a tag. Let's do it!

Filtering Bookmarks

CanJS makes filtering a breeze with the filter function that it adds to can.Observe.List, available by loading can/observe/list.js. By calling filter and passing a function that returns true or false to determine which bookmarks to keep, we get back a filtered bookmark list that we can then pass to our bookmark list control.

First, we create a filter object, which is an observe with a filter tag and a filter function:

canjs/public/app/tagfilter/app.js

```
var filterObject = new can.Observe({
  filterTag: "" // the filter tag is initially blank
});
var filterFunction = function(bookmark) {
  var tagList = bookmark.attr("tagList");
  var filterTag = filterObject.attr("filterTag");
  var noFilter = (!filterTag) || (filterTag.length == 0);
  var tagListContainsFilterTag = tagList && tagList.indexOf(filterTag) > -1;
  return noFilter || tagListContainsFilterTag;
};
```

The filter function returns true or false to indicate whether the bookmark should be included in the list given the current filter tag. The function returns true if there is no filter tag or if the bookmark's tag list includes the filter tag.

Next, we can create a filtered bookmark list by calling filter and passing it our filter function. We then pass the filtered list to the bookmark list control:

canjs/public/app/tagfilter/app.js

```
TaggedBookmark.findAll({}, function(bookmarks) {
  var eventHub = new can.Observe({});
  // Pass filterObject to the controls
  var options = {eventHub:eventHub, bookmarks:bookmarks,
    filterObject:filterObject};

  // Create the filtered bookmark list
  var filtered = bookmarks.filter(filterFunction);

  // Create an options object with the filtered bookmark list
  var filteredOptions = can.extend({}, options, {bookmarks:filtered});
  // ...
  // Create the bookmark list control with the filtered bookmark list
  new TagFilterBookmarkListControl("#bookmark_list_container", filteredOptions);
  // ...
});
```

Finally, we can filter the bookmark list when a user clicks on a tag. All we have to do is extend the bookmark list control, overriding the view so that we display the tag list with the links and adding a listener that responds to clicks on the links. The listener retrieves the tag and sets the filter on the filter object:

```
canjs/public/app/tagfilter/app.js
var TagFilterBookmarkListControl = BookmarkListControl.extend({
  // Use the bookmark list view with the tag links
  view: "/app/tagfilter/bookmark_list",
  // Listen for clicks on tag links, set filterTag on filterObject
  "a.tag click": function(el, evt) {
    var tag = String(el.data("tag"));
    this.options.filterObject.attr("filterTag", tag);
  }
});
```

Notice how again, because we are using an observe as the filter object, the code remains neatly decoupled. As depicted in the following diagram, the control only needs to set the filter tag on the filter object. The control does not need any reference to the bookmark list, nor do we need to do any manual refreshing of the view. The bookmark list automatically updates to the new filter.

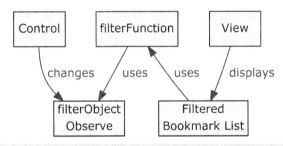

Figure 8—Using an observe to filter the bookmark list

We can now add a tag filter control to display the current filter and a link to clear it and show all bookmarks. The control displays the view with the filter object as a view model and resets the filter tag when the user clicks on the clear link:

```
canjs/public/app/tagfilter/app.js
var TagFilterControl = can.Control.extend({
  defaults: {
    view: "/app/tagfilter/tag_filter"
  }
}, {
  init: function(element, options) {
```

```
      this.element.html(options.view, options.filterObject);
    },
    "a.clear click": function(el, evt) {
      this.options.filterObject.attr("filterTag", "");
    }
});
```

Again, the control only has a reference to the filter object and only needs to reset the filterTag attribute to clear the filter. Depending on the current filter, the view displays either "Filtered by tag," with a link to clear the filter, or "All bookmarks":

canjs/public/app/tagfilter/tag_filter.mustache
```
<h3>
{{#if filterTag}}
  Filtered by tag: {{filterTag}}
  | <a class="clear" href="#">Clear filter</a>
{{else}}
  All bookmarks
{{/if}}
</h3>
```

We add an element on the page where we want to display the filter control:

canjs/views/index.mustache
```
<div id="bookmark_form_container"></div>
<div id="filter_container"></div>
<div id="bookmark_list_container"></div>
          <!-- ... -->
```

Finally, we add the filter control to the app by instantiating the control and associating it to the element that we added on the page:

canjs/public/app/tagfilter/app.js
```
TaggedBookmark.findAll({}, function(bookmarks) {
  var eventHub = new can.Observe({});
  // Pass filterObject to the controls
  var options = {eventHub:eventHub, bookmarks:bookmarks,
    filterObject:filterObject};
  // ...
  new TagFilterControl("#filter_container", options);
});
```

Voilà! That was easy. As you can see, controls give us a nice way of organizing functionality into self-contained, narrowly focused modules. We have bookmarks where each has its own list of associated tags. We've seen how we can create a filtered list by tag. From the original bookmark list, we can also create another list: the list of unique tags, each with the number of bookmarks that are associated with the tag.

Creating a Tag List

We've learned how to create a filtered list of bookmarks using the filter function. We can also extend can.Model.List to synthesize the data in the list. What we'll do is go through the bookmark list and construct a list of unique tags with the number of bookmarks for each tag. We'll use this data to display the tag list shown on the right side of the page in Figure 5, *The complete CanJS bookmarking application*, on page 44.

To build the list of tags, we iterate over the bookmarks and keep track of tags with bookmark counts. Then we sort the tags before returning the tag list:

```
canjs/public/app/tagfilter/app.js
var TaggedBookmark = ValidatingBookmark.extend({
  // ...
});
TaggedBookmark.List = ValidatingBookmark.List.extend({
  // Returns a list of tags, each with label and bookmarkCount
  tags: function() {
    // Keep track of how many bookmarks per tag
    var bookmarkCounts = {};

    // Loop through each bookmark in the list
    this.each(function(bookmark) {
      var tagList = bookmark.attr("tagList");

      if (tagList) {
        // Loop through each tag associated to the bookmark
        tagList.each(function(tag) {
          var existing = bookmarkCounts[tag];
          // Either increase the existing count, or initialize to 1
          bookmarkCounts[tag] = existing ? existing + 1 : 1;
        });
      }
    });

    // The keys in bookmarkCounts are the tag labels
    var labels = Object.keys(bookmarkCounts);

    // Sort the tag labels
    labels.sort();

    // Return a list of tags with label and bookmark count
    return can.map(labels, function(label) {
      return {label:label, bookmarkCount:bookmarkCounts[label]};
    });
  }
});
```

What we've effectively done here is add a tags attribute to the bookmark *list* instead of to each individual bookmark. This makes the tag list view very simple: iterate over the tags attribute of the bookmark list object, displaying each tag with its label and bookmark count:

```
canjs/public/app/tagfilter/tag_list.mustache
Tags:
<ul>
  <!-- Use the dot notation to get the tags attribute -->
  {{#bookmarks.tags}}
    <li>
      <a class="tag" href="#" {{data "tag"}}
      >{{label}} ({{bookmarkCount}})</a>
    </li>
  {{/bookmarks.tags}}
</ul>
```

The tag list control simply displays the view and responds to link clicks, setting the tag filter on the filter object:

```
canjs/public/app/tagfilter/app.js
var TagListControl = can.Control.extend({
  defaults: {
    view: "/app/tagfilter/tag_list"
  }
}, {
  init: function(element, options) {
    this.eventHub = options.eventHub;
    var model = {bookmarks:options.bookmarks};
    element.html(options.view, model);
  },
  "a.tag click": function(el, evt) {
    var tag = el.data("tag");
    this.options.filterObject.attr("filterTag", tag.label);
  }
});
```

Gathering the list of unique tags from all the bookmarks, each tag indicates how many bookmarks have the tag. Thanks to live binding, the tag list and the bookmark counts automatically update when a bookmark's tags are changed, when a bookmark is created, or when one is deleted. Try it out!

Managing the Browser's Location with Routing

When a user clicks on a tag link, the bookmark list filters by that tag. Clicking on another tag link filters it again. What happens if a user clicks the browser's Back button? It would be nice if we showed the previously filtered bookmark list. Let's make it happen.

can.route

can.route is a special can.Observe that is associated with the browser's hash—that is, the part at the end of the URL starting with #. When you set an attribute on can.route, the hash is modified. Conversely, when the hash is changed, the attributes of can.route are updated:

```
canjs/public/concepts/concepts-test.js
location.hash = "#!action=filter"
can.route.attr("action"); // returns "filter"
can.route.attr("tag", "Frameworks");
location.hash; // returns "#!&action=filter&tag=Frameworks"
```

By being able to listen for changes on the browser's hash, we can make single-page JavaScript applications that handle the use of the browser's Back and Forward buttons without reloading the whole page. We can even make pages of the application bookmarkable!

Since can.route is an observe, controls can listen to changes and react appropriately. To listen to can.route, use the special string "<pattern> route" syntax as the event handling string, and use a function that receives a single parameter. The <pattern> is a URI pattern much like those we used in Sinatra, like filter/:tag:

```
canjs/public/app/routing/app.js
var RoutingControl = can.Control.extend({
  "filter/:tag route": function(data) {
    this.options.filterObject.attr("filterTag", data.tag);
  }
});
```

This handles hash values such as #!filter/Frameworks and filters the bookmark list by the given tag, Frameworks. The event handling function receives a single object that contains attributes matching the variable parts of the URI pattern—those that start with :.

Notice that we also get nicer-looking URIs: #!filter/Frameworks instead of #!action=filter&tag=Frameworks.

Two more important details about routes:

- To handle an empty hash (#, #!, or no hash at all), just use route, with no URI pattern, in the control.

- To force a hash change event when the app starts, trigger a hashchange event in the control's init function. This effectively handles browser bookmarks or entering a URL in the browser's location bar.

With that in mind, here is the routing control:

```
canjs/public/app/routing/app.js
var RoutingControl = can.Control.extend({
  init: function() {
    $(window).trigger("hashchange");
  },
  "route": function() {
    this.options.filterObject.attr("filterTag", "");
  },
  "filter/:tag route": function(data) {
    this.options.filterObject.attr("filterTag", data.tag);
  }
});
```

We pass the same options object as we've been passing to other controls;
namely, it contains the filterObject. For the control's element, we don't need a
particular element on the page. We simply use document.body:

```
canjs/public/app/routing/app.js
new RoutingControl(document.body, options);
```

Now going to a URI such as #!filter/Frameworks filters the bookmark list by the
Frameworks tag. We can take advantage of this by having links that point to
hashes instead of handling clicks in the controls. For example, here are the
links in the tag list:

```
canjs/public/app/routing/tag_list.mustache
Tags:
<ul>
  {{#bookmarks.tags}}
    <li>
      <a href="#!filter/{{label}}">{{label}} ({{bookmarkCount}})</a>
    </li>
  {{/bookmarks.tags}}
</ul>
```

The tag list control no longer needs the a.tag click function at all. The links
cause a hash change that is handled by RoutingControl.

A link pointing to #! clears the filter:

```
canjs/public/app/routing/tag_filter.mustache
<h3>
{{#if filterTag}}
  Filtered by tag: {{filterTag}}
  | <a href="#!">Clear filter</a>
{{else}}
  All bookmarks
{{/if}}
</h3>
```

We're using a different approach to trigger filtering when the user clicks on a tag. Instead of having controllers listen for the click and trigger the filter, we're just changing the hash and letting the routing controller handle the event.

Another nice routing feature is that a user can *bookmark* a page. For example, a user might often look at the bookmark list filtered by a particular tag and want to bookmark that to go directly to the filtered list.

What We Learned on Day 3

Today we explored more ways of using CanJS observes and models: we added validation, tag lists, and filtering. Most importantly, we learned how we can extend models and add functionality that controls and views can use. In keeping with the "Update the observe and let everything else refresh" tenet, we built a filter object that any component can change. The filtered bookmark list automatically updates.

Finally, we learned a different way of triggering events using can.route. This gives us the possibility of managing browser navigation, bookmarks, and manually entered URLs within a single-page CanJS application.

Day 3 Self-Study

Find:

- The list of additional CanJS utilities and plugins that you can use in your projects

- EJS, the other templating engine supported by CanJS—contrast with Mustache.

- can.compute and how it can bring live binding to computed values

Do:

- Explain why the true flag is needed in tagList.attr(notEmpty.sort(), true); when updating the tag list to match the ones entered by the user. What happens if you omit the flag?

- Add a sort function on the bookmark list so that you always display a sorted list of bookmarks.

- Finish modifying the routing version of the bookmarking application by changing the bookmark list view to use links with hashes.

- Redo one of the views to use EJS.

- Implement *two-way* live binding between views and models. That is, when you enter a value in a form input field, the corresponding attribute on the model automatically gets set to the new value.

An Interview with Justin B. Meyer, Creator of CanJS

Us: What made you decide to create CanJS?

Justin: In 2006, Brian Moschel and I set out to build a service-as-a-service platform. With a GUI, developers could create a rest service layer and build the UI with JavaScript. To power it, we built the first version of JavaScriptMVC, which might have been the first framework with dependency loading, event delegation, declarative event binding, RESTful models, and templates. At that point, our company changed direction and we became a full-time JavaScript consulting company—Bitovi.

CanJS is derived from JavaScriptMVC. We released CanJS because JavaScriptMVC's size was a barrier for entry to CanJS's greatness. So we focused on creating a small, tight core with only the essential features.

Us: What do you feel are the best features of CanJS? What makes CanJS unique?

Justin: I'll answer these together because there's so much overlap between what sets CanJS apart and what are the best features of CanJS.

CanJS is the best of the Backbone and Ember worlds and largely is better at both. Like Backbone, it's small and relatively unassuming with regard to the structure of your application. But CanJS contains the modern features of Ember, like live binding and computed values. Yet CanJS's live binding is faster, its Mustache implementation more accurate, and its computed values implementation prettier.

For example, Ember makes you write which properties you are binding to:

```
var fullName = Ember.computed(function() {
  return this.get('first') + " " + this.get('last');
}).property('first', 'last');
```

While you can just write them like this with CanJS:

```
var fullName = can.compute(function() {
  return me.attr('first') + " " + me.attr('last');
});
```

But CanJS's can-do-it-ness doesn't stop there. The framework puts a special emphasis on preventing memory leaks by providing templated event handlers and a reference counting model store. It works directly with jQuery, Zepto, MooTools, YUI, and Dojo, allowing you to use a can.Control to bind to widgets made with these libraries. And CanJS provides a large collection of first-party plugins.

Us: What do you have in mind for the future of CanJS?

Justin: One of CanJS's great strengths is that Bitovi is fully committed to it as a technology. Someone using JavaScriptMVC 1.0 five years ago has an upgrade path *to all the great modern features in today's CanJS. CanJS will always be adapting, improving, and adding new features.*

There are currently four initiatives underway for CanJS, three of which I can talk about.

First, libraries like AngularJS and Knockout have made HTML-centric development popular again. Although this approach has some disadvantages—for example it's harder to weave in multiple behaviors on one element—using controls produced like Web Components is conceptually easier. For 1.2, we're looking to add can.Component. It will unify a custom element tag, a can.Control, a template, and a can.Observe.

Second, we've been working on a super-model plugin. For many CRUD situations, it will provide drop-in client-side caching, live updating, and instantaneous writes.[9]

Third, we're completely overhauling CanJS's website and documentation. We're aiming to have the best documentation of any major JS framework.

Wrapping Up

We have seen how CanJS offers a really nice way of structuring a JavaScript application into models, views, and controllers. Models are not just data containers; they drive the application by signaling changes to other parts of the application and by synchronizing with the server. Views, with the simplicity of the Mustache syntax, are easy to read, and they automatically update themselves to reflect model changes. Controllers combine models and views into components that handle UI events.

CanJS's Strengths

CanJS gives an excellent balance of functionality and transparency. That is, you get great features without sacrificing clarity: your code remains straightforward JavaScript, with no black magic going on.

The library is lightweight without sacrificing features. You get support for exchanging data with the server via Ajax, model-view live binding, controls with scoped UI event handling, and several plugins for many other useful functionalities.

Finally, CanJS is modular: it's not an all-or-nothing proposition. The core contains functionality that most applications need, and the rest is separated into add-ons that you can include as needed.

---

9. http://bitovi.com/blog/2013/03/weekly-widget-instantaneous-web-apps.html

CanJS's Weaknesses

The decision to keep CanJS straightforward and transparent means that you may end up having to write more code than with other frameworks that rely more heavily on conventions and task automation. Whether this is undesirable is a matter of taste; some developers want to get things done with the least amount of code possible, while others prefer not to use a framework that does *too much.*

Final Thoughts

It's a fantastic time to be a JavaScript developer. There is no shortage of exciting frameworks, and CanJS is a solid contender. Development is very active, with new releases coming out frequently. The community is friendly and helpful, and newcomers often say that after learning CanJS, it becomes their framework of choice.

CHAPTER 3

AngularJS

Do you remember the game Simon Says? The person leading the game says, "Simon says jump up and down," and all the players have to jump up and down. However, if the leader says to do something without prefixing with "Simon says," players have to refrain from doing the action. What makes the game fun for everyone is that the focus is on either following the instructions or not moving, rather than on the physical ability of doing the prescribed action. *How* you perform an action does not matter; *what* you do (move or stay still) is what keeps you in the game or gets you eliminated.

AngularJS is like a game of Simon Says.[1] As the instructor, you describe *what* to do without needing to know the details about *how* the actions are performed. As such, AngularJS applications are developed in a *declarative* manner. CanJS, the framework we discussed in the previous chapter, was an example of a more *imperative* approach, which tends to be more explicit about how the program works. Which approach is better? Just as in the Vim versus Emacs debate,[2] that's for you to decide. The best tools in the universe are those that make *you* the most productive.

The Big Picture

AngularJS is a model-view-controller, client-side JavaScript framework that works especially well with a server that offers a REST/JSON interface. Dependency injection, HTML directives, and two-way binding are just some of the features that make AngularJS compelling.

---

1. http://angularjs.org
2. http://en.wikipedia.org/wiki/Editor_war

AngularJS is a framework of many moving parts. Before diving into the details, let's look at the big picture. The following diagram illustrates the features that we'll discover on our AngularJS adventure:

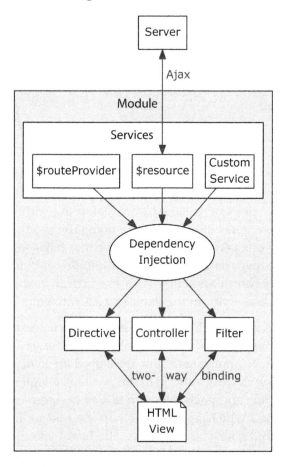

Figure 9—Overview of some AngularJS concepts

In AngularJS, a *module* is the starting point of your application. Encompassed within a module are components, such as services, controllers, directives, filters, and others.

AngularJS features *dependency injection*, which automatically wires up blocks of code, or *services*. You can define services and give them names and then use these names to indicate dependencies. AngularJS takes care of connecting services together. This gives you a nice way of keeping your code loosely coupled.

AngularJS also provides several services out of the box. A *resource* is a built-in service that synchronizes models with the server. A *route provider* lets you define URIs for navigating within your application without refreshing the whole page.

Controllers prepare the model for the view and make callback functions available for the view to call. You write controllers to provide the connections between the model and the view. Controllers are also the place where you handle view events.

Directives are special attributes on HTML elements to manipulate the DOM and render dynamic values. AngularJS has many built-in directives, and you can also write your own. The same goes for *filters*, which are functions that directives can use to filter data within a view.

Two-way live binding is another nifty AngularJS feature that automatically refreshes views when models change. Conversely, changes in the view also automatically update the model.

Day 1 will be dedicated to dependency injection, services, resources, and automated tests. On Day 2, we'll cover controllers, views, directives, and two-way live binding. Day 3 wraps up the chapter with data manipulation using filters and browser navigation support with AngularJS's route provider.

We have many exciting features to explore, so let's get started.

Day 1: Using Dependency Injection

Today we begin learning about AngularJS by looking at dependency injection and services. After discussing those foundations, we'll jump right into building a sample application. We'll define resources that talk to the server and even write automated tests that exercise our code. We've got a big day ahead of us!

One of the most distinguishing features of AngularJS is its dependency injection container. Without it, direct function calls between components tie them together for life. Instead, you define services and indicate what other services are needed by each service, keeping a clean separation of concerns.

Dependency injection goes a long way in keeping your code modular and testable. Each service is a block of code—a *module*, if you will—that indicates its dependencies but is blissfully unaware of how those dependencies are created. They are just passed in to the service as function arguments. A service fills a role for a client, and the client doesn't care which service does the work so long as the role is filled.

That is also tremendously helpful in making the code testable. When you are testing a service, you want to test *its* capabilities, not those of its dependencies. To take the dependencies out of the equation and focus only on the service being tested, you can pass mock objects that just act as you need them to for the purposes of the test. As far as the service is concerned, a test is just another one of the service's clients.

Let's have a quick look at what all this means in terms of code. Say you have a service, MyService, that needs another service, MyHelper, and calls the helper's doSomething function. In the following code, MyService takes care of creating an instance of MyHelper:

angularjs/public/concepts/concepts-test.js

```
var MyService = function() {
  var myHelper = new MyHelper();
  var result = myHelper.doSomething("test");
  // ...
};
```

The problem with this code is that it's not easily testable. The MyService function uses an instance of the *real* MyHelper class, along with everything that MyHelper might bring along. That makes it hard to write a test that focuses solely on what MyService is supposed to accomplish.

Using dependency injection, MyService is no longer responsible for creating an instance of MyHelper. Instead, the instance of MyHelper is passed in as an argument to the MyService function:

angularjs/public/concepts/concepts-test.js

```
var MyService = function(myHelper) {
  var result = myHelper.doSomething("test");
  // ...
};
```

That makes MyService simpler and much easier to test. We can create a separate instance of MyHelper that responds to doSomething in whatever way we need for the purposes of the test and then pass it to the MyService function. In the application code, an instance of the real MyHelper class would be passed to MyService. AngularJS takes care of that with dependency injection.

Now that we've seen how dependency injection makes code more modular and testable, let's turn it up a notch and create an AngularJS application. We'll get a sneak preview of how the different pieces of an AngularJS application fit together.

Hello, AngularJS

Dependency injection and two-way live binding are essential to any AngularJS application. Let's set up a basic example to see it all in action. By all means, go ahead and use this application as a starting point to experiment with your own code.

Open the angularjs/public folder from the sample code bundle. You will find a file named index-basic.js that contains the following JavaScript code:

```
angularjs/public/index-basic.js
① var app = angular.module("BasicApp", []);

② app.service("greeter", function() {
     this.name = "";
     this.greeting = function() {
       return (this.name) ? ("Hello, " + this.name + "!") : "";
     };
   });

③ app.controller("BasicController", function($scope, greeter) {
     $scope.greeter = greeter;
   });
```

Let's break it down piece by piece.

❶ The call to angular.module creates your AngularJS application. You choose a name, such as BasicApp in this example, and indicate the list of required plugins or just an empty list, [].

❷ Next, you call functions on the returned value (the variable called app here) to define services, controllers, and so on. We've defined a service named greeter that has a name property and a greeting function that returns a greeting based on the name.

❸ Finally, we have a controller named BasicController that needs the $scope and our greeter service. The $scope is provided by AngularJS to make objects available to the view. In general, AngularJS-provided objects have the $ prefix to differentiate them from your own code. Now we've defined a greeter property on the scope to be our greeter service. This gives the view access to greeter.

Next, let's look at the view. Open the file named index-basic.html. It contains the following HTML code:

```
angularjs/public/index-basic.html
   <!doctype html>
① <html lang="en" ng-app="BasicApp">
     <head>
```

```
      <meta charset="utf-8">
      <title>AngularJS Basic</title>
    </head>
❷  <body ng-controller="BasicController">
      <div>
        What is your name?
❸        <input type="text" ng-model="greeter.name">
      </div>
      <div>
❹        {{greeter.greeting()}}
      </div>
    </body>
❺  <script src="lib/angularjs/1.0.8/angular.js"></script>
    <script src="index-basic.js"></script>
  </html>
```

It looks a lot like plain HTML. What makes this an AngularJS view are the attributes that start with ng- and the code between the double braces, {{ }}. Let's look at each piece in more detail:

❶ The ng-app attribute on the <html> element page starts up the application. Notice that the value of the attribute matches the name that we gave our application, BasicApp, when we called the angular.module function in the JavaScript code.

❷ Next, we use the ng-controller attribute on the element of the page where we want to use a controller, BasicController in this case. A page can have multiple controllers; we don't have to worry about conflicts between two controllers because each one is confined to the corresponding element with the ng-controller attribute and the element's children.

❸ Within the controller's element and the element's children, we can use the properties that the controller associated with the $scope. In our case, that is greeter. First, we have a text input that is bound to greeter.name using the ng-model attribute.

❹ Second, we have an output displaying the result of calling greeter.greeting() using the {{ }} syntax. Although this looks like the Mustache or Handlebars syntax, it is actually parsed by AngularJS's own template engine.

❺ Finally, the page loads the angular.js script as well as the script for our code, index-basic.js.

Open the index-basic.html file in your browser. You should see the "What is your name?" message with a text box. After typing a name, you should see the greeting appear, as shown here:

Notice how the greeting changes *as you type* in the text box. That is Angular-JS's live binding at work.

Although the example is simple, we accomplished several interesting Angular-JS tasks. We defined a service, used dependency injection, created a controller, used directives in a view, and took advantage of two-way live binding. That is pretty good for a first application. Now that we've seen a quick overview of how these pieces work together, let's discuss each concept in more detail. We'll start with services.

Creating Services

In an AngularJS application, *services* are blocks of code that provide functionality to various parts of the application: controllers, filters, other services, and so on. With dependency injection, AngularJS takes care of wiring services together. Services and dependency injection are an awesome combination, because writing your code in services keeps your application modular and dependency injection saves you from having to write boilerplate code that instantiates and connects services.

Once you've defined a module, use the service function to create a service. Indicate the service name and function that contains the service. If the service needs other services, specify parameters to the function with names that match the names of the required services. Here's an example:

```
angularjs/public/concepts/concepts-test.js
var app = angular.module("TestApp", []);
app.service("serviceA", function() {
  this.name = "A";
});
app.service("serviceB", function() {
  this.name = "B";
});
app.service("serviceC", function(serviceA, serviceB) {
  serviceA.name; // returns "A"
  serviceB.name; // returns "B"
});
```

When creating serviceC, serviceA and serviceB get injected because the parameter names of the function match the names of the services.

Using String Names Instead of Parameter Names

Matching parameter names to service names is concise. That strategy also lets you add, remove, or reorder parameters without worrying about keeping another part of the code in sync. It is the easiest way to specify dependencies; in fact, we'll use this method in our sample code.

However, relying on argument names can break when you minify your code. Indeed, code minification may involve changing argument names to shorten them and reduce code size. To address this issue, AngularJS offers another strategy: specifying service names with strings. This solves the code minification problem because strings remain intact.

The first way of indicating services by string names is to define an $inject property on the service function, with an array of strings indicating the service names to inject:

```
angularjs/public/concepts/concepts-test.js
app.service("serviceA", function() {
  this.name = "A";
});
app.service("serviceB", function() {
  this.name = "B";
});
➤ var svcC = function(svcA, svcB) {
  svcA.name; // returns "A"
  svcB.name; // returns "B"
};
➤ svcC.$inject = ["serviceA", "serviceB"];
app.service("serviceC", svcC);
```

When defining svcC, the parameter names svcA and svcB do not match the service names, serviceA and serviceB. The mismatch could be the result of minification or simply your own choice of variable names. When creating the $inject property, we've indicated the dependencies to inject by their names. The order of the service names must match the order of the function's parameters because that is how they will be matched up.

You can now change the function's parameter names without breaking dependency injection. On the other hand, you need to take care of keeping the $inject string array synchronized with the service names to inject and make sure they match the *order* and *number* of parameters defined in the function.

From the previous code example, you can see how using $inject forces you to create a service in three steps instead of one: associate the function to a variable, define $inject on that variable, and call the service function to create the service.

Using String Names More Concisely

The second way of indicating injected dependencies by string names eliminates the need to use a temporary variable and adding the $inject property. Instead, you can once again define a service in a single step. When calling the service function, specify the service name followed by an *array* instead of a function. In this array, indicate dependencies using strings followed by the service function:

```
angularjs/public/concepts/concepts-test.js
app.service("serviceA", function() {
  this.name = "A";
});
app.service("serviceB", function() {
  this.name = "B";
});
app.service("serviceC", ["serviceA", "serviceB", function(svcA, svcB) {
  svcA.name; // returns "A"
  svcB.name; // returns "B"
}]);
```

That was more concise than the $inject strategy while still being resistant to code minification changes. You still need to match the service name order to the function parameter order; however, maintenance is easier with this method because the service names and function parameters are close to each other in the code.

Using the service function is actually just one way of creating a service. The factory function is another way. Let's see the difference between the two and how you choose one or the other.

Using Service and Factory

When we use service, we assign properties to this within our service function. AngularJS then creates the service by using new on the function that we wrote. This works well when our service is an object. The factory function also creates a service, but it directly uses the result that we return instead of calling new. Use factory when you want your service to be a function or be the result of calling another function instead of an object that will be created with new and on which you add properties with this.

Let's look at a simple example. If we wanted a service to be a function, we'd define it with factory:

```
angularjs/public/concepts/concepts-test.js
app.factory("deleteBookmark", function() {
  return function(bookmark) {
    // delete the bookmark...
  };
});
```

To use the deleteBookmark service, we'd simply inject it into another service and call it directly as a function:

```
angularjs/public/concepts/concepts-test.js
app.service("someService", function(deleteBookmark) {
  var bookmark = ...;
  deleteBookmark(bookmark);
});
```

The service and factory functions offer two convenient ways of creating services. We'll be using both in our code examples.

Now let's shift gears again and start building the application that we'll grow over the rest of the chapter.

Our Bookmarking Application Front End from Another Angle

Using services, dependency injection, and other AngularJS features, we'll create the bookmark application front end shown in the following screenshot. The application connects to the bookmark server from Chapter 1, *Sinatra*, on page 1, and is very similar to the application we created in Chapter 2, *CanJS*, on page 35. Again, we'll exchange data from the server, taking care of rendering the view and handling user interaction. We're building the same application with AngularJS as we did with CanJS so that you can easily compare these two JavaScript frameworks.

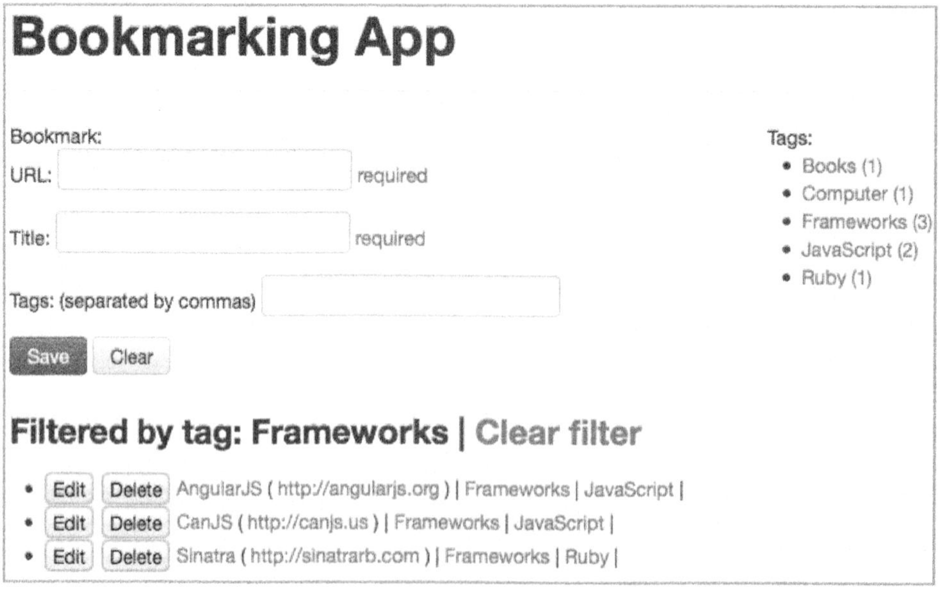

Figure 10—The complete AngularJS bookmarking application

We'll begin by retrieving the bookmark list from the server. Using the Angu-larJS resource service, we'll automate the handling of Ajax requests and responses to exchange data with the server. This is very handy, as it greatly reduces the amount of code that we have to write to connect our client to the server. We'll also create services to save and delete a bookmark. We'll end the day by writing automated tests that verify the behavior of our code.

Using the Resource Service

When we need a way to exchange data between client and server, Ajax is the norm. With AngularJS's resource service, we don't have to bother with low-level Ajax requests and responses. We can just define a resource with a URI. When paired with a REST API such as the one provided by our Sinatra bookmark server, we can let AngularJS handle the data exchanges.

To use the resource service, the first thing we need to do is load the corre-sponding JavaScript file. This is because the service is not part of the AngularJS core:

```
angularjs/views/index.mustache
<script src="/lib/angularjs/1.0.8/angular.js"></script>
<script src="/lib/angularjs/1.0.8/angular-resource.js"></script>
```

Next, we need to specify ngResource as a dependency when we create our application module:

```
angularjs/public/app/base/app.js
angular.module("App_base", ["ngResource"])
```

Armed with the factory function and dependency injection, we can define a service named Bookmark that creates, reads, updates, and deletes bookmarks between the client and the server:

```
angularjs/public/app/base/app.js
app.factory("Bookmark", function($resource) {
  return $resource("/bookmarks/:id", {id:"@id"});
});
```

We're using $resource, which is the resource service provided by AngularJS. Remember that the AngularJS API generally uses the $ prefix to easily distin-guish framework code from application code.

The first parameter to $resource is the URI. Notice that we can use parameters in the URI, prefixed with :, just as we did with Sinatra and CanJS. In our case, the URI has an :id parameter.

To specify a value, we include an object with an id attribute when we call a resource function. Here's our example:

```
var bookmark = Bookmark.get({id:42}); // GET /bookmarks/42
bookmark.title = "changed";
bookmark.$save({id:bookmark.id});   // POST   /bookmarks/42
bookmark.$delete({id:bookmark.id}); // DELETE /bookmarks/42
```

After we obtain the bookmark object from the server, the value of bookmark.id is 42. When we called the $save and $delete functions, we specified the id parameter using {id:bookmark.id}. That repetition can be eliminated. When calling the $resource function, we specify a second argument, indicating the default values to use for the URI parameters. For example, $resource("/bookmarks/:id", {id:1}) would use an id of 1 if it was not otherwise specified. Of course, hardcoding a value is not particularly useful. Instead, we can use a string prefixed with @, as we are doing above with $resource("/bookmarks/:id", {id:"@id"}), to tell AngularJS to use the value of the id attribute from the object on which $save or $delete is called. Our example then becomes this:

```
var bookmark = Bookmark.get({id:42}); // GET /bookmarks/42
bookmark.title = "changed";
bookmark.$save();   // POST   /bookmarks/42
bookmark.$delete(); // DELETE /bookmarks/42
```

The results are the same, but we no longer have to specify {id:bookmark.id} when calling $save() and $delete(). That is now done automatically because we have {id:"@id"} as the default value for the :id parameter of the URI.

We now have a Bookmark service that defines a resource for exchanging bookmark data with the server. We can retrieve the bookmark list by calling the query() function on Bookmark. We'll use dependency injection to get the Bookmark service and produce the bookmark list as another service named bookmarks:

`angularjs/public/app/base/app.js`
```
app.factory("bookmarks", function(Bookmark) {
  return Bookmark.query();
});
```

We now have the bookmark list provided by the bookmarks service. Although the list contains bookmark resource objects that we can use to send requests to the server, the bookmark *list* is not automatically updated when adding or deleting bookmarks. When we save a new bookmark, we need to manually add it to the list. After deleting a bookmark, we also have to remove it from the list. We do not need to do anything after making changes to a previously existing bookmark, since it is already in the list.

Using the $save function on a bookmark object, we can save the bookmark back to the server. Since the bookmark is a resource, calling $save automatically issues a POST request. To determine whether the bookmark is new, so that we know if we need to add it to the bookmark list, we check the existence of the id value:

```
angularjs/public/app/base/app.js
app.factory("saveBookmark", function(bookmarks) {
  return function(bookmark) {
    if (!bookmark.id) {
      bookmarks.push(bookmark);
    }
    bookmark.$save();
  };
});
```

To delete a bookmark, we can call the $delete function on the bookmark. This sends a DELETE request to the server. We'll also delete the bookmark from the bookmark list:

```
angularjs/public/app/base/app.js
app.factory("deleteBookmark", function(bookmarks) {
  return function(bookmark) {
    var index = bookmarks.indexOf(bookmark);
    bookmark.$delete();
    bookmarks.splice(index, 1);
  };
});
```

We've created services to create, read, update, and delete bookmarks between the client and the server. Although we don't have a user interface yet, it would be nice to verify that our code works at this point. A great way to do that is to write automated tests. When you're ready, let's do that next.

Writing Automated Tests for Services

The AngularJS community is big on writing automated tests to verify that application code is working properly. The framework offers tremendous testing support, and the documentation examples often have accompanying tests. Test-driven development is emphasized in AngularJS for good reason. With TDD, you develop a suite of tests alongside your code. Running your tests ensures that your code works. This safety net gives you the freedom to refactor your code with confidence, because your automated tests tell you right away if your changes caused a regression.

Several tools exist for running JavaScript tests. In the following examples, we'll use Jasmine because it is easy to set up, has no dependencies, and offers a capable, intuitive API.[3] Moreover, tomorrow we'll be using AngularJS's

---

3. http://pivotal.github.io/jasmine

end-to-end testing tools, which follow Jasmine's syntax. Today we're writing unit tests. Let's begin with an HTML page for running Jasmine:

angularjs/public/index-test.html
```
<html lang="en">
  <head>
    <meta charset="utf-8">
    <title>Jasmine Spec Runner</title>
    <link rel="stylesheet" type="text/css" href="lib/jasmine-1.3.1/jasmine.css">
  </head>

  <body>
  </body>

  <script src="/lib/jasmine-1.3.1/jasmine.js"></script>
  <script src="/lib/jasmine-1.3.1/jasmine-html.js"></script>

  <script src="/lib/angularjs/1.0.8/angular.js"></script>
  <script src="/lib/angularjs/1.0.8/angular-resource.js"></script>
➤ <script src="/lib/angularjs/1.0.8/angular-mocks.js"></script>

  <script src="/app/base/app.js"></script>
➤ <script src="/app/base/app-test.js"></script>

  <script src="/test/test-runner.js"></script>
</html>
```

The page loads the CSS and JavaScript files for Jasmine, as well as the JavaScript files for AngularJS and for our application. In particular, notice the angular-mocks.js and app-test.js files. The former is a library of mocks to simulate AngularJS services. The latter is where we'll write our unit tests.

To write Jasmine tests, we start with the following structure:

angularjs/public/app/base/app-test.js
```
describe("base/app-test.js", function() {
  beforeEach(function() {
    module("App_base");
  });

  // Add tests here
});
```

The describe and beforeEach functions are provided by Jasmine. With describe, we create a container for a set of tests. The beforeEach function, as its name suggests, runs code before each test. Here, we're loading our application with the module function provided by the angular-mocks library.

We're ready to add some tests. Within the describe block, we can add another, nested describe block for testing the bookmark resource. We'll verify that the bookmarks service retrieves the list of bookmarks from the server by issuing a GET request. To test for Ajax requests and provide a mock response for the benefit of our test case, the AngularJS mock library provides the $httpBackend service:

```
angularjs/public/app/base/app-test.js
describe("Bookmark resource", function() {
  var mockBookmarks = null;
  beforeEach(inject(function($httpBackend, Bookmark) {
    mockBookmarks = [
      new Bookmark({id:1}), new Bookmark({id:2}), new Bookmark({id:3})
    ];
    $httpBackend.expectGET("/bookmarks").respond(mockBookmarks);
  }));
  it("should retrieve bookmarks", inject(function($httpBackend, bookmarks) {
    $httpBackend.flush();
    expect(bookmarks.length).toBe(mockBookmarks.length);
  }));

  // add more tests here
});
```

❶ In the call to the beforeEach function, we can use the inject function to benefit from dependency injection in our test code. Here, we're injecting the $httpBackend service and our own Bookmark model. We're using the latter to create a mock list of bookmarks for the purposes of our test.

❷ The $httpBackend service provides methods for indicating which requests to expect and how to respond to them. Because we'll be using our bookmarks service, which retrieves the list of bookmarks from the server, we expect a GET request to the /bookmarks URI. In response, we return the mock list of bookmarks.

❸ The it function comes from the Jasmine library and represents a test case. The first parameter is a string for describing the test case. The it function was given its name so that, combined with the description that follows, the line of code reads like an English sentence.

Just as with beforeEach, we can use the inject function to retrieve dependencies. Within the body of the it function, we're calling flush() on $httpBackend to explicitly flush pending requests. Remember that Ajax requests are asynchronous. Writing test code that deals with asynchronous function calls is difficult and error-prone. To make things easier, the mock $http-Backend object holds on to pending requests and lets us control when to execute them with the flush() function. This keeps our test code linear and easy to follow.

❹ Within the it block, calls to Jasmine's expect are where we indicate what is required for the test to pass. After passing the *actual* value, we call another function, called a *matcher*, and pass it the *expected* value. The toBe matcher asserts that the two values are the same. Jasmine provides several matchers, and you can also write your own.

From the source code bundle, go to the angularjs directory and start the web server by running the ruby app.rb command. Then, using your browser, navigate to http://localhost:4567/index-test.html. The Jasmine test runner executes the tests and generates a report of the results, similar to this screenshot.

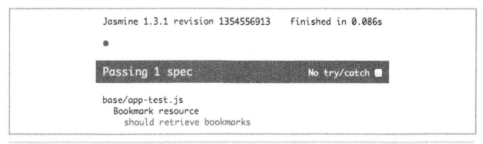

Figure 11—The Jasmine test runner

Let's add a test for saving a bookmark:

angularjs/public/app/base/app-test.js
```
it("should save a bookmark", inject(
  function($httpBackend, Bookmark, bookmarks, saveBookmark) {
    $httpBackend.flush();

    $httpBackend.expectPOST("/bookmarks").respond({id:4});
    saveBookmark(new Bookmark({url:"http://angularjs.org", title:"AngularJS"}));

    $httpBackend.flush();
    expect(bookmarks.length).toBe(mockBookmarks.length + 1);
  }
));
```

We've created another it block for the test case. After flushing the $httpBackend to get the bookmarks list, we indicate that we expect a POST request and that we'll respond with an ID for the created bookmark. The call to saveBookmark is what should send the POST request. Finally, after flushing the $httpBackend again, this time for saving the bookmark, we verify that the bookmarks list has one more bookmark.

We can add a test for deleting a bookmark in a similar fashion:

```
angularjs/public/app/base/app-test.js
it("should delete a bookmark", inject(
  function($httpBackend, bookmarks, deleteBookmark) {
    $httpBackend.flush();
    var bookmark = bookmarks[0];

    $httpBackend.expectDELETE("/bookmarks/" + bookmark.id).respond(200);
    deleteBookmark(bookmark);

    $httpBackend.flush();
    expect(bookmarks.length).toBe(mockBookmarks.length - 1);
  }
));
```

This time, we grab the first bookmark from the list and set up the $httpBackend to expect a DELETE request with the ID of the bookmark. To that, we'll simply respond with a 200 OK HTTP status code. After deleting the bookmark, we expect one less bookmark in the bookmarks list.

After making changes to the test code, simply refresh the browser to reload http://localhost:4567/index-test.html and see the results.

Unit tests are an excellent way to verify code behavior. With Jasmine's expressive API and AngularJS's mock library, we can easily write and run unit tests for our AngularJS services.

What We Learned on Day 1

Our first day of discovering AngularJS revealed some of the aspects that make AngularJS unique. We learned about modules, services, dependency injection, resources, and automated tests. We certainly covered a lot of ground!

Day 1 Self-Study

Find:

- The AngularJS API documentation

- Two other ways to define services besides service and factory

- The angular-seed project, which you can use as a template for your AngularJS applications

Do:

- Take advantage of the REST API from our Sinatra server and write a service that retrieves bookmarks with tags using the /bookmarks/:tag URI.

- Write Jasmine tests that verify the behavior of your service and run them in your browser.

Day 2: Creating Controllers and Views

Just as in the MVC architecture, AngularJS controllers orchestrate data flow between models and views. We'll spend our second day learning all about controllers and how to make views dynamic with directives. We'll have a closer look at the $scope, which is the glue between controllers and views. To put what we learn into practice, we'll create a view for the bookmark list and a form for creating and editing bookmarks. When we're done, we'll have a front end as shown in the figure.

So far we've retrieved data from the server with a resource to produce data objects. Today we'll complete the flow of data down to the view, injecting the data into controllers and making it available to view directives with the scope, as depicted in Figure 12, *Data flow from server to view*, on page 91. Let's ramp up our day by learning how we create controllers.

Creating Controllers and Using View Directives

Now we'll build a controller and a view for the bookmark list. This will start giving a user interface to our application. The view will display the bookmarks, each with an Edit and a Delete button next to it, and the controller will provide callback functions to handle the events triggered by the buttons. Just like the service and factory functions create services, the controller function creates a controller with a name as well as a function that indicates dependencies by the names of the parameters:

```
angularjs/public/app/base/app.js
app.controller("BookmarkListController",
  function($scope, bookmarks) {
    $scope.bookmarks = bookmarks;
  }
);
```

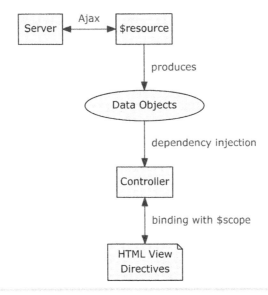

Figure 12—Data flow from server to view

The controller receives the $scope and our list of bookmarks by dependency injection. Provided by AngularJS, the $scope is the bridge of communication between controllers and views. Assigning the bookmarks property to the $scope makes it available to the view.

To use the controller in the view, we use the ng-controller directive with the controller's name, BookmarkListController:

```
angularjs/views/base.html
<div
  ng-controller="BookmarkListController"
  ng-include src="'/app/base/bookmark_list.html'">
</div>
```

The ng-controller directive associates the controller with the <div> element. Everything within this <div> can reference the attributes that the controller assigned to the $scope object.

The ng-include directive loads a template from a URI. Since directive attribute values are code expressions, we need to surround the URI with single quotes to get a literal string value. Here we're loading the bookmark_list.html template. Using ng-include is optional; we could just as well have included the HTML template directly within the <div> element. We're using ng-include because it allows us to break up templates into separate files, making our code easier to manage.

The bookmark_list.html template renders the bookmark list, with Edit and Delete buttons next to each bookmark:

```
angularjs/public/app/base/bookmark_list.html
<ul>
  <li class="bookmark" ng-repeat="bookmark in bookmarks">
    <button ng-click="editBookmark(bookmark)">Edit</button>
    <button ng-click="deleteBookmark(bookmark)">Delete</button>
    <a href="{{bookmark.url}}">{{bookmark.title}}</a>
  ( <a href="{{bookmark.url}}">{{bookmark.url}}</a> )
  </li>
</ul>
```

We're using some interesting directives: the ng-repeat directive iterates over the bookmarks list, which comes from the $scope. The directive renders an <li> element for each iteration and assigns the current bookmark to the bookmark variable. Within the <li> element, we have the Edit and Delete buttons, each with an ng-click directive that calls a function, passing the bookmark as an argument. (We'll set up the editBookmark and deleteBookmark callback functions in a moment.) Finally, we have links to the bookmark's URL, one with the bookmark's title and the other with the bookmark's URL. Notice how we refer to the bookmark object by using the {{ }} syntax.

The following figure summarizes how we link the controller and the scope in the JavaScript code to the directives in the HTML view:

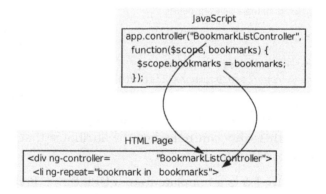

Figure 13—Connections between a controller and a view

When the user presses the Edit or Delete button next to a bookmark, the ng-click directives call the editBookmark and deleteBookmark functions. To make them available to the view, we just need to specify them as dependencies in the controller and assign them to the scope:

```
angularjs/public/app/base/app.js
app.controller("BookmarkListController",
  function($scope, bookmarks, deleteBookmark, editBookmark) {
    $scope.bookmarks = bookmarks;
    $scope.deleteBookmark = deleteBookmark;
    $scope.editBookmark = editBookmark;
  }
);
```

The deleteBookmark service is the one that we created earlier. The editBookmark service does not exist yet; let's build it now.

Taking Advantage of Two-Way Data Binding

When the user clicks on the Edit button next to a bookmark, we want to edit the corresponding bookmark in the bookmark form. When the user saves the bookmark, we want to save the changes back to the server and update the bookmark list. Finally, when the form is blank or when the user clears the form, we want to create a new bookmark. Let's see how we can achieve all of this very cleanly by taking advantage of AngularJS's two-way data binding.

We'll start with a service named state that defines an object where we'll store properties to which other services can bind. Think of this object as being to services what the scope is to controllers and views—the tie that binds:

```
angularjs/public/app/base/app.js
app.service("state", function(Bookmark) {
  this.formBookmark = {bookmark:new Bookmark()};
  this.clearForm = function() {
    this.formBookmark.bookmark = new Bookmark();
  };
});
```

We've added a formBookmark property, initialized to an object with a blank bookmark, and a clearForm function that resets formBookmark.bookmark to a blank bookmark. These will be convenient for the bookmark form.

Now that we have the state object, we're ready to write the editBookmark service:

```
angularjs/public/app/base/app.js
app.factory("editBookmark", function(state) {
  return function(bookmark) {
    state.formBookmark.bookmark = bookmark;
  };
});
```

Editing a bookmark merely consists of setting the formBookmark.bookmark property on the state object to the bookmark being edited. When we create the bookmark form, we'll just need to bind the form's input fields to the properties of the formBookmark on the state object, and two-way live binding will take care of communicating changes back and forth. Let's do that now, shall we?

Creating the Bookmark Form

Creating forms in AngularJS is easy, thanks to two-way binding. As with other view templates, the form is plain HTML with AngularJS directives. The ng-model directive binds an input field to a model property, and ng-submit on the <form> element calls a function when the user submits the form.

Let's create the form for creating and editing bookmarks in the bookmark_form.html file. The template for the form is as follows:

```
angularjs/public/app/base/bookmark_form.html
Bookmark:
<form ng-submit="saveBookmark(formBookmark.bookmark)">

  <label>
    URL:
    <input type="text" ng-model="formBookmark.bookmark.url" name="url">
  </label>

  <label>
    Title:
    <input type="text" ng-model="formBookmark.bookmark.title" name="title">
  </label>

  <input type="submit" class="btn btn-primary" value="Save">
  <input type="button" class="btn" ng-click="clearForm()" value="Clear">

</form>
```

Thanks to the ng-model directive, when the value changes in the input, AngularJS automatically updates the value in the model and vice versa. We don't need any code to transfer values to and from the form.

To save the bookmark, all we need is the ng-submit directive on the <form> element. This calls the saveBookmark function that we'll make available in the controller for the bookmark form. We also have the ng-click directive on the Clear button that calls the clearForm function from the controller.

Let's go ahead then and write the bookmark form controller. We'll need to set the formBookmark, saveBookmark, and clearForm properties on the $scope:

```
angularjs/public/app/base/app.js
app.controller("BookmarkFormController",
  function($scope, state, bookmarks, saveBookmark) {
    $scope.formBookmark = state.formBookmark;
    $scope.saveBookmark = saveBookmark;
    $scope.clearForm = state.clearForm;
  }
);
```

We've hooked up the scope's formBookmark and clearForm properties to the same properties on the state object. The interesting part of that story is that when we change the binding of formBookmark.bookmark on the state object, the scope *automatically* picks up the change—and so does the form in the view, along with the input fields. With that in place, editing a bookmark *just works*, because the editBookmark function sets the bookmark to edit on the formBookmark.bookmark property of the same state object.

Remember that we already have a saveBookmark service that adds the bookmark to the bookmarks list if it is new. Now, after saving the bookmark on the server with $save, we'll also clear the form:

```
angularjs/public/app/base/app.js
➤ app.factory("saveBookmark", function(bookmarks, state) {
    return function(bookmark) {
      if (!bookmark.id) {
        bookmarks.push(bookmark);
      }
      bookmark.$save();
➤    state.clearForm();
    };
  });
```

Now that we have everything in place for the BookmarkFormController, we can use it in the view:

```
angularjs/views/base.html
<div
  ng-controller="BookmarkFormController"
  ng-include src="'/app/base/bookmark_form.html'">
</div>
```

Fantastic! With the scope and the state object, live binding keeps everything synchronized. Our code remains cleanly decoupled: for example, pressing the Edit button on the bookmark list sets the bookmark on the form, but the bookmark list is not directly tied to the form. As shown in Figure 14, *The Bookmark Form Controller*, on page 96, our state object acts as an intermediate to keep components separate.

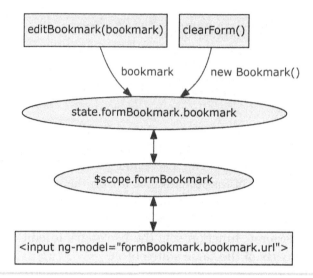

Figure 14—The Bookmark Form Controller

In a framework without live binding, the bookmark list would contain code to populate the bookmark form in order to edit the selected bookmark and would contain more code to pull data out of the form and back into the bookmark object in order to save the bookmark. With our state object and two-way live binding, however, we don't need any plumbing code.

An Important Note About the Scope

It's worth having a closer look at how we defined the formBookmark property on the scope and on the state object, because there lurks a trap into which many an AngularJS developer has fallen.

You may have wondered why we assigned an object with a bookmark property to the formBookmark variable, forcing us to use formBookmark.bookmark to refer to the bookmark. Why not assign the bookmark directly to formBookmark?

Refer to the following diagram. In this scenario, we've assigned a blank bookmark to formBookmark. Both the state object and the $scope point to the same object. When editing an existing bookmark, we assign the bookmark to the formBookmark property on the state object, hoping that the $scope picks up the change. We're in for a disappointment, though. The problem is that by reassigning formBookmark, we've changed the *reference* to a different object. As you can see at the bottom of the diagram, after the change, we've broken the link between the state and the $scope. Their formBookmark properties now point to two different objects.

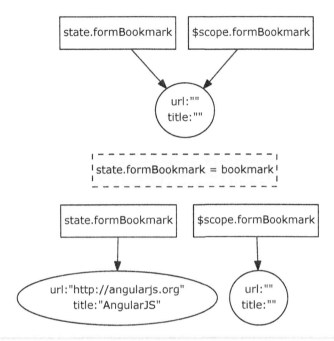

Figure 15—The $scope should not refer to a top-level object.

Because of the disconnect, changes to state.formBookmark in one part of the code will not be seen by the controller's $scope.formBookmark. In our application, that would result in breaking the Edit button: editing a bookmark would not populate the bookmark form.

Now look at Figure 16, *The $scope should refer to a nested object*, on page 98. By having formBookmark point to an object with a bookmark property and having *that* property point to the bookmark, we can change the formBookmark.bookmark reference and still preserve the link between the state and the $scope:

The key is not changing the top-level reference, formBookmark. Instead, we change a *nested* property, formBookmark.bookmark. After doing that, both the state and the scope still point to the same object with their formBookmark property. It is that object's bookmark property that is now referring to a different object.

The takeaway is that *there should be at least one dot* in the expression when sharing references to model objects between the scope and the other parts of the application.

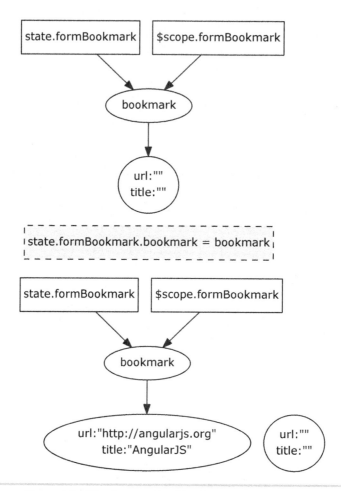

Figure 16—The $scope should refer to a nested object.

Writing End-To-End Automated Tests

Yesterday we wrote some unit tests with Jasmine. Today we'll write some higher-level tests that exercise our application on an end-to-end basis. We'll test what should happen in the browser rather than in individual units of code. This type of testing is closer to what you would do were you to test the application manually: going to a URI, filling out and submitting a form, and looking at the results in the browser.

AngularJS provides a library and an API for writing end-to-end tests. To set up a test runner, all we need is to load the angular-scenario.js file and add the ng-autotest directive on the <script> tag. We'll also load a file where we'll write our tests. This could be any file; we've named it e2e-tests.js:

angularjs/public/e2e-test-runner.html

```
<html lang="en">
  <head>
    <meta charset="utf-8">
    <title>AngularjS End-to-End Test Runner</title>
  </head>
  <body>
  </body>
➤ <script src="/lib/angularjs/1.0.8/angular-scenario.js" ng-autotest></script>
➤ <script src="/e2e-tests.js"></script>
</html>
```

We're ready to write our tests in the e2e-tests.js file. We don't need to learn a new syntax, because AngularJS follows the Jasmine style for its end-to-end testing API. As you can see here, the setup for an end-to-end test looks very much like a Jasmine test:

angularjs/public/e2e-tests.js

```
describe("Bookmark list", function() {
  beforeEach(function() {
➤   browser().navigateTo("/");
  });
  it("should display a bookmark list", function() {
➤   expect(repeater("li.bookmark").count()).toBeGreaterThan(0);
  });
});
```

We have the same describe, beforeEach, and it functions as we had in our Jasmine unit tests. The difference with end-to-end tests is that we're using the AngularJS scenario library to call functions such as browser, which makes a request, and repeater, which inspects the content of the web page. This is a higher level of testing than what we wrote in our unit tests. Here, we're expecting the page to display a list of bookmarks, which means the page has at least one <li> element with the bookmark class.

Let's write a test for creating a bookmark by filling out and submitting the form. The test checks how many bookmarks were in the list and then verifies that the list contains one more bookmark after submitting the form:

angularjs/public/e2e-tests.js

```
   it("should add a new bookmark", function() {
❶    var bookmarkCount = repeater("li.bookmark").count();
     bookmarkCount.execute(function() {});
     var previousCount = bookmarkCount.value;

❷    input("formBookmark.bookmark.url").
       enter("http://docs.angularjs.org/guide/dev_guide.e2e-testing");
     input("formBookmark.bookmark.title").
       enter("AngularJS end-to-end testing guide");
```

```
③   element("input:submit").click();
④   expect(repeater("li.bookmark").count()).toBe(previousCount + 1);
    });
```

❶ We want to count the bookmarks at the beginning of the test. We'll be able to use that value to compare with the number of bookmarks after submitting the form to create a new bookmark. Now, the repeater.count does not return a value directly; it returns what's known as a *future*. We need to call execute to get the value. What's more, we are *required* to provide a callback function; otherwise the test runner will skip the test. That's why we are passing a blank function to execute.

❷ With the input and enter functions, we can simulate entering a value in an input field. The code we wrote fills in values for the bookmark's URL and title.

❸ The element function uses a jQuery-style selector to find an element. After finding the form's submit button, we call click() to simulate a button click.

❹ The expect(...).toBe(...) syntax is the same as with Jasmine. In this case, we do not have to call execute on repeater.count; the expect function takes care of that for us. We're counting the number of bookmarks in the list and verifying that we have one additional bookmark. If the test passes, we've confirmed a basic scenario involving the creation of a new bookmark.

To run the tests, start the server with the ruby app.rb command and open your browser to http://localhost:4567/e2e-test-runner.html. You'll see the test results as illustrated in the following figure.

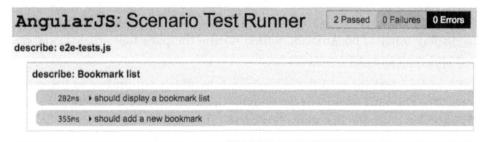

Figure 17—The AngularJS end-to-end test runner

We've written a test that fills out a form, submits it, and verifies the result on the web page. With the duo of unit tests and end-to-end tests, we're well equipped to write automated test suites that ensure the health of our AngularJS applications.

What We Learned on Day 2

On our second day, we moved from services on to controllers and views. We discussed how controllers, scopes, and view directives work together to develop user interfaces. We created a view of the bookmark list and a form for creating and editing bookmarks. We took advantage of two-way live binding to keep everything synchronized between the form, the bookmark list, and the server. Finally, we continued discovering AngularJS's strong testing support by writing end-to-end automated tests. It has been a productive day indeed.

Day 2 Self-Study

Find:

- The list of AngularJS directives
- The API for the AngularJS end-to-end testing library

Do:

- Try using different view directives and verify the results in your browser. For example, use ng-mouseenter and ng-mouseleave to show and hide a bookmark's tags when moving the mouse.

- Write end-to-end tests to verify the behavior of the view directives.

- Run your tests with Karma, a test runner created by the AngularJS team.

Day 3: Building Filters and Routes

Today we conclude our exploration of AngularJS by discovering more ways to benefit from AngularJS's exceptional data binding. In doing so, we'll wrap up our bookmarking application by adding tags, filtering, and routing. With data binding, it's not only possible, it's smooth sailing to implement these features while keeping our components cleanly decoupled. The majority of the code we write focuses on the model; AngularJS takes care of updating the view.

The first thing we'll do today is improve our application by adding tag list support to the bookmarks. That involves adding an input field for the user to enter the bookmark's tags (separated by commas) and splitting the string on commas to obtain a list. We also want to show the tags next to each bookmark in the bookmark list. Finally, we'd like to build a list of unique tags along with the number of bookmarks. The following screen capture gives you an idea of the result that we are shooting for.

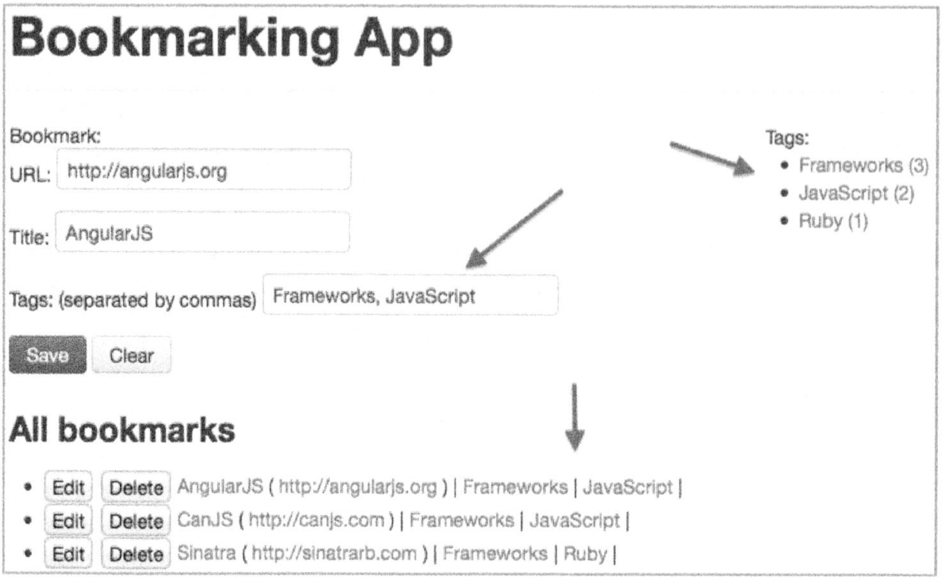

Bookmarking App

Bookmark:

URL: http://angularjs.org

Title: AngularJS

Tags: (separated by commas) Frameworks, JavaScript

Save   Clear

Tags:
- Frameworks (3)
- JavaScript (2)
- Ruby (1)

All bookmarks

- Edit Delete AngularJS (http://angularjs.org) | Frameworks | JavaScript |
- Edit Delete CanJS (http://canjs.com) | Frameworks | JavaScript |
- Edit Delete Sinatra (http://sinatrarb.com) | Frameworks | Ruby |

Figure 18—Adding tags to bookmarks

Adding Tags to Bookmarks

We'll start by adding an input to the bookmark form for the user to enter tags:

```
angularjs/public/app/tagfilter/bookmark_form.html
<label>
  Tags: (separated by commas)
  <input type="text" ng-model="formBookmark.bookmark.tagList" ng-list
    name="tagList">
</label>
```

We've bound the input to the bookmark's tagList property. Notice the ng-list directive in the <input> tag: this converts the comma-separated string that the user enters in the input box to a list of strings in the tagList property. For example, if the user enters Frameworks, JavaScript, the tagList property will contain ["Frameworks", "JavaScript"].

Saving a bookmark now includes the tagList property when sending data to the server, so the bookmark's tags are saved. The server also sends the tagList when we retrieve bookmarks; when editing an existing bookmark, we need to convert the tagList property back to the comma-separated string to populate the input box. It turns out that the ng-list directive already does that for us, so we're done.

We've added support for tags on bookmarks. Now we'd like to display the list of unique tags, each with the number of bookmarks that have the tag, as shown on the right side of the screen in Figure 18, *Adding tags to bookmarks*, on page 102.

Building a Tag List

Building the tag list involves going through all the bookmarks and keeping track of tags and bookmark counts. We'll start with a service that returns a function for building the tag list from the list of bookmarks:

angularjs/public/app/tagfilter/app.js
```
app.factory("buildTagList", function() {
  return function(bookmarks) {
  };
});
```

We'll be able to call this as a function, buildTagList(bookmarks), to get a list of tags with labels and bookmark counts.

Within the function, we'll create a bookmarkCounts object that contains the number of bookmarks per tag:

angularjs/public/app/tagfilter/app.js
```
var bookmarkCounts = {};

bookmarks.each(function(bookmark) {
  var tagList = bookmark.tagList;

  tagList.each(function(tag) {
    var existing = bookmarkCounts[tag];
    bookmarkCounts[tag] = existing ? existing + 1 : 1;
  });
});
```

Once we're done iterating over the tag list, the keys in the bookmarkCounts object are the tag labels. We'll sort the labels and return a list of objects with labels and corresponding bookmark counts:

angularjs/public/app/tagfilter/app.js
```
var labels = Object.keys(bookmarkCounts);
labels.sort();
return labels.map(function(label) {
  return {label:label, bookmarkCount:bookmarkCounts[label]};
});
```

Our tag list is ready. To display it in a view, we need a controller that sets the tag list on the scope. We also want the tag list to be updated when the bookmark list changes. Remember that we have to manually manage the bookmark list; it is not automatically hooked up for live binding. To listen for changes on a property, the $scope has a $watch function that takes the property name as a string and a callback function that receives the updated value. In our tag list controller, we'll watch the bookmarks property and update the tags on the scope by calling our buildTagList service:

angularjs/public/app/tagfilter/app.js
```
app.controller("TagListController",
  function($scope, state, bookmarks, buildTagList) {
    $scope.bookmarks = bookmarks;
    $scope.$watch("bookmarks", function(updatedBookmarks) {
      $scope.tags = buildTagList(updatedBookmarks);
    }, true); // true compares objects for equality rather than by reference.
  }
);
```

We now have the tags property on the $scope, ready to be displayed in the view. We can render the tag list with the ng-repeat directive:

angularjs/public/app/tagfilter/tag_list.html
```
Tags:
<ul>
  <li ng-repeat="tag in tags">

    <a href="#"
      ng-click="filterBy(tag)">{{tag.label}} ({{tag.bookmarkCount}})</a>
  </li>

</ul>
```

We're now showing each tag's label and bookmark count. Congratulations, we've achieved our first goal of the day!

Notice that we've made each tag clickable. When the user clicks on a tag, we want to filter the bookmark list and show only the bookmarks that have the selected tag. That's our next mission.

Manipulating Data with Filters

The links on the tags call a filterBy(tag) function on the $scope. We want that function to filter the bookmark list by tag. But we also want the tags next to each bookmark to do the same thing. By now, we've learned that the best way to achieve such functionality while keeping the code simple and the components loosely coupled is to reap the benefits of data binding. We already have a state object that acts as the communication hub between the different parts of our application, so let's add a property for the bookmark filter:

```
angularjs/public/app/tagfilter/app.js
app.service("state", function(Bookmark) {
  this.formBookmark = {bookmark:new Bookmark()};
  this.clearForm = function() {
    this.formBookmark.bookmark = new Bookmark();
  };
  this.bookmarkFilter = {filterTag:""};
});
```

We can now define the filterBy function on the $scope and add it to our tag list
controller. All the function does is set the value of bookmarkFilter.filterTag on the
state object:

```
angularjs/public/app/tagfilter/app.js
app.controller("TagListController",
  function($scope, state, bookmarks, buildTagList) {
    $scope.bookmarks = bookmarks;
    $scope.$watch("bookmarks", function(updatedBookmarks) {
      $scope.tags = buildTagList(updatedBookmarks);
    }, true); // true compares objects for equality rather than by reference.

    $scope.filterBy = function(tag) {
      state.bookmarkFilter.filterTag = tag.label;
    };
  }
);
```

As you can probably anticipate, filtering the tag list involves binding to that
property on the state object and filtering the bookmarks list. To accomplish the
task, we'll use another weapon from AngularJS's arsenal: filters. Much like
with services and controllers, we just need to specify a name and a function
with any dependencies to the filter function:

```
angularjs/public/app/tagfilter/app.js
app.filter("filterByTag", function() { // no dependencies
});
```

Within this function, we need to return another function that takes a list of
bookmarks and returns another list with just the bookmarks to keep after
the filter has been applied. The function can also accept any other parameters
it needs to do its work. In our case, the filter needs the tag by which to filter
the bookmarks:

```
angularjs/public/app/tagfilter/app.js
return function(bookmarks, filterTag) {
  return bookmarks.filter(byTag(filterTag));
};
```

The function filters the bookmarks by tag. What the bookmarks.filter function needs is a function of a *single* bookmark that returns true or false to indicate whether to include the bookmark in the filtered list. That is what the byTag function provides:

angularjs/public/app/tagfilter/app.js
```
var byTag = function(filterTag) {
  return function(bookmark) {
    var tagList = bookmark.tagList;
    var noFilter = (!filterTag) || (filterTag.length == 0);
    var tagListContainsFilterTag = tagList &&
      tagList.indexOf(filterTag) > -1;
    return noFilter || tagListContainsFilterTag;
  };
};
```

To determine whether to keep the bookmark, the function looks at the filter tag and the bookmark's tags. If the filter tag is not present or blank, there is no filter and the bookmark is kept. Otherwise, the bookmark's tag list must contain the filter tag for the bookmark to be kept.

Using the Filter in the View

Our filterByTag filter is ready. To use the filter in the view template, we need to *pipe* the bookmark list to the filter with the | character, like so:

angularjs/public/app/tagfilter/bookmark_list.html
```
<li class="bookmark"
  ng-repeat="bookmark in bookmarks | filterByTag:bookmarkFilter.filterTag">
```

We're filtering the bookmark list with our filterByTag function and specifying an additional argument by adding : followed by the tag by which to filter, the value of bookmarkFilter.filterTag. AngularJS takes care of applying our filter and rendering just the filtered list of bookmarks in the view. Even better, because the scope's bookmarkFilter.filterTag is bound to our state object, whenever other parts of the application change the state object's bookmarkFilter.filterTag, AngularJS reflects the change by refreshing the filtered list.

To connect the selected filter tag from the tag list to the bookmark list, we grab the bookmarkFilter from our state object and make it available to the view by binding it to the $scope in the bookmark list controller:

angularjs/public/app/tagfilter/app.js
```
app.controller("BookmarkListController",
  function($scope, state, bookmarks, editBookmark, deleteBookmark) {
    $scope.bookmarks = bookmarks;
    $scope.bookmarkFilter = state.bookmarkFilter;
```

```
➤     $scope.filterBy = function(tag) {
        state.bookmarkFilter.filterTag = tag;
      };
      // ...
    }
);
```

We've also made the filterBy callback function available. Not surprisingly, that modifies the bookmarkFilter object on the state object. Now when rendering the list of tags next to each bookmark, we can link them so that clicking them also filters the bookmark list:

angularjs/public/app/tagfilter/bookmark_list.html
```
<span ng-repeat="tag in bookmark.tagList">
  <a href="#" ng-click="filterBy(tag)">{{tag}}</a> |
</span>
```

Our filter is now fully available from the view.

Clearing the Filter

We have one more detail to address. Sure, users can now filter the bookmark list by clicking on tags, but they also need to be able to *clear* the filter so that the complete list is shown once again. That's just a matter of setting bookmark-Filter.filterTag to a blank string on the state object. Let's do that in a controller for the tag filter:

angularjs/public/app/tagfilter/app.js
```
app.controller("TagFilterController", function($scope, state) {
  $scope.bookmarkFilter = state.bookmarkFilter;

  $scope.clearFilter = function() {
    state.bookmarkFilter.filterTag = "";
  };
});
```

In the view, we'll either show the current tag by which the list is filtered, along with a link to clear the filter, or we'll just display *All bookmarks* when no filter is being applied. We can use the ng-show directive to show or hide part of the view template based on a condition:

angularjs/public/app/tagfilter/tag_filter.html
```
<h3 ng-show="bookmarkFilter.filterTag">
  Filtered by tag: {{bookmarkFilter.filterTag}}
  | <a href="#" ng-click="clearFilter()">Clear filter</a>
</h3>
<h3 ng-show="!bookmarkFilter.filterTag">All bookmarks</h3>
```

We've completed our mission. Go ahead and try it. Run the server from the angularjs directory with ruby app.rb and open the http://localhost:4567/example/tagfilter

URL in your browser. Add some bookmarks with tags, edit the tags, filter the list, delete a bookmark, and notice how everything refreshes consistently, all thanks to AngularJS's two-way data binding.

Defining Routes

As we did with CanJS, we'd like to make the AngularJS application support browser navigation with the Back and Forward buttons, and with bookmark-able pages as well. Client-side frameworks don't usually include a solution to this problem, but AngularJS offers a *route provider* to make this possible.

With the route provider, we can associate controllers and templates with URIs. The route URIs can have parameters, and controllers can easily access the values of those parameters. Let's use these features to navigate between different tag filters and to go back to displaying all bookmarks.

To use the route provider, we add a third parameter to the angular.module function call. Remember that the first parameter is the module name, the second, the list of dependencies. The third parameter is a function that gets called when creating the module. The function can use dependency injection, so we'll get the $routeProvider, which is the service provided by AngularJS that we can use to define routes:

```
angularjs/public/app/routing/app.js
angular.module("App_routing", ["ngResource", "App_tagfilter"],
  function($routeProvider) {
    var params = {
      controller: "BookmarkListController",
      templateUrl:"/app/routing/bookmark_list.html"
    };
    $routeProvider.
      when("/", params).
      when("/filter/:tag", params);
  }
)
```

We've associated both the default URI and the /filter/:tag URI to the BookmarkList-Controller. The template is also specified in the route provider. We no longer need ng-include src="'/app/tagfilter/bookmark_list.html'" in the view. Instead, we use ng-view=:

```
angularjs/views/routing.html
<div
  ng-controller="BookmarkListController"
  ng-view>
</div>
```

When a route matches one that we've declared in the route provider, AngularJS renders the corresponding template within the element that has the ng-view directive.

To use routes, controllers use dependency injection to obtain the $routeParams object, which contains attributes that match the parameters in the URI. For example, when the user goes to a URI that matches /filter/:tag, $routeParams.tag is the value present in the place of :tag in the URI. We can set this value to the bookmark filter tag on the state object, like so:

angularjs/public/app/routing/app.js
```
app.controller("BookmarkListController",
  function($scope, $routeParams, state,
    bookmarks, editBookmark, deleteBookmark) {
    $scope.bookmarks = bookmarks;
    $scope.bookmarkFilter = state.bookmarkFilter;
    state.bookmarkFilter.filterTag = $routeParams.tag;
    $scope.editBookmark = editBookmark;
    $scope.deleteBookmark = deleteBookmark;
  }
);
```

We can do the same in the TagListController:

angularjs/public/app/routing/app.js
```
app.controller("TagListController",
  function($scope, $routeParams, state, bookmarks, buildTagList) {
    $scope.bookmarks = bookmarks;
    state.bookmarkFilter.filterTag = $routeParams.tag;
    $scope.$watch("bookmarks", function(updatedBookmarks) {
      $scope.tags = buildTagList(updatedBookmarks);
    }, true);
  }
);
```

This works in the TagFilterController as well:

angularjs/public/app/routing/app.js
```
app.controller("TagFilterController",
  function($scope, $routeParams, state) {
    $scope.bookmarkFilter = state.bookmarkFilter;
    state.bookmarkFilter.filterTag = $routeParams.tag;
  }
);
```

Again, everything goes through our state object. This time, we're binding bookmarkFilter.filterTag to the value of the route's tag. When the URI changes, be it by clicking on a link, entering a URL in the browser's location bar, or using a bookmark, the value of the tag gets set on the state object and everything else on the page automatically reflects the change.

Now instead of having ng-click="filterBy(tag)" on the tag links in the bookmark list, we can just link to #/filter/{{tag}}:

```
angularjs/public/app/routing/bookmark_list.html
<span ng-repeat="tag in bookmark.tagList">
  <a href="#/filter/{{tag}}">{{tag}}</a> |
</span>
```

We make a similar change in the tag list:

```
angularjs/public/app/routing/tag_list.html
Tags:
<ul>
  <li ng-repeat="tag in tags">
    <a href="#/filter/{{tag.label}}">{{tag.label}} ({{tag.bookmarkCount}})</a>
  </li>
</ul>
```

To clear the filter, the link just needs to point to #:

```
angularjs/public/app/routing/tag_filter.html
<h3 ng-show="bookmarkFilter.filterTag">
  Filtered by tag: {{bookmarkFilter.filterTag}}
  | <a href="#">Clear filter</a>
</h3>
<h3 ng-show="!bookmarkFilter.filterTag">All bookmarks</h3>
```

These changes not only make the links simpler, they also result in less code in the controllers. We can remove the filterBy function from the BookmarkListController and the TagListController, as well as the clearFilter function from the TagFilterController. Once more, dependency injection and data binding have made our task a breeze.

What We Learned on Day 3

Our final day of learning AngularJS was spent taking advantage of data binding to build powerful features. We were able to concentrate on the model and on making connections in controllers, letting AngularJS take care of refreshing views.

Day 3 Self-Study

Find:

- The list of built-in filters provided by AngularJS
- The angular-ui and angular-utils projects.

Do:

- Experiment with AngularJS filters, such as limitTo, lowercase, and orderBy.
- Write a custom filter for getting the list of bookmarks that have no tags.
- Try out the ng-grid component from the angular-ui project.

An Interview with Miško Hevery, creator of AngularJS

Us: What made you decide to create AngularJS? What was missing from existing frameworks at the time?

Miško: There were several reasons that conspired together to make Angular a reality.

1. *I realized that making web apps was just one big marshaling problem of how do you get data from the DB to the browser and then back again. After building many web apps, I was not looking forward to building another one the old way.*

2. *I wanted to bring static web pages to life by adding just a bit more markup. This explains the directives, which are very core to Angular and which are also very unique in the JS framework space. I wanted to have a basic <form> come to life just by adding few extra attributes, without having to write any more imperative code.*

3. *I wanted to learn JavaScript, and building a framework sounded like a good idea as a first JS project. I did not know about any other JS frameworks other than JQuery.*

The original Angular was a service in the cloud that would allow you to build very simple CRUD applications with nothing but markup, and the data would be persisted in the cloud DB as a service. Over time Angular lost the DB as a service and become a general web framework, rather than a purely declarative extension of HTML.

Us: What do you feel are the best features of AngularJS? What makes AngularJS unique?

Miško: Three things make Angular unique:

1. *Having the ability to extend the vocabulary of HTML through directives. The idea of extending the HTML is very powerful, and it allows the developer to express the goal of the code in a declarative fashion rather than with imperative steps.*

   While embedding declarative information in HTML is done by other frameworks, the vocabulary of those frameworks is fixed. Angular allows the declarative vocabulary to be extended, which allows the developer to turn the HTML into domain-specific language, or DSL.

2. *Dependency injection is common on the server side, but Angular pioneered it on the client side. Angular was the first framework to fully take advantage of DI. The result is that Angular applications do not need main methods or other code responsible for assembling the application.*

3. *Angular was designed with testability in mind. We (the Angular team) are big believers in TDD; we built Angular with TDD, and we want to enable developers to build their applications with TDD. Many design decisions in Angular were driven with testing in mind. Angular comes with end-to-end test runners and with mocks for unit tests.*

Us: *What do you have in mind for the future of AngularJS? What are you most excited about, looking forward?*

Miško: *Angular has become a test bed for design ideas, many of which are making it to standards—for example, Object.Observe and MDV. Our hope is that we can use Angular as a proving ground for these ideas, and if they turn out to be useful, we can turn these ideas into web standards and push them into the browser.*

Wrapping Up

AngularJS has a unique approach to web application development. Using dependency injection in JavaScript code and directives in HTML templates, AngularJS applications are *declarative.* Two-way live binding means everything automatically stays synchronized, and we focus on what the application *does* rather than worrying about communicating events between components.

AngularJS's Strengths

AngularJS offers a lot out of the box. You get a dependency injection container, a template compiler that parses and organizes directives, an end-to-end testing library, and much more. This enables you to organize your code in services, controllers, filters, and other well-organized components. You can add attributes to plain HTML to make a page dynamic, rather than writing a lot of plumbing code. Finally, you can write tests to verify that it all works perfectly.

The features provided by AngularJS greatly simplify the creation of bread-and-butter CRUD applications. A considerable amount of real-world web development is geared toward that type of application, making AngularJS a good choice for many projects.

AngularJS also has a lot of momentum. Perhaps because it is backed by Google, and certainly because of its powerful features, the number of people using AngularJS is very large and keeps growing. This in turn results in more online resources: tutorials, articles, presentations, blog posts, and answers to questions on forums.

AngularJS's Weaknesses

The declarative approach is a nice one, but it can easily get out of hand in large applications if you are not careful. If you abuse dependency injection, your code can become hard to follow. You gain a loose coupling mechanism at the expense of having less of a direct line between a function call and the source of the function. Similarly, getting carried away with directives and expressions can make templates difficult to read and maintain.

Because of the amount of magic involved for AngularJS to provide dependency injection, two-way binding, view directives, and so on, you might find it harder to debug your application should you hit a roadblock. It might not be as easy to figure out why something does not work in your AngularJS application than with other frameworks that are simpler and more straightforward under the hood.

Beyond the basics, the learning curve for AngularJS tends to be somewhat steeper than that of other frameworks that use a more traditional approach. If you get stuck, it may be challenging to find a solution.

Final Thoughts

There is a lot of excitement surrounding AngularJS. If its philosophy appeals to you and you decide to go further with AngularJS, you will find a large and enthusiastic community that shares your interest.

Ring

A bucket of LEGOs can be anything you want it to be. You can build a house, a car, or a spaceship, or just keep stacking them one on top of the other until you run out. Many different kinds of blocks exist, but every block works together, thanks to a simple, underlying design for connecting two blocks.

Functional languages like Clojure are a bucket of LEGOs. Each brick is simple; every brick can be used effortlessly with other bricks; bricks can be combined in many different and useful ways; and there are no hidden mechanisms or components to complicate your constructions.

Ring is how web libraries in Clojure are connected together. Like all LEGOs, Ring and its related libraries can be stacked and combined in endless ways to build the perfect web application. There's no master plan, few rules, and each construction is personal and unique.

Introducing Ring

Ring is not a web framework; it is a simple abstraction of HTTP interactions. While there are quite a few web libraries and even some web frameworks in Clojure, they all seem to build on Ring's foundations. In this chapter, we'll explore Ring and some of the most commonly used libraries that leverage it.

Ring models HTTP requests and responses as data. This data is easily manipulated and transformed by all of the standard Clojure tools. In a language designed for the manipulation of data, elevating HTTP to the level of data gives web developers using Ring enormous amounts of power. As Alan Perlis, a American computer scientist well known for his work on programming languages, once said, "It is better to have 100 functions operate on one data structure than 10 functions on 10 data structures."[1]

---

1.   http://www.cs.yale.edu/quotes.html

Throughout this chapter, you'll see how Ring's data is manipulated and transformed to provide URL routing, handle response generation, build middleware, and ease testing. Unlike many other frameworks and libraries, there's little magic to how it works. Inspecting the value of items in a dictionary, adding and removing items from lists, and similar mundane operations are all that lies behind the scenes.

On top of Ring, we'll look at libraries for handling common tasks. We'll explore these by using them to write a bug tracking application, complete with a REST API and the usual trimmings.

On the first day, we'll explore HTML generation with Hiccup, which turns HTML into data ready for slicing and dicing with Clojure. We'll see how Korma, a library for working with SQL databases, makes SQL more programmatic and reusable. Compojure will tie these pieces together by orchestrating which requests go where.

On Day 2, we'll turn to working on the REST API. We'll use data.json to deal with incoming and outgoing JSON data. To ensure the data is always what we expect, we'll employ Valip to do validation. We'll also come back to Compojure for a deeper look at URL routing.

Finally, on Day 3, we'll go behind the scenes of Ring itself to learn about middleware and how to write our own. We'll get a different perspective on HTML as data by investigating Enlive, one of the coolest templating libraries in any language. Last, but not least, we'll see one of the many ways to test Ring applications with clojure.test and Kerodon.

There's a lot to cover, but a picture may help put everything into perspective. Figure 19, *Ring application overview*, on page 117 shows a typical Ring application's architecture and how the pieces relate to one another.

Like Ring itself, many of these components elevate their domains to the level of data. This is a unique perspective on programming that is common in Clojure but reusable in almost any language. For web applications built on Ring, it's data all the way down.

Day 1: Basic Towers

Today we'll explore Ring and its friends in the context of Zap, a bug tracking application we're going to build. As with other bug trackers you may have used, Zap will record bugs for multiple projects, allow users to comment on bugs, and track the status of bugs as they are found and fixed. The architecture of Zap should be quite familiar; there is a database to store the bugs and other data, a way to map URLs to views, and helpers to generate HTML.

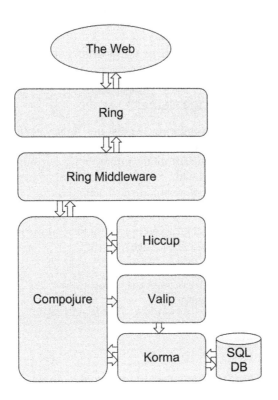

Figure 19—Ring application overview

Another thing to keep in mind today is that almost every component you will see is replaceable with something else. Later this week you'll see one of these alternatives.

Getting Started

Clojure is an interesting language because it is really just a library. There is no need for you to install Clojure as you would with most other languages. Instead, you only need a JVM and the Leiningen build tool.

You can find a JVM for your platform in your system's package manager or at http://www.oracle.com/technetwork/java/javase/downloads/index.html. Leiningen can be found at http://leiningen.org/. Please make sure you install Leiningen version 2, and not the older 1.x release.

All the dependencies your project needs will be declared in Leiningen's project.clj configuration file, including the version of Clojure your application will use.

Leiningen takes care of all the hard work of finding, downloading, and managing these dependencies. And if you've ever used Java or another JVM language before, you'll be relieved to know that Leiningen also handles the classpath for you.

Leiningen? What a Strange Name!

Leiningen is named after "Leiningen Versus the Ants," a short story by Carl Stephenson. This is a playful challenge to Java's classic build tool, Ant. The tool's primary author, Phil Hagelberg, contributes a number of interesting tools and libraries to the Clojure community, all with similarly imaginative names. For example, his Slamhound and Robert Hooke libraries are also quite nice.

Leiningen looks for dependencies in Clojars and the Maven Central Repository.[a] Clojars is a Ring application, and if you're looking for real world examples of Ring apps in production, its code is a good place to start.[b]

---

a.   https://clojars.org/ and http://search.maven.org/, respectively.
b.   https://github.com/ato/clojars-web

Hello, World!

Your first task is to create a new Leiningen project. In whatever directory you use to hold your projects, run the following command to create the initial project skeleton.

```
$ lein new hello
Generating a project called hello based on the 'default' template.
To see other templates (app, lein plugin, etc), try `lein help new`.
```

Now you'll need to edit project.clj to add in the dependencies for your first Ring app. Make it similar to the following:

clojure/hello/project.clj
```
(defproject hello "0.1.0-SNAPSHOT"
  :description "Hello World"
❶  :dependencies [[org.clojure/clojure "1.5.1"]
                 [ring/ring-core "1.1.8"]
                 [compojure "1.1.5"]]

❷  :plugins [[lein-ring "0.8.3"]]

❸  :ring {:handler hello.core/app})
```

❶ These are the project's dependencies. They are written [GROUP-ID/ARTIFACT-ID "VERSION"]. These identifiers are often specified in a library's README. If both the GROUP-ID and ARTIFACT-ID are the same, the GROUP-ID can be omitted.

❷ The :plugins keyword defines Leiningen plugins to activate in this project. The format is the same as for the :dependencies section. In this case, lein-ring provides some handy helpers for packaging and running Ring applications.

❸ The :ring section is the configuration for the lein-ring plugin. :handler points to the top-level Ring handler that defines the application. The value is a namespace-qualified symbol. The part before the slash is a namespace, and the part after is the symbol bound to the application.

The last thing to do for this simple app is to write the code.

Source code in Leiningen projects is stored under src. The filesystem heirarchy under src exactly mirrors the namespace heirarchy. For example, the code for the namespace hello.core would be in src/hello/core.clj. The code for com.prag-prog.7web.zap.views would be found in src/com/pragprog/7web/zap/views.clj. If you're familiar with Java namespaces and packages, you should feel right at home.

> ## Clojure Naming Issues
>
> In Clojure, it is idiomatic to use dashes to separate parts of names instead of under-scores or camel case. For example, you'd use :project-name instead of :project_name or :projectName. This is true whether the name is a keyword, symbol, or namespace.
>
> Unfortunately, since Clojure namespaces are Java packages and dashes are not legal in Java identifiers, this can cause some problems if you aren't careful. The solution is to use underscores in filenames but use the dashes in the namespace names. For example, the namespace hello.people-of-earth would be defined in the file:
>
> src/hello/people_of_earth.clj
>
> The Clojure compiler automatically transforms the dashes into underscores behind the scenes, but it expects the files to use the underscores.

Leiningen's default project template already created the file src/hello/core.clj defining the hello.core namespace. Replace the example code with this minimal application:

clojure/hello/src/hello/core.clj
```
(ns hello.core
  (:use compojure.core))
(defroutes app
  (GET "/" []
    "Hello, World!"))
```

❶ The (:use ...) form in the namespace declaration pulls in all the symbols from compojure.core, so they are easily available in the current namespace. This is needed for the defroutes and GET symbols used later.

❷ defroutes defines routes for the application. It is similar to other def-like forms in Clojure; you provide a symbol for it to bind the routes to. You'll notice the symbol is app and the current namespace is hello.core, which means this matches the Ring plugin configuration in projects.clj that pointed to hello.core/app. The routes are listed in order, and the routing logic will check each route in turn, moving on to the next if a given route does not match.

❸ The only route listed defines a handler for the HTTP GET method to the root path. The empty vector, [], will be discussed later and is used to bind path parameters given in the route. The value returned here is a simple string; Compojure will handle the transformation of strings into suitable HTTP 200 responses.

The only thing left to do is to start the application and test it out. This is where Clojure's leverage of the Java ecosystem and Leiningen's plugin capabilities really shine. Run the following command in your hello project directory.

```
$ lein ring server
2013-03-02 21:34:21.040:INFO:oejs.Server:jetty-7.6.1.v20120215
Started server on port 3000
```

This command starts up a local server on port 3000 and opens your default web browser to the root URL of your application. If you are running this on a server without a windowing system, you can use lein ring server-headless instead to skip opening the browser.

Your output might differ from the output shown before, as Leiningen may need to download the various dependencies needed to run the server and your application.

If everything went to plan, you should see the words "Hello, World!" greeting you in your browser. Congratulations! You've now written your first Ring application. Next, we'll start creating the bug tracker, Zap, and learning about other useful libraries for web applications.

Tasty Data with Korma

There are as many ways to build web applications as there are programmers. Some start by designing URL structures, some by mocking up HTML for the user interface, and some by organizing data. We're going to start from the data and build up from there to views and routing. One advantage of this method is that when we get to views, we won't have to create or worry about dummy data; we'll have models already created to play with.

What's in a Bug Tracker?

Our fictional users have a set of features they'd like to see in Zap. They have multiple projects they'd like to track. Every issue will have a title and a description as well as the ability for others to add comments. An issue can have several statuses, like "open" or "fixed." This is a pretty simple design, but it should be plenty for the first iteration. Your users will have many feature and change requests once we've put a working project in their hands.

The data can be easily realized in a relational model, and so we'll use a relational database to store it. Any of the well-known databases will work for our purposes, but in order to reduce the number of moving parts you'll have to deal with, we'll choose SQLite.

Many frameworks in other languages allow you to create your data model with code, avoiding SQL entirely. Clojure does not have a similar tool yet, so we'll have to make do with writing the schema directly in SQL.

Spend a few moments thinking about the different pieces and how they'd fit together, and then take a look at the following to see the schema we'll be working with throughout this chapter:

clojure/zap/day1/resources/data/schema.sql

```
-- zap schema

CREATE TABLE project (
  id INTEGER PRIMARY KEY,
  name TEXT NOT NULL
);

CREATE TABLE issue (
  id INTEGER PRIMARY KEY,
  project_id INTEGER REFERENCES project(id) NOT NULL,
  title TEXT NOT NULL,
  description TEXT NOT NULL,
  status INTEGER REFERENCES status(id) NOT NULL
);

CREATE TABLE status (
  id INTEGER PRIMARY KEY,
  name TEXT NOT NULL
);

CREATE TABLE comment (
  id INTEGER PRIMARY KEY,
  issue_id INTEGER REFERENCES issue(id) NOT NULL,
  content TEXT NOT NULL
);
```

```
-- status enums
INSERT INTO status (id, name) VALUES (1, 'open');
INSERT INTO status (id, name) VALUES (2, 'fixed');
INSERT INTO status (id, name) VALUES (3, 'wontfix');
INSERT INTO status (id, name) VALUES (4, 'invalid');
```

Aside from the four needed tables, we've also inserted the statuses needed for the app. Now, in your project directory, create the database and load the schema. Most systems these days ship with a copy of SQLite, but if yours doesn't—Windows for example—then you can grab a copy from the SQLite website.[2]

```
$ sqlite3 -init resources/data/schema.sql zap.db .quit
-- Loading resources from resources/data/schema.sql
```

With our new database created, we can dive into how to access it from Clojure.

Building Models

We'll be using the Korma library to work with our database.[3] Unlike object relational mapping (ORM) systems in other frameworks, Korma sticks close to the concepts in SQL. However, it exposes SQL in a way that is composable, and you'll see why this is useful shortly.

First, we'll have to tell Korma about our database and the things in it. Korma calls the tables in the database *entities*. Just as Clojure has def and defn for defining symbols and functions and Compojure used defroute to define routes, Korma has defdb and defentity, which do exactly what they sound like:

clojure/zap/day1/src/zap/models.clj
```
(ns zap.models
   (:refer-clojure :exclude [comment])
   (:use korma.db korma.core)
   (:require [clojure.string :as string]))

(defdb zap
   (sqlite3 {:db "zap.db"}))

(defentity project
   (entity-fields :id :name))

(declare comment)
(defentity issue
   (entity-fields :id :project_id :title :description :status)
   (has-many comment))
```

_____

2. https://www.sqlite.org/
3. http://sqlkorma.com/

```
(defentity status
  (entity-fields :id :name))

(defentity tag
  (entity-fields :id :issue_id :tag))

(defentity comment
  (entity-fields :id :issue_id :content)
❺ (belongs-to issue))
```

❶ This line might look a little odd if you haven't seen :refer-clojure before. Since the ns macro automatically refers all the symbols in clojure.core, we have to tell it to exclude comment since it clashes with one of our entities.

❷ Here we define the database. For SQLite the configuration is quite simple; but for a real database, this is where you'd find the username, password, and host parameters.

❸ entity-fields tells Korma what fields to return by default in queries. It's not required, but it's useful to have in case your schema changes later.

❹ Korma has support for defining relationships between entities. The has-many relationship means there are zero or more comments associated with each issue. This information can be used in queries to do some types of automatic joins.

❺ belongs-to is the inverse of has-many.

This may look familiar to model definitions in other frameworks you've seen. Note that there's no behavior here, only description of the data.

Exploring with the REPL

Before we dive into implementing the models, let's play with Korma at the REPL. You can launch the REPL with lein repl from your project directory and then use the in-ns function to switch to the zap.models namespace after loading it:

```
nREPL server started on port 54315
REPL-y 0.1.9
Clojure 1.4.0
«help text»
user=> (require 'zap.models)
«omitted output»
nil
user=> (in-ns 'zap.models)
#<Namespace zap.models>
zap.models=>
```

Let's start by adding some projects into the database. Like SQL, Korma uses insert to create new rows:

```
zap.models=> (insert project (values {:name "Zap"}))
«omitted output»
{:last_insert_rowid() 1}
zap.models=> (insert project (values {:name "Website"}))
{:last_insert_rowid() 2}
```

Queries are done using select. You can choose what fields to include (overriding the default specified by entity-fields) using fields. where works as you expect but with Clojure expressions:

```
zap.models=> (select project)
[{:name "Zap", :id 1} {:name "Website", :id 2}]
zap.models=> (select project (fields :name))
[{:name "Zap"} {:name "Website"}]
zap.models=> (select project (where {:id 1}))
[{:name "Zap", :id 1}]
zap.models=> (select project (where (or (> :id 1) (= :name "Zap"))))
[{:name "Zap", :id 1} {:name "Website", :id 2}]
```

Passing a map to where is a shortcut syntax. Each key is a field name, and the value is the expression that must hold. All the keys and values in the map must match for the where to match. The Korma documentation goes into more detail on this.

In addition to where clauses, you can also have order, group, and join, which correspond directly to their SQL counterparts. Deleting rows and updating columns works very similarly to select, and you'll see those as we write the model code for Zap.

Model Functions

We still need to define our model functions that the rest of the web app needs. We'll need to create projects, issues, and comments; list projects and issues; get details about an issue; and change issue status. Let's start with the project-related functions. If you like, you can also experiment with these functions at the REPL.

clojure/zap/day1/src/zap/models.clj
```
(defn all-projects []
  (select project))

(defn create-project [proj]
  (insert project (values proj)))

(defn project-by-id [id]
  (first (select project (where {:id id})))))
```

❶ select always returns a list, even if the query returns a unique row. We use first here to return the result. If the result list is empty, first returns nil.

The issue-related functions are slightly more complex:

clojure/zap/day1/src/zap/models.clj
```
❶ (defn- issue-query []
❷   (-> (select* issue)
❸       (fields [:issue.id :id]
                  :project_id
                  :title
                  :description
                  [:status.id :status_id]
                  [:status.name :status_name])
❹       (join status (= :issue.status :status.id)))))

(defn issues-by-project [id]
❺   (-> (issue-query)
        (where {:issue.project_id id})
❻       exec))

(defn issue-by-id [id]
    (-> (issue-query)
        (where {:issue.id id})
        exec
        first))
```

❶ This is a helper function that returns a partial query. Since multiple model functions will need the right fields joined with the corresponding status row, those bits are factored out here.

❷ Unlike SQL, Korma's functions allow you to build queries incrementally without resorting to hacks like string concatenation. Here Clojure's threading operator builds a basic select query using select* and then augments it with the desired fields and a join. Other Korma functions also have *-versions that build queries incrementally. Some other frameworks have similar support, but Korma's is particularly elegant.

❸ Passing a vector instead of a keyword as a field creates an alias. In this case the id column of the issue table will appear as :id in the result list.

❹ Joining a second table is easy too. Here we match up the issue's status with the status table.

❺ Our query starts off with the partial query we built in our helper.

❻ Partial queries, like those created with select*, don't execute until passed to exec.

Comment and status functions are very similar.

Our users have requested the ability to search for specific bugs, and implementing find-issues gives us a chance to show off a few more interesting bits of Korma:

clojure/zap/day1/src/zap/models.clj
```
(defn find-issues [q]
  (let [q (str "%" (string/lower-case q) "%")]
    (-> (issue-query)
        (where (or (like (sqlfn lower :issue.title) q)
                   (like (sqlfn lower :issue.description) q)))
        exec)))
```

First, the query string is built. SQL requires % to be used for matching any surrounding text. Then, our issue-query helper is used once again. This composability thing is really starting to pay off. Finally, notice the use of like, which maps to its SQL counterpart of the same name, and sqlfn, which sets up a call to a built-in function in SQL so that the search is case insensitive.

With the models working, we can move on to the views.

HTML Is Data with Hiccup

Our views will be responsible for generating the HTML output for our application. We'll be using Hiccup to turn Clojure data into HTML output.[4] Leveraging Clojure's amazing data manipulation functions makes quick work of an otherwise tedious task.

The basic idea of Hiccup is simple. HTML elements are represented as vectors with a keyword for the element name, an optional map of attributes, and zero or more child elements or lists of child elements in the same format. Here are some examples:

clojure/examples/src/examples/hiccup1.clj
```
[:h1 "Zap Issue Tracker"]

[:div {:class :content}
 [:p "Do you have issues? Zap can help!"]
 [:p "Zap is a simple issue tracking solution ..."]]
```

This is just a less verbose syntax for the same content you'd write in HTML—hardly amazing. The trick is that any function that returns similar data structures can be used as well. This allows you to harness the full power of Clojure to automate the writing of HTML.

---

4. https://github.com/weavejester/hiccup

```
clojure/examples/src/examples/hiccup2.clj
[:ul
 (for [item items]
   [:li (:name item)])])]

[:body
 [:div {:class :header}
  (include-header)]

 [:div {:class :content}
  [:h1 "Welcome!"]
  [:p "..."]]]]
```

Hiccup provides a macro html to turn this data into actual HTML output. Let's run the first set of examples through Hiccup's html function.

```
clojure/examples/src/examples/hiccup1.clj
(require '[hiccup.core :refer [html]])

(html [:h1 "Zap Issue Tracker"])
;;=> "<h1>Zap Issue Tracker</h1>"

(html
 [:div {:class :content}
  [:p "Do you have issues? Zap can help!"]
  [:p "Zap is a simple issue tracking solution ..."]])
;;=> "<div class=\"content\"><p>Do you have issues? Zap can help!</p><p>Zap is a
;;    simple issue tracking solution ...</p></div>"
```

Hiccup is so simple that it is a bit deceiving. Turning HTML into data allows you to do all sorts of creative things. You might write a function that inserts headers or footers in pages, rewrites URLs, or filters sets of elements to be placed in a different page. And you'd do this the same way you'd insert elements into a vector, map over collections, or filter and concatenate any sequence.

Let's use Hiccup to generate our main page:

```
clojure/zap/day1/src/zap/views.clj
❶ (defn base-page [title & body]
    (html5
     [:head
❷     (include-css "/css/bootstrap.min.css")
      (include-css "/css/zap.css")
      [:title title]]
     [:body
      [:div {:class "navbar navbar-inverse"}
       [:div {:class :navbar-inner}
        [:a {:class :brand :href "/"} "Zap!"]
        [:form {:class "navbar-form pull-right"}
```

```
            [:input {:type :text :class :search-query :placeholder :Search}]]]]
```
❸   `[:div.container (seq body)]]]))`

```
(defn projects []
  (base-page
   "Projects - Zap"
   [:div.row.admin-bar
    [:a {:href "/projects/new"}
     "Add Project"]]
   [:h1 "Project List"]
   [:ol
```
❹
```
    (for [p (models/all-projects)]
      [:li [:a {:href (str "/project/" (:id p) "/issues")} (:name p)]])]])))
```

❶ base-page is a helper function that generates the main site template, inserting the title and the page content where appropriate.

❷ Hiccup includes several helpers like include-css to make your life easier. It simply generates the appropriate <link> tag.

❸ Since body might be a list or a vector, seq is used to turn it into a sequence. Hiccup will treat a vector as a literal element, but it treats a sequence as a list of children.

❹ You can read this as "for every project, p, generate a list item with p's information."

Here's the view for creating a new issue. Notice the form-generating functions that Hiccup provides:

clojure/zap/day1/src/zap/views.clj
```
(defn new-issue [id]
  (let [proj (models/project-by-id id)]
    (base-page
     (str "New Issue for " (:name proj) " - Zap")

     [:h1 "New Issue for " (:name proj)]
     (form-to
      [:post (str "/project/" (:id proj) "/issues")]
      (text-field {:class "span8"
                   :type :text
                   :placeholder "Title"} :title)
      [:br]
      (text-area {:class "span8"
                  :placeholder "Description"
                  :rows 5} :description)
      [:br]
      (submit-button {:class "btn btn-primary"} "Create Issue")))))
```

We won't show the other views here since they are all very similar. Check out src/zap/views.clj to see the rest of them.

We have almost all the pieces for a complete application. The last component is mapping URLs to views.

Routing with Compojure

Most web frameworks try to abstract routing logic to make it easy to create and manage the many URLs every web application needs. Quite a few choices for this component exist in Clojure, each with its own flavor and focus. We'll be using Compojure in Zap, which is one of the oldest and most popular of these routing libraries.

In addition to routing, we'll also need to take care of some plumbing relating to how incoming HTTP requests are processed. For example, it would be convenient if form parameters and query parameters were dealt with in a uniform way so that our code did not have to care about the difference. For this task, we'll be taking a brief look at some of the middleware that ships with Ring.

URLs and Views

In *Hello, World!*, you saw one example of a URL mapping to a view. Compojure's defroutes macro takes a series of such mappings and turns them into code that finds and executes the correct view for a given input URL. The easiest way to learn is to dive right into the routing for Zap:

```
clojure/zap/day1/src/zap/core.clj
(defroutes app-routes
❶  (GET "/" []
    (views/index))
  (GET "/projects" []
    (views/projects))
  (GET "/projects/new" []
    (views/new-project))
  (POST "/projects" [& params]
    (views/make-project params))

❷  (GET "/project/:id/issues" [id]
    (views/issues-by-project id))
  (GET "/project/:id/issue/new" [id]
    (views/new-issue id))
❸  (POST "/project/:id/issues" [id & params]
    (views/make-issue id params))

  (GET "/issue/:id" [id]
    (views/issue id))
```

```
(POST "/issue/:id/comments" [id & params]
  (views/make-comment id params))
(POST "/issue/:id/close" [id & params]
  (views/close-issue id params)))
```

❶ This is similar to the route you saw before, except that instead of returning a string, it returns the result of a function. In addition to GET routes, there are routes for all the common HTTP methods: POST, PUT, DELETE, and so on.

❷ As in function declarations, routes take a parameter list. The parameters, represented as keywords, are matched to their placeholders in the URL string. In this case, the keyword :id stands in for the second path element. It is mapped to a symbol of the same name, id, and made available to the code in the route's body.

❸ Sometimes your routing logic or your view will need access to other parts of the HTTP request data. The query parameters are passed into the function as keyword arguments, which you can collect into a map with the & params syntax. You could also use :as req to bind the entire request map to the req variable and access what you need from the request map.

The preceding routes are a complete set of routes for Zap. They aren't very complicated, mostly delegating the response to our view functions and passing in parameters where necessary. Compojure supports some input sanitization in the routes, such as limiting parameters to strings that conform to regular expressions or to integers in certain ranges. See the API documentation for more details.

We'll see some more advanced Compojure tricks tomorrow. For now, let's deal with the incoming data from clients, such as the information about an issue when the issue is being created.

Dealing with Input and Middleware

Compojure allows us to access the request map in our routing functions, but what data is in the request map and how can we get at it? The answer is that all the HTTP request data is there, but it is not always easily accessible.

The following snippet shows an example request map:

clojure/examples/src/examples/request.clj
```
{:remote-addr "127.0.0.1"
 :scheme :http
 :request-method :get
❶ :query-string "a=1&b=2"
 :route-params {}
 :content-type nil
 :uri "/foo"
```

```
:server-name "0.0.0.0"
:params {}
:headers {"accept-charset" "ISO-8859-1,utf-8;q=0.7,*;q=0.3"
          "accept-language" "en-US,en;q=0.8"
          "accept-encoding" "gzip,deflate,sdch"
          "user-agent" "Mozilla/5.0 ..."
          "accept" "text/html,..."
          "connection" "keep-alive"
          "host" "0.0.0.0:3000"}
:content-length nil
:server-port 3000
:character-encoding nil
:body #<Input org.mortbay.jetty.HttpParser$Input@4251b296>}
```

❶ The query string contains all the query parameters, but they aren't decoded at all.

❷ The input data stream may contain form parameters, but they aren't decoded either.

It wouldn't be very much fun to decode all this data yourself, and fortunately, Ring can do this kind of work for you. You might imagine yourself writing a function that transforms this request map into a slightly different one. Perhaps it decodes :query-string into its own map, :query-params. It could also do the same for the request input data. You could go even further and add new keys to the map to make web browser user agents easy to deal with.

Ring calls functions that transform the request map *middleware*. Middleware is also used to transform the response map in the same way. This simple idea is very powerful, since all of these small, simple functions can be composed together to achieve many different goals.

The hypothetical middleware to deal with query parameters and form parameters actually exists as part of Ring itself. ring.middleware.params/wrap-params and ring.middleware.keyword-params/wrap-keyword-params convert the raw data into the parameter maps :keyword-params and :form-params, combine those into a single and easy-to-use :params map, and finally convert all the keys from strings to Clojure keywords.

Since Ring middleware consists of simple data transformation functions, we can string them together along with our Compojure routes to put together an entire application. Here's the main application definition for Zap:

clojure/zap/day1/src/zap/core.clj
```
(def app
  (-> app-routes
      (wrap-resource "public")
      wrap-keyword-params
      wrap-params))
```

❶ app-routes is bound to Zap's routes, which were defined in defroutes.

❷ wrap-resource serves static files from the resources directory of your application. Zap uses this for CSS and images.

Due to some details that we'll explore on Day 3, middleware composition reads from bottom to top. First wrap-params will decode parameters, and then wrap-keyword-params will turn strings into keywords, any URLs matching static files will be served, and if none are found, our application routes will be tried. By the time Zap's routes are invoked, the request map is in beautiful shape.

With easy access to user input in the form of query and form parameters, let's write the view that creates new issues:

clojure/zap/day1/src/zap/views.clj
```
(defn make-issue [id params]
  (let [iss (merge params {:project_id id :status 1})]
    (models/create-issue iss)
    (response/redirect-after-post (str "/project/" id "/issues"))))
```

The code adds some default parameters to the user input and passes it off to the model function to create the issue. Since this is an HTTP POST method, we generate a redirect back to the list of issues instead of returning a normal response. Ring includes several helpful response generators like this one in the ring.util.response namespace.

What We Learned on Day 1

The first day is always the toughest, but here you are at the end—great job! If you've not used Clojure much before, it might have been challenging to follow along with everything, but a cure for that is to spend some time at the REPL playing with individual pieces. Clojure programmers often build simple functions that obviously work and build more sophisticated constructions from there. Since most components shown today are, at their core, simple data transformations, it's that much easier to explore them interactively.

We went on a whirlwind tour of a basic, but quite functional, Ring application. Starting from data design, we built models with Korma, a library that turns SQL into composable functions. Hiccup made creating views to present the data as easy as writing down data structures. Compojure helped by matching URLs to views tying everything together. Finally, we explored Ring middleware, which helped transform user input into easy-to-use structures.

Each of these pieces primarily operates on simple data. Clojure's tool chest is sparse compared to many other languages, but it packs a wallop few can match.

Day 1 Self-Study

Find:

- James Reeves's blog and his talks on Clojure web development
- Other Ring applications on GitHub
- Alternative routing libraries

Do:

- Add bug counts to the project page.
- Add the ability to edit projects, bugs, and comments.
- Play with Korma's composable query capability.
- Move the database to MySQL or PostgreSQL.

Day 2: Patterns of Bricks

Master LEGO builders have internalized an enormous amount of architectural patterns that turn simple-looking bricks into specialized constructions. Certain bricks allow you to build sideways; well-placed hinges create off-axis surfaces; and novel uses of normal bricks add visual interest to a model. Clojure is a language of simple bricks that can be arranged into powerful patterns, and these patterns help you construct powerful web applications.

Let's put some of Clojure's common patterns to use to build the public API for Zap.

Defining the API

Before we build the API, we should have some idea of what it will do. We'll assume you've got some experience using or creating RESTful web APIs so that we can get straight to the fun bits—the implementation.

We'll need some way to list projects and issues, as well as a way to get detailed information on both. We'll also want to create, modify, and delete these resources as well.

Let's start with project operations (Table 1, *Project Operations*, on page 134). Next, we can define the issue operations (Table 2, *Issue Operations*, on page 134).

Comments will be returned together with the issue details instead of on their own. There's no need for a separate GET method for those.

In all cases the API will return data in JSON format and will accept input with standard form parameters.

Request	Description
POST /projects	Add a new project
GET /projects	Enumerate all projects
GET /project/ID	Get details for project *ID*
DELETE /project/ID	Delete project *ID*
PUT /project/ID	Update project details for *ID*

Table 1—Project Operations

Request	Description
POST /project/PID/issues	Create an issue for a project
GET /project/PID/issues	Enumerate all issues for a project
GET /project/PID/issue/IID	Get details about issue *IID*
DELETE /project/PID/issue/IID	Delete issue *IID*
PUT /project/PID/issue/IID	Update details for issue *IID*
POST /project/PID/issue/IID/comments	Add a comment for issue *IID*
DELETE /project/PID/issue/IID/comment/CID	Delete comment *CID*

Table 2—Issue Operations

With that out of the way, we can start implementing the API specification. We'll need to start by learning how to manipulate JSON data in a Ring app.

Dealing with JSON

Like every other programming language these days, the Clojure ecosystem contains multiple libraries for dealing with JSON-formatted data, and thanks to its first-class Java interop support, it has direct access to any of the Java JSON libraries available.

Since we're building a JSON-based API, we'll need some way to transform Clojure's data structures into JSON. The most straightforward way to do this is to use the data.json library, which is a part of Clojure's contrib libraries.

data.json is fairly flexible, but its workhorse functions are read-str and write-str. read-str takes a JSON string and returns the corresponding Clojure data structure, and write-str takes Clojure data and emits JSON strings.

Let's see an example:

clojure/examples/json.clj
```
(require '[clojure.data.json :as json])
(json/write-str {:foo 1 :bar 2})
;;=> "{\"foo\":1,\"bar\":2}"

(json/read-str "{\"foo\":1,\"bar\":2}")
;;=> {:foo 1 :bar 2}
```

The model functions we created yesterday closely parallel the API we want, and they already return Clojure data structures. This means that creating the read-only parts of the Zap API is just a matter of calling the model functions we already have and translating them to JSON.

Let's define the API's routes beginning with the project list by adding the following to the defroutes call in zap/core.clj:

clojure/zap/day2/src/zap/core.clj
```
(GET "/api/projects" []
  (json/write-str (models/all-projects)))
```

You can just add to the defroutes you made yesterday. This time, the handler function calls the appropriate model function and then emits a JSON string of the results instead of generating an HTML response.

The other read-only API calls are very similar:

clojure/zap/day2/src/zap/core.clj
```
(GET "/api/project/:id" [id]
  (if-let [proj (models/project-by-id id)]
    (json/write-str proj)
    {:status 404 :body ""}))
(GET "/api/project/:pid/issues" [pid]
  (json/write-str (models/issues-by-project pid)))
(GET "/api/project/:pid/issue/:iid" [pid iid]
  (json/write-str (models/issue-by-id iid)))
```

Notice the repeating parts in the route bodies. You can refactor this tomorrow when we learn more about writing our own Ring middleware.

Now that the read-only parts are out of the way, let's work on the parts that add, modify, or delete data.

Validating Inputs

In order to accept input from the API's consumers, we need to validate that it is correct before storing it in the database. One way to do this is to write a series of guard clauses in the API views that test for various error conditions on the data. Is the name of the project nonempty? Is the status of the issue one of the four legal values? Are all the required fields of the issue provided?

This approach has several problems. The first is that the validation code might be repeated in different places; for example, the create project and edit project actions will both need to validate project data. The second problem is that a large tree of nested if expressions is hard to read and to maintain.

The normal solution to this problem is to factor out the validation routines into their own functions, such as valid-project? and valid-issue?. However, this only solves the first of the two problems.

The Clojure solution is to use the power of the language to abstract away the nested if expressions. Imagine a declarative language like the following one, where you specify a list of rules, each containing a field name, a simple validation, and an error message. Then when checking input data against this rule set, the result is a list of errors broken out by key:

```
(defvalidator valid-project?
  [:name present? "name must be specified"]
  [:name (min-length 1) "name must not be blank"])

(valid-project? {:foo "bar"})
;;=> {:name ["name must be specified" "name must not be blank"]}
```

This is even better than just factoring out the validation logic, as now it also returns an easy-to-use list of problems that you can use to build a good error message for the API's consumer or for a user.

Decomposing problems this way is common in functional languages like Clojure, and it allows the sum of the parts to become greater than the whole as they are combined in new and interesting ways.

Designing this hypothetical DSL is pretty easy in practice. A simple Clojure macro enables the extra bit of syntax, and the validation logic is simply iterating over the rules and checking them while building up the validation result. Fortunately for us, several such DSLs exist for Clojure already, and for Zap we'll be using Valip, yet another great library written by James Reeves.[5]

Using Valip

Valip consists of two simple parts. The first is the validate function, which takes a map structure to validate and the validation rules. The second part is the predicates that are used within the rules.

Here's the previous example translated into Valip:

---

5.   https://github.com/weavejester/valip

```
clojure/examples/src/examples/valip.clj
(require '[valip.core :refer [validate]]
         '[valip.predicates :refer [present? min-length]])

(defn valid-project [proj]
  (validate proj
    [:name present? "name must be specified"]
    [:name (min-length 1) "name must not be blank"]))
```

Besides present? and min-length, Valip includes other useful predicates such as max-length, matches (which tests the field against a regular expression), url?, numeric?, between, and even dns-lookup (which verifies a given hostname is resolvable). Writing your own predicates is also very easy. Here's the min-length predicate from Valip's src/valip/predicates.clj:

```
clojure/examples/src/examples/valip.clj
(defn min-length
  "Creates a predicate that returns true if a string's length is greater than
          or equal to the supplied minimum."
  [min]
  (fn [s] (>= (count s) min)))
```

Let's create a few validations for Zap:

```
clojure/zap/day2/src/zap/validations.clj
(ns zap.validations
  (require [valip.core :refer [validate]]
           [valip.validations :refer [present?]]))

(defn valid-project? [proj]
  (validate proj
    [:name present? "name must be specified"]
    [:name (min-length 1) "name must not be blank"]))

(defn valid-issue? [iss]
  (validate iss
    [:title present? "title must be specified"]
    [:title (min-length 1) "title must not be blank"]
    [:description present? "description must be specified"]
    [:description (min-length 1) "description must not be blank"]
    [:status (between 1 4) "status id must be between 1 and 4"]))
```

Validating comments is left for you to finish during today's self-study.

Now that validations are handled, all that's left is to use them in our API views.

Finishing Off the API

Once again our task is relatively easy thanks to the model code that we created yesterday. Let's start with the create-project view, which is called when POST /api/projects is called to create a new project entry:

```
clojure/zap/day2/src/zap/views.clj
(defn create-project [params]
  (let [errors (valids/valid-project? params)]
    (if errors
      {:status 400
       :body (json/write-str {:errors errors})}
      (do
        (models/create-project params)
        {:status 200 :body ""}))))
```

First the validator runs and collect the errors. If there are any, a 400 status response is returned for the bad request along with the list of errors in JSON format. If there were no errors, the project is created.

Let's look at something slightly more complex, the edit-project view. Unlike create-project, this view might be invoked for an invalid project ID. In that case, we'll need to return a 404 Not Found error message. Other than that, the logic is largely the same:

```
clojure/zap/day2/src/zap/views.clj
(defn edit-project [id params]
  (let [errors (valids/valid-project? params)]
    (if errors
      {:status 400
       :body (json/write-str {:errors errors})}
      (if-let [proj (models/project-by-id id)]
        (do
          (models/update-project id params)
          {:status 200 :body ""})
        {:status 404 :body ""}))))
```

Notice that valid-project? might be doing a lot of complicated validations on the data if our bug tracker was itself more complicated. The code here would not need to change much to support that—perhaps only to provide better error messages—and our validation logic would remain the same clear list of rules, albeit somewhat longer.

The rest of the API's views will be similar to the ones shown before for project-related actions. Think about how you might abstract some of this away; Clojure makes it easy!

With API views under control, we should revisit routing to see if we can make some improvements.

Composable Routes

Yesterday we used the defroutes macro to create a set of URL routing rules for Zap. One way to add the new routes needed for Zap's API would be to add more routing rules to the list; this is what the API has used so far. For non-trivial applications, this list of routes is likely to be very long, and it would be better if the routing logic could be built up in smaller pieces that are then composed together into a master list of routes. The defroutes macro has a syntax for this: the context route.

The arguments to context are the same as those to GET and POST. Instead of writing the routing actions directly, you can just pass the name of the set of routes you created elsewhere. The defroutes macro creates a Ring handler that can be used directly in route bodies.

The way context works behind the scenes is very simple. It just tests for the path prefix you specified as the second argument, trims that prefix off the path, and passes the modified request into the handler given as the last argument.

Let's see a simple example:

```
(defroutes sub-routes
  (GET "/bar" [] "Bar")
  (GET "/baz" [] "Baz")

(defroutes app-routes
  (GET "/" [] "Root")
  (context "/foo" [] sub-routes))
```

First, a set of routes is defined, sub-routes, handling a related group of routing rules. Then the context syntax is used to include that group of rules under the path /foo. Now retrieving path / will return Root, /foo/bar will return Bar, and /foo/baz will return Baz.

Note that the routes in sub-routes don't need any knowledge of where in the path they'll ultimately end up. If you later decide to move this group of routes under /legacy/foo, it is as simple as changing the prefix given to context.

A complex application might have many different groups of routing rules defined, each group being relatively simple. The main application routes are then just a list of context definitions tying it all together.

Since Zap is relatively simple, we'll split the routing logic into two groups. The first group will be the routes we created yesterday, and the second will be the API routes. Finally, the app-routes will just compose the two groups along with the static resources and error handlers:

clojure/zap/day2/src/zap/core.clj

```clojure
(defroutes api-routes
  (GET "/projects" []
    (json/write-str (models/all-projects)))
  (GET "/project/:id" [id]
    (if-let [proj (models/project-by-id id)]
      (json/write-str proj)
      {:status 404 :body ""}))
  (GET "/project/:pid/issues" [pid]
    (json/write-str (models/issues-by-project pid)))
  (GET "/project/:pid/issue/:iid" [pid iid]
    (json/write-str (models/issue-by-id iid)))

  (POST "/projects" [& params]
    (views/create-project params))
  (DELETE "/project/:id" [id]
    (views/delete-project id))
  (PUT "/project/:id" [id & params]
    (views/edit-project id params)))

(defroutes app-routes
  (GET "/" []
    (views/index))
  (GET "/projects" []
    (views/projects))
  (GET "/projects/new" []
    (views/new-project))
  (POST "/projects" [& params]
    (views/make-project params))

  (GET "/project/:id/issues" [id]
    (views/issues-by-project id))
  (GET "/project/:id/issue/new" [id]
    (views/new-issue id))
  (POST "/project/:id/issues" [id & params]
    (views/make-issue id params)))

(defroutes all-routes
  (context "" [] app-routes)
  (context "/api" [] api-routes))

(def app
  (-> app-routes
      (wrap-resource "public")
      wrap-keyword-params
      wrap-params))
```

Now the two sections are completely separated, and each section contains only pertinent entries. Extraneous things like static resources and request processing are handled entirely in the piece that glues everything together.

Notice also that it's not just one function calling a bunch of helpers. Routes are composable in that they can call each other, delegate to other functions, be combined with other routes, or be wrapped by Ring middleware. Since each route is itself a Ring handler, you may invoke it directly, passing in a request map and getting a response map in return. This property makes them extremely easy to test.

This composition is not by any means limited to routes either. Korma, the library we used yesterday for talking to our SQL data store, puts SQL into a composable form, allowing reuse of WHERE clauses and field specifications. There's no need to do fancy string concatenation; you can just combine the simple parts into a bigger whole, reusing or delegating as is convenient.

Composition and its complement, separation of concerns, is one of the core building blocks of Clojure applications. Rich Hickey, in his talk "Simple Made Easy,"[6] used the word *complected*, meaning interleaved or braided, to describe code that is not simple. By separating complected components, you simplify your code and enable the individual pieces to be reused and combined in new and interesting ways. Think of how useful the simple LEGO bricks are compared to a brick shaped like a car. You can build a car from the simple bricks fairly easily, but building anything else from a car brick is going to be frustrating at best.

What We Learned on Day 2

The Ring stack is a collection of simple, useful, reusable pieces that can be put together in many configurations to solve problems. Today we looked at more compositional patterns in the context of designing the public API for Zap.

We defined what methods and paths the Zap API would contain, sticking to common best practices.

We looked at how easy it is to work with JSON data in Clojure. JSON comes particularly easily for Clojure since it has a rich set of data structures and data structure literals that are even more powerful and convenient than JSON itself.

We also looked at one way of handling data validation using the Valip library. Valip made validations clear and simple with its handy DSL, decomposing the validation logic.

---

6. http://www.infoq.com/presentations/Simple-Made-Easy

Finally, we showed how composition of routing is used to define small, separate bits of the application's routing logic and then combine them easily into a greater whole.

Tomorrow we'll look at another way to generate HTML and delve deeper into Ring handlers and middleware. And, of course, there will be more examples of composition.

Day 2 Self-Study

Find:

- The Compojure API documentation
- The data.json API documentation
- Alternative validation libraries

Do:

- Implement comment validation.
- Finish the rest of the API views.
- Refactor the API to support both XML and JSON output formats.
- Add support for paging to the API using offset and limit parameters. (Hint: Take a look at Clojure's take and drop functions.)

Day 3: Other Ways to Build

Our tour thus far has been of a typical stack a Ring app would use. We'll now explore a few side alleys and an alternative templating library to give you a flavor of the myriad of options available. Clojure programmers have been refining ideas from other languages and frameworks, as well as striking out on paths less travelled in their search for web programming enlightenment.

You saw Ring middleware briefly on previous days, and today we'll dive a little deeper so that you can write your own middleware. The pattern used by Ring middleware appears in other Clojure libraries as well—notably in nREPL, the network REPL library—and it is a useful one to know.

Hiccup templating is convenient and fast for Clojure programmers, but it probably isn't the best interface for designers. We'll look at Enlive, the other big name in Clojure templating libraries, and see what solutions it can offer to this problem.

Testing is important, and we'll wrap up with a basic example test. Let's jump right in!

Ring Middleware

On the first day of your Ring journey, we suggested thinking about Ring middleware as simple data transformation functions that modified either the request or response maps provided by Ring. The reality is slightly more complicated, due to the fact that instead of transforming maps directly, we're building a pipeline of transformations to be executed whenever requests are handled. Because Clojure is a functional language, it probably won't surprise you that middleware actually manipulates *functions*.

Functional programming has function right there in its name, so you know it must be important. In functional languages, functions themselves are first-class values just like integers or objects. This means that functions can return functions, variables can be bound to functions, and functions can be passed as arguments to other functions. This is a very powerful concept, and you may have gotten a taste of it from other languages that have borrowed ideas from Lisp.

Let's look at some examples of functions returning functions. To motivate the example, we'll start with a simple goal: write a function that modifies an input list by changing strings to keywords.

clojure/examples/src/examples/function_return.clj
```
(defn keywordize [l]
  (for [elem l]
    (if (string? elem)
      (keyword elem)
      elem)))

(keywordize [1 2 "foo" 3 "bar"])
;;=> (1 2 :foo 3 :bar)
```

Pretty straightforward, right? Imagine that you've been handed some function that transforms a list, and you'd like to add the keywordize transformation as well. Easy! Just call the original function on the list and then pass that result to keywordize.

clojure/examples/src/examples/function_return.clj
```
(keywordize (other-transform [1 2 "foo" 3 "bar"]))
;; or
(-> [1 2 "foo" 3 "bar"]
    other-transform
    keywordize)
```

A problem occurs if you don't have the input on hand and ready. Given a transforming function, we'd like to modify it by adding more transformations and then return a new transforming function that can be used by other parts of the code—sometime later, when input is available. To do this, we need to return a function instead of simply applying a function:

clojure/examples/src/examples/function_return.clj
```
(defn wrap-keywordize [f]
  (fn [l]
    (keywordize (f l))))
```

If wrap-keywordize is called on a transforming function, it returns a new function that runs the original transformation and then runs keywordize on the result. You'll notice that keywordize is operating on f's output, but what if we wanted it to operate on its input? Perhaps f's transformations already expect strings to be replaced by keys.

clojure/examples/src/examples/function_return.clj
```
(defn wrap-keywordize-output [f]
  (fn [l]
    (keywordize (f l))))

(defn wrap-keywordize-input [f]
  (fn [l]
    (f (keywordize l))))
```

With the -output and -input versions of the wrappers, we can now wrap either way. And nothing stops you from wrapping both input and output.

This function manipulation is mind-bending stuff, so go through the steps a few times if it hasn't quite sunk in fully. The change from applying functions to returning functions is simple, but it is disproportionately powerful. Instead of adding a wing to an airplane, it can add the power to fly to anything you give it.

If you've made it this far, then congratulations—you understand how Ring middleware works! Of course, instead of lists as input, Ring passes the request map, and instead of lists as output, the function at the center of the transformation generates a response map. Ring middleware can choose to transform one or both of these maps, just as our wrapping functions transformed the input and output.

We can put middleware to use to solve a problem in Zap. All of the API routes need to serialize their response to JSON. It would be nice if we could wrap API functions with middleware that did that transformation for us.

Think for a bit about how you might do this, and then take a peek at the following solution:

```
clojure/examples/src/examples/function_return.clj
(defn wrap-json-response [f]
  (fn [req]
    (let [resp (f req)
          body (:body resp)]
      (assoc req :body (json/write-str body)))))
```

Adding wrap-json-response to the list of Ring middleware for your application will change responses that are normal Clojure data structures into their JSON representations. We no longer need to call json/write-str in every route.

Enlive

Let's climb up from the bottom of the stack in the caves of Ring, right up to the mountain summit that is HTML templating. In *HTML Is Data with Hiccup*, we played with Hiccup by writing HTML in Clojure data structures. Let's look now at Enlive, which manipulates existing HTML content to produce output.

Enlive is HTML origami, and it is just as clever and beautiful. You first create a mockup of the HTML output you'd like, and then you use that mockup directly as the HTML template, transforming it via simple changes to the output you want. For example, the mockup HTML might contain a list of dummy projects. In the transformation, the first <li> element would be used as a template to populate with a single project's data, and then one list item would be created for each project, replacing the dummy items.

Even better, the transformations are written using CSS selectors and Hiccup-like data structures. Instead of dealing with partials, which are just templates of pieces of HTML instead of whole HTML documents, templates can be extracted from the mockup output and reused anywhere. HTML designers never have to use anything but HTML, and their mockups never need to be translated into templates at all. Instead, you write the transformations needed to change the mockup into real output in situ.

Before we can transform anything, we need some HTML to work on. Let's pretend that an amazing designer friend of ours has handed us a mockup of the Projects page for Zap:

```
clojure/zap/day3/resources/templates/projects.html
<!DOCTYPE html>
<html>
  <head>
    <link href="/css/bootstrap.min.css" rel="stylesheet" type="text/css">
    <link href="/css/zap.css" rel="stylesheet" type="text/css">
    <title>Projects - Zap</title>
  </head>
```

```
<body>
  <div class="navbar navbar-inverse">
    <div class="navbar-inner">
      <a class="brand" href="/">Zap!</a>
      <form class="navbar-form pull-right">
        <input class="search-query" placeholder="Search" type="text">
      </form>
    </div>
  </div>

  <div class="container">
    <div class="row admin-bar">
      <a href="/projects/new">Add Project</a>
    </div>

    <h1>Project List</h1>

    <ol>
      <li>
        <a href="/project/1/issues">Zap</a>
      </li>
      <li>
        <a href="/project/2/issues">Website</a>
      </li>
    </ol>
  </div>
</body>
</html>
```

Enlive provides a macro deftemplate that creates a template function from an
HTML file and a list of transformation rules. Let's look at a simple template
that just changes the page title:

clojure/examples/src/examples/enlive.clj
```
(use 'net.cgrand.enlive-html)

(deftemplate page-with-title "templates/projects.html"
  [title]

  [:title] (content (str title " - Zap")))
```

deftemplate is similiar to defn. It takes a name for the new function, the path to
the template relative to the project's resources directory, the parameters for the
function, and finally the body. The body of a template consists of transformations, each of which is a CSS selector and transformation function pair. CSS
selectors are written as keywords in a vector. This example selects all elements
whose tag is title. The content transformation function replaces the content of
the matched elements.

Enlive supports most CSS selectors. A selector of #content .big a would be written [:#content :.big :a]. Enlive's selector syntax reference contains more details.[7] With these, you can easily express targets for transformations.

In addition to the function content, Enlive also provides set-attr for setting attributes on elements, add-class for adding new CSS classes to elements, remove-attr, and do->, which strings together several transformations at once. You can also wrap any of these functions in normal Clojure expressions like if or cond to get dynamic behavior.

You can also make *snippets* in Enlive, which are like templates but created from an extracted piece of a document. Let's make a snippet we can reuse for the project list's <li> elements:

clojure/examples/src/examples/enlive.clj
```
(defsnippet project-item
❶  "templates/projects.html" [:.container :ol [:li first-child]]
   [proj]

❷  [:a] (do->
         (set-attr :href (str "/project/" (:id proj) "/issues"))
         (content (:name proj))))
```

❶ The only difference between deftemplate and defsnippet is the extra selector to choose what elements to extract from the base HTML. Notice the new selector notation [:li first-child] in the snippet definition; this is equivalent to CSS's li:first-child. In order to express this compound selector in Enlive, it gets wrapped in its own vector. Enlive's first-child selector predicate is just one of many choices. Some other interesting predicates are nth-child, attr?, and text-pred.

❷ Here's do-> in action combining several transformations into a single one.

That covers the basics of Enlive. Let's put it to use and rewrite the whole project list view for Zap:

clojure/zap/day3/src/zap/views.clj
```
❶ (deftemplate base-page "templates/projects.html"
   [title & body]
   [:title] (content title)
   [:.container] (content body))

(defsnippet admin-bar
   "templates/projects.html" [:.container :.admin-bar]
   [links]
```

---

7. http://enlive.cgrand.net/syntax.html

```
❷    [:a (but first-child)] nil
❸    [:a] (clone-for [[url title] links]
           (do->
             (set-attr :href url)
             (content title))))

(defsnippet project-item
  "templates/projects.html" [:.container :ol [:li first-child]]
  [proj]
  [:a] (do->
         (set-attr :href (str "/project/" (:id proj) "/issues"))
         (content (:name proj))))

(defn projects []
  (base-page
   "Projects - Zap"

   (admin-bar {"/projects/new" "Add Project"})
❹   (html [:h1 "Project List"])
   (map project-item (models/all-projects))))
```

❶ The base page is created from the mockup, replacing just a few key sections.

❷ The predicate but negates a predicate. Here all children but the first are deleted so that only one element is actually cloned by the next rule.

❸ clone-for clones an element once for each item in a collection. It mirrors Clojure's for syntax, except the body in this case is a transformation.

❹ html creates new DOM nodes in Enlive using Hiccup syntax.

The end result is slightly more verbose than straight Hiccup code, but your designer can now work completely independently in a familiar medium. Integration work only requires agreement on page structure, and it's easy to change CSS selectors in the code if the page structure changes.

A Little About Testing

As the final leg of our tour, let's look very quickly at one way you can test your Ring app. Clojure has great testing facilities, including clojure.test for unit testing, as well as test.generative, which generates random test cases from simple rules. For testing Ring applications, there is Kerodon.[8]

Kerodon adds the ability to interact with Ring apps inside of tests in a convenient way. You can simulate browsing to pages, filling in forms, pressing buttons, and even following redirects. Here's a small example:

8.　https://github.com/xeqi/kerodon

clojure/zap/day3/test/zap/basic.clj

```
(deftest projects-page-exists
  (-> (session zap/app)
      (visit "/projects")
      (has (status? 200) "page exists")
      (within [:h1]
        (has (text? "Project List") "header is there"))))
```

You can run your tests with lein test:

```
$ lein test
lein test zap.basic

Testing zap.basic

Ran 1 tests containing 2 assertions.
0 failures, 0 errors.
```

This test visits /projects, checks the HTTP status code of the response, and ensures some known text is present in the page. Behind the scenes Kerodon is building Ring request maps on your behalf and checking that the response maps meet your expectations. Other libraries for testing Ring exist as well, and several other styles of testing frameworks are also available, so try a few and find your favorite.

What We Learned on Day 3

Today was a quick overview of some interesting pieces of the Ring ecosystem. The Clojure community innovates rapidly, and many libraries are competing for their place in your toolbox. There are too many such tools to cover in an entire book, let alone a single chapter, but you should now have a taste for what's out there.

We looked at Ring middleware, which is an important layer in the application stack, stringing together transformations of HTTP requests and responses. Ring middleware is yet another place where Clojure's power of composition shines brightly. The compositional patterns in Clojure can be tricky to wrap your mind around if you aren't used to that level of abstraction.

Enlive is a radical departure from traditional templates in other frameworks, but it is one that works well, especially in teams where HTML is written by nondevelopers. It expresses CSS selectors as data, giving you easy access to manipulate HTML.

Last, but certainly not least, we looked at one approach to testing. Since Ring applications are, at heart, simple functions that take and return maps, testing them is surprisingly easy, even without the help of great libraries like Kerodon.

Day 3 Self-Study

Find:

- More Enlive tutorials
- Other templating frameworks to compare with Hiccup and Enlive

Do:

- Check out the list of Ring's included middleware.
- Convert more views to Enlive.
- Write tests for adding new issues and closing them.

Interview with James Reeves

James Reeves is a one-man software company and a driving force in the Clojure web ecosystem. It's hard to do anything in Clojure relating to the web without using code that he wrote. He created or maintains several of the libraries we'll see in this chapter, including Ring, Compojure, and Hiccup.

Us: *What do you feel are Ring's strengths for programming web applications?*

James: *Ring is based upon a single, simple abstraction that allows developers to write web applications using nothing but functions and standard Clojure data structures. This means Ring can play to Clojure's strengths and make it easier to develop larger applications from small, independent functions.*

Ring produces relatively performant applications, running a little slower than statically typed languages like Java or Go, but typically much quicker than interpreted languages like Ruby or Python. Ring seems to be most often used for RESTful web services, perhaps because Ring makes it easy to factor out common functionality.

Us: *What's your favorite thing about using Ring for the Web?*

James: *Ring lets me work with HTTP using pure functions and maps, without requiring any custom types or classes. There are fewer barriers to working with Ring, and because of that it's easier to leverage the tools the language provides. I find myself using more higher-level functions in Ring (like middleware) because they're so easy to put together.*

Us: *What are your thoughts on à la carte collections of libraries versus full-stack frameworks like Rails or Django?*

James: *Full-stack frameworks span a comfortable middle ground between applications that are too small for a framework to be necessary and applications that are too large for full-stack frameworks to make much of a dent in overall complexity and development time.*

There are, I think, two pressures coming to bear on full-stack frameworks. The first is that developers are beginning to favor distributed systems made of smaller services, which lend themselves to more lightweight libraries. The second is that as libraries become better, we can build more without needing as much of an application skeleton as a framework provides.

I suspect there will always be a place for frameworks like Rails and Django, at least in the foreseeable future, but my guess is that they'll be used less, or perhaps used in a more piecemeal fashion.

Wrapping Up

Ring is a simple data abstraction for HTTP requests and responses, but this simplicity gives it much of its power. Turning HTTP, SQL, HTML, and routing into data structures means they can be manipulated and combined to your heart's content with the powerful tools in Clojure. Each library is like a kind of LEGO brick, and each Ring app is a unique construction from these simple pieces. Ring data ties everything together.

We concentrated on traditional web application architecture in order to show off Ring and friends without leaving you lost in a sea of new knowledge. Libraries exist for a variety of alternative architectures, including integration with queuing systems, WebSockets, and all the other amenities one finds in large web applications.

Ring's Strengths

Ring and Clojure go together, and many of Ring's strengths come directly from strengths in the underlying language. Lisps are often regarded as among the most powerful of programming languages, and Clojure is as capable as any of its parenthetical ancestors. Clojure is not just a powerful language; it's a practical response to the lack of advanced and high-level tooling around modern programming problems.

The Java ecosystem is vast, and Java code has been created to solve nearly every problem you can imagine. It's been a popular choice for web applications, especially in the enterprise. The JVM in particular is a piece of remarkable engineering and is nearly unbeatable for performance without resorting to a native language like C or C++.

Clojure embraces the Java platform and the JVM. Integration with Java code is seamless and easy. It's so easy that it's often easier to write Java code in Clojure than directly in Java due to Clojure's dynamic nature. Clojure code can call Java code; Java code can call Clojure; and many practical additions to the language make working with Java easy. For example, Clojure collections all implement the standard Java collection interfaces.

Ring and the libraries we looked at take full advantage of this integration. Ring builds on top of Java servlets and Jetty. Enlive uses the Tag Soup library, which is written in Java. Korma builds on top of Java's database connectivity infrastructure. Your application will not want for libraries; practically anything you can imagine already exists in Java land.

Working with data is easier in Clojure than in nearly any other language you can find. It has syntactic support not just for lists and maps but also for sets and vectors. The threading operators make chaining transformations as easy as Unix command pipelines.

By turning HTTP, CSS selectors, HTML elements, and even code into data, Clojure's wonderful toolbox can be put to use on these problems directly. This is a powerful concept that becomes second nature after awhile. Ring and related projects make extensive use of this idea to great effect.

Functional languages are studies in composition. Functions are first-class values and can be passed around, returned, and bound to variables. This allows you to combine functions together and build higher-level abstractions to solve problems. You might have a taste for this already from languages like JavaScript or Ruby, but the tools available for this in Clojure are finely honed.

Ring middleware is a great example of composition. Each middleware function does something simple—converting string keys to keywords or parsing query and form parameters—but all can be combined in many ways to build custom web request processing. Compojure uses composition to layer and combine routing rules.

Composition is quite a different tool than OOP's inheritance. Instead of extending, you combine. You'll find it much easier to use and reason about composition, and it's a natural companion to web applications, which are often compositions of resources themselves. Ring's apps are compositions themselves, each piece of which also makes use of composition.

Ring's Weaknesses

All frameworks, libraries, and languages have their warts, and no tool is perfect at all things. While Ring apps excel at many things, keep a few things in mind before you begin your journey as a Ring app developer.

While access and integration with the Java platform is a huge win for Ring and Clojure, you need some familiarity with Java to take advantage of this. Many web developers who've worked in Ruby and Python have shunned Java for years, and whether or not this was reasonable, learning some Java is an important part of using Clojure to its full potential. If you're new to Java and Clojure, it makes the learning curve a little bit steeper.

Most of the Ring platform is à la carte. While there are a few upstart full-stack frameworks in Clojure, most of the platform revolves around libraries that do a small set of things and work well with the rest of the platform. Ring's data abstractions are responsible for much of this interoperability.

While this means you can build custom solutions and pay only for what you use in terms of overhead and performance, it also means you must be cognizant of the choices and how pieces fit together. You may have to try a few options before you find one that suits your needs. Also, there may be little if any documentation on some combinations of tools, since there are so many possible combinations.

Final Thoughts

Clojure brings the power of Lisp to bear on web problems, and Ring takes this power and runs with it. You can view a web application as a set of data transformations, and in that perspective, Clojure certainly has a lot of advanced tooling to make your life easier. The dynamic nature of Clojure will make Ruby, JavaScript, and Python programmers feel right at home, and the access to the Java platform will satisfy any pointy-haired bosses in your life. Like a pile of LEGOs, you can create whatever you want in infinite combinations, but it also demands some imagination and creative thinking.

CHAPTER 5

Webmachine

Webmachine is quite different than other frameworks and libraries you may have seen before. It works a bit like the Socratic method or a Choose Your Own Adventure book. Webmachine asks your application questions, and the answers determine a path through the HTTP decision tree.

Does this URL exist? If no, return a 404; if yes, keep going. What kind of content does this URL support? What encodings does it support? When was it last modified? In each case, you provide simple answers, but Webmachine turns these into sophisticated handling of HTTP requests that few other systems can match.

All of this comes on top of the battle-hardened reliability and concurrency support that Erlang itself provides. The combination is potent, and other languages and frameworks are starting to draw from Webmachine's inspiration.

Introducing Webmachine

HTTP is often discussed as a simple protocol, but the truth is that it's quite complicated. Most frameworks expose it only on a very basic level, using the ability to route requests based on methods and URLs and to return a few types of responses. They hide the full machinery, which has support for content negotiation, encodings, and caching.

Figure 20, *Simple HTTP processing*, on page 156 shows how most web frameworks expose the HTTP protocol.

It is simple to understand but hides most of HTTP's power. If you want caching or content negotiation, you must implement the decision logic yourself in the controller. Sometimes frameworks come with extension points—for example, see *Ring Middleware*, on page 143—for handling other HTTP logic. This

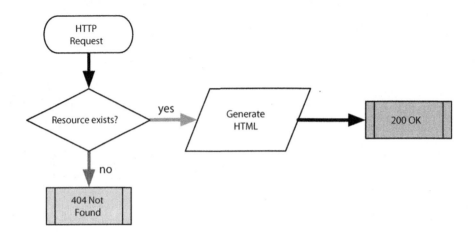

Figure 20—Simple HTTP processing

middleware is limited in functionality and can only modify the HTTP request and response data; your resource must still inspect the middleware's data and make its own decisions.

Webmachine exposes a more complete HTTP protocol. The following figure should give you an idea of how complicated HTTP really is. Each diamond is a decision point, where Webmachine will ask your code a question. The double arrows and shaded diamonds in the figure show what happens to an HTTP request as it is processed in a normal flow ending with 200 OK. Notice how many decisions must be made.

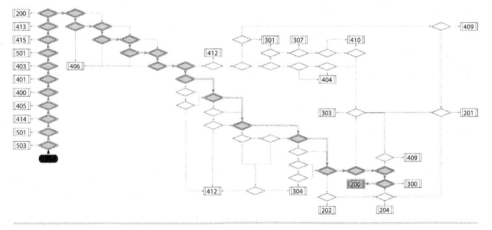

Figure 21—HTTP processing flowchart

Most web applications don't need to make this many decisions, but instead of hiding these decisions from the programmer or predetermining their answers, Webmachine exposes them and affords complete control. It simplifies everything through well-chosen default answers, but the hooks are there if your application requires different behavior.

One advantage of this approach is that the decision logic is separated from the code that generates individual answers. Another advantage is that you no longer need to remember HTTP status codes. What's the difference between 301 and 302? Should you return a 401 or a 403? Webmachine will provide the correct response given your answers to more tractable questions.

On the first day we'll look at our first Webmachine app and start exploring Webmachine's resource functions. Next, we'll look at how Webmachine dispatches HTTP requests.

During Day 2 we'll implement the first version of Petite, a link-shortening application that will make use of the extra control over HTTP that Webmachine provides. We'll also play with templating and content negotiation.

Day 3 is all about controlling caching and authorization, two important pieces of many modern apps that are often neglected by other frameworks.

Let's dive right in.

Day 1: HTTP Request as State Machine

Webmachine excels at making complex HTTP processing simple, and its sweet spot is very much on the back end of web systems. It is used to power APIs such as Opscode's Chef Server API as well as HTTP interfaces to distributed systems like Basho's Riak database. We'll look at Webmachine through the lens of a link-shortening service, and by the end of today, you'll be ready to make your very own link shortener.

Link shorteners have proliferated since they first appeared around 2002,[1] turning lengthy URLs into compressed sequences of alphanumerics that fit in limited space or require less typing. They work by redirecting from the shortened link to the destination by using a big lookup table. They don't quite fit the normal flow of web applications that most frameworks cater to—the focus is on altering HTTP flow, not on manipulating application state—but they are right at home in Webmachine.

---

1.   http://en.wikipedia.org/wiki/URL_shortening

Getting Started

Webmachine is built in Erlang, a robust, concurrent, and functional language originally designed for use in telecommunications applications. You'll need to install a copy of the Erlang runtime and development libraries. Packaged versions of these can be found in most system's package managers on Linux or in Homebrew on Mac OS X; Windows binaries are available from the Erlang site (http://www.erlang.org/). Any recent version of Erlang should work fine.

Once you have Erlang installed, you can check that all is working by starting up the Erlang console. It should print out the version number and leave you at an Erlang prompt.

```
$ erl
Erlang R15B03 (erts-5.9.3.1) [source] [64-bit] [smp:8:8] [async-threads:0]
    [hipe] [kernel-poll:false] [dtrace]

Eshell V5.9.3.1  (abort with ^G)
1>
```

You can quit the Erlang console by pressing Ctrl-C twice.

Next, you need to download Webmachine from GitHub. The easiest way to do this is to clone the Webmachine repository with Git. It doesn't need to be installed anywhere special, as it will create a self-contained Webmachine project for us in the location of our choosing. In the directory you'd like to work in, run the following commands:

```
$ git clone https://github.com/basho/webmachine.git
Cloning into 'webmachine'...
remote: Counting objects: 2542, done.
remote: Compressing objects: 100% (1291/1291), done.
remote: Total 2542 (delta 1468), reused 2247 (delta 1210)
Receiving objects: 100% (2542/2542), 1.80 MiB | 39 KiB/s, done.
Resolving deltas: 100% (1468/1468), done.
```

All the pieces are in place, and we can start making Webmachine apps. There's no need to install or configure Webmachine like we do with other frameworks. Erlang's virtual machine and the Rebar package manager make getting started easy.

Hello, World

Webmachine comes with a script, new_webmachine.sh, that creates a new project for you, complete with a simple resource, basic routes, and build scripts. You pass it the name of your project and, optionally, the path the project should be created at:

```
$ webmachine/scripts/new_webmachine.sh hello
==> priv (create)
Writing /Users/jack/src/hello/README
Writing /Users/jack/src/hello/Makefile
Writing /Users/jack/src/hello/rebar.config
Writing /Users/jack/src/hello/rebar
Writing /Users/jack/src/hello/start.sh
Writing /Users/jack/src/hello/src/hello.app.src
Writing /Users/jack/src/hello/src/hello.erl
Writing /Users/jack/src/hello/src/hello_app.erl
Writing /Users/jack/src/hello/src/hello_sup.erl
Writing /Users/jack/src/hello/src/hello_resource.erl
Writing /Users/jack/src/hello/priv/dispatch.conf
```

Most of these files are part of any Erlang application or are simple placeholders. It's only important to know that running start.sh will launch the application,
and src/hello_resource.erl and priv/dispatch.conf define the main resource and URL
routes, respectively.

We can build and run the app by running make and start.sh. By default, the
application will listen on port 8000 so you can point your browser to
http://localhost:8000/ to be greeted by Webmachine.

```
$ make
==> hello (get-deps)
Pulling webmachine from {git,"git://github.com/basho/webmachine","HEAD"}
Cloning into 'webmachine'...
«omitted output»
==> hello (compile)
Compiled src/hello_app.erl
Compiled src/hello_resource.erl
Compiled src/hello.erl
Compiled src/hello_sup.erl

$ ./start.sh
Erlang R15B03 (erts-5.9.3.1) [source] [64-bit] [smp:8:8] [async-threads:0]
    [hipe] [kernel-poll:false] [dtrace]
«omitted output»
=PROGRESS REPORT==== 2-May-2013::22:52:15 ===
        application: hello
         started_at: nonode@nohost
```

You can quit the Erlang virtual machine by pressing Ctrl-C twice.

Let's look at the two most important files, dispatch.conf and hello_resource.erl.

The dispatch.conf file is a sequence of Erlang terms, each ending with a period.
These are the dispatch rules that map URLs to resources.

webmachine/hello/priv/dispatch.conf
```
{[], hello_resource, []}.
```

Our file contains a single simple rule that has three parts: a path specification, the resource module, and the arguments for the resource. An empty list, [], for the path specification represents the root path. hello_resource is the module—defined in a corresponding erl file—implementing the Webmachine resource, and it takes no arguments, so [] is an empty argument list. This file is pretty bare, but we'll see more complicated sets of dispatch rules later.

hello_resource.erl defines an Erlang module called hello_resource, which implements a resource. Each of the exported functions of a resource will be called by Webmachine's state machine to answer the questions that will determine how the HTTP request is processed.

webmachine/hello/src/hello_resource.erl
```
   -module(hello_resource).
❶ -export([init/1, to_html/2]).
❷ -include_lib("webmachine/include/webmachine.hrl").

❸ init([]) -> {ok, undefined}.

❹ to_html(ReqData, State) ->
       {"<html><body>Hello, new world</body></html>", ReqData, State}.
```

❶ These are the exported resource functions. Notice that they end in /1 or /2, which is the function's signature in Erlang; functions with the same name and different numbers of arguments are distinct functions in Erlang. init gets called when the resource is initialized, and it's passed the arguments given in the dispatch rules. to_html is the default content function, which Webmachine calls to answer the question of what content, or *representation*, to return to the user. We'll see lots more resource functions as we go along.

❷ All Webmachine resources must include webmachine.hrl, which defines the request data structures.

❸ The init function sets up the resource's state for the request. This state will be threaded through each of the resource functions. For example, it's passed as the second argument to to_html. Since this resource has no internal state, it returns undefined.

Data in Erlang is immutable, so functions typically take the old state and return a new version of the state, which then gets passed to the next function. This threading of immutable state makes functional programs very easy to reason about.

❹ Resource functions return a three-tuple of result, request data, and the new internal state. The result of a content function is usually an iolist, which is a string, a binary, or a list of iolists.

As you can see, it takes a little bit of infrastructure to get a Webmachine app running, but the actual resource module and dispatch rules are pretty minimal. Of course, this is just the beginning. The real fun starts when we start to add more resource functions to our resource's module.

Working with Resource Functions

Webmachine resources can have over thirty resource functions that customize various parts of the HTTP request–handling behavior. Webmachine calls a resource function to ask a question, and your resource provides a simple answer—often just true or false. Your resource modules don't need to implement every one of these functions because Webmachine provides default behavior for each of them. The list of all resource functions, their default behaviors, and the legal answers are all spelled out in the documentation.[2]

The most basic of these resource functions is content_types_provided, which answers Webmachine's question about what representations (or content types) your resource will be providing. By default Webmachine assumes a single HTML representation defined in a function called to_html, but by implementing content_types_provided yourself, you can add alternate representations or change which function Webmachine will call for a given representation.

The next example shows how you can return both a plain text and an HTML representation for the same resource by implementing content_types_provided and two representation functions, to_html and to_text:

webmachine/hello2/src/hello2_resource.erl
```
-module(hello2_resource).
-export([init/1,
         content_types_provided/2,
         to_html/2,
         to_text/2]).

-include_lib("webmachine/include/webmachine.hrl").

init([]) -> {ok, undefined}.

❶ content_types_provided(ReqData, State) ->
    {[{"text/html", to_html},
      {"text/plain", to_text}], ReqData, State}.
```

---

2.   https://github.com/basho/webmachine/wiki/Resource-Functions

```
to_html(ReqData, State) ->
    {"<html><body>Hello, HTML world</body></html>\n", ReqData, State}.

to_text(ReqData, State) ->
    {"Hello, text world\n", ReqData, State}.
```

❶ Here we add a handler, to_text, for the text/plain content type in addition to to_html.

❷ This handler is almost identical to to_html, except that it returns text.

With this simple change, our little app will change its behavior based on the Accept header given by the HTTP client. Clients pass the list of media types they understand in the Accept header, and Webmachine uses this information to choose an appropriate content handler. Notice that you don't have to implement content negotiation yourself; you only need to answer Webmachine's simple question about what representations are available. We can imitate this behavior with curl at the command line:

```
$ curl --header 'accept: text/html' http://localhost:8000/
<html><body>Hello, HTML world</body></html>

$ curl --header 'accept: text/plain' http://localhost:8000/
Hello, text world
```

Most frameworks don't expose this information, which is why you see many APIs encoding format selection into the URL itself. For example, Twitter's public API chooses the format based on the extension given in the API URL—statuses/public_timeline.json returns JSON data, and statuses/public_timeline.atom returns an Atom feed. This amounts to minor abuse of the HTTP protocol. The two Twitter endpoints are just different representations of the same resource, and in Webmachine, this structure is preserved.

Existential Resource Functions

Let's take a look at some resource functions that will be very useful for our link shortener. Our link-shortening app doesn't actually contain the content the user ultimately wants. Webmachine asks a resource whether or not it is available by calling resource_exists. Normally, Webmachine assumes this is true, but in the case of a shortened link, it definitely isn't.

In the hello2 project, create src/uncertain_resource.erl, which is a slightly modified version of our original "Hello, World!" example:

webmachine/hello2/src/uncertain_resource.erl
```
-module(uncertain_resource).
-export([init/1,
         to_html/2]).
```

```
-include_lib("webmachine/include/webmachine.hrl").
init([]) -> {ok, undefined}.
to_html(ReqData, State) ->
    {"nothing to see here", ReqData, State}.
```

You'll also need to modify the dispatch rules to add a path for the new resource, priv/dispatch.conf:

webmachine/hello2/priv/dispatch.conf
```
{[], hello2_resource, []}.
{["uncertain"], uncertain_resource, []}.
```

Compiling and running hello2 and visiting http://localhost:8000/uncertain should work as you expect. Now let's implement resource_exists; it's quite easy since it only has two possible answers:

webmachine/hello2/src/uncertain_resource.erl
```
%% remember to add resource_exists/2 to the export list

resource_exists(ReqData, State) ->
    {false, ReqData, State}.
```

Recompile and try the URL again. You should see that it now returns a 404 Not Found error. This is exactly what should happen when resources don't exist, but notice that we didn't modify the content functions of the resource, nor did we specify anywhere that the request should return a 404. We just answered a simple question, and Webmachine took care of the details.

Webmachine, inquisitive as it is, asks our resource even more questions. Try adding an implementation for previously_existed:

webmachine/hello2/src/uncertain_resource.erl
```
%% remember to add previously_existed/2 to the export list

previously_existed(ReqData, State) ->
    {true, ReqData, State}.
```

Let's see what Webmachine does now:

```
$ curl -i http://localhost:8000/uncertain
HTTP/1.1 410 Gone
Server: MochiWeb/1.1 WebMachine/1.10.0
Date: Sun, 12 May 2013 04:12:09 GMT
Content-Type: text/html
Content-Length: 0
```

Did you know that there was an HTTP status code for this case? You have probably never used status code 410 in your own applications, but Webmachine always knows exactly the right status to pick because it models the whole HTTP state machine.

If the resource doesn't currently exist but it used to exist, where has it gone? Webmachine inquires by calling moved_permanently and moved_temporarily. Since the former is more appropriate for a link shortener, let's implement moved_permanently and see what Webmachine will do:

```
webmachine/hello2/src/uncertain_resource.erl
%% remember to add moved_permanently/2 to the export list

moved_permanently(ReqData, State) ->
    {{true, "http://pragprog.com/"}, ReqData, State}.
```

```
$ curl -i http://localhost:8000/uncertain
HTTP/1.1 301 Moved Permanently
Server: MochiWeb/1.1 WebMachine/1.10.0
Location: http://pragprog.com/
Date: Sun, 12 May 2013 04:25:36 GMT
Content-Type: text/html
Content-Length: 0
```

Webmachine has again figured out exactly what to do. This part of the Webmachine state machine for making decisions is shown in Figure 22, *Webmachine's existential state machine logic*, on page 165.

The other resource functions work very similarly, although some have more complex answers than just true and false. We'll see more of these later, but for now, let's talk about dispatching.

Dispatching Requests

Dispatching is the process of deciding which Webmachine resource to use for a given incoming request. You may want to send all /user URLs to one resource or switch between two resources based on whether you're dealing with individual items or collections. Almost any logic is possible, but Webmachine makes common patterns quite easy, and we'll concentrate on those.

Create a new Webmachine project called dispatcher and examine priv/dispatch.conf.

```
webmachine/dispatcher/priv/dispatch.conf
{[], dispatcher_resource, []}.
```

You've seen this dispatch rule before, but let's break it down and examine it more closely.

Each rule is either a three-tuple or a four-tuple. In this three-tuple version, the first element is the path specification, the second is the Erlang module implementing the resource that should match this rule, and the last element contains the arguments that get passed to the resource's init function.

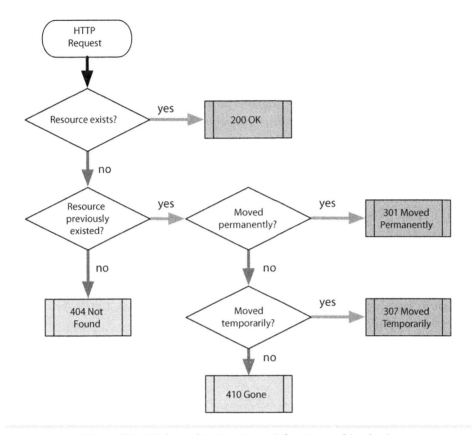

Figure 22— Webmachine's existential state machine logic

The path specifier is [], which represents the root path, /. Each item in this list is a path term, and Webmachine breaks up the requested path into pieces by splitting on slashes and then tries to match each piece against the corresponding path term. For example, ["hello", "world"] would match /hello/world.

A resource can inspect the path by using the wrq:path(ReqData) function. Modify src/dispatcher_resource.erl to print the path, add the ["hello", "world"] dispatch rule, and then build and run the dispatcher app.

```
webmachine/dispatcher/src/dispatcher_resource.erl
-module(dispatcher_resource).
-export([init/1, to_html/2]).
-include_lib("webmachine/include/webmachine.hrl").

init([]) -> {ok, undefined}.
to_html(ReqData, State) ->
    {["you asked for ", wrq:path(ReqData), "\n"],
     ReqData, State}.
```

```
webmachine/dispatcher/priv/dispatch.conf
{["hello", "world"], dispatcher_resource, []}.
```

```
$ curl http://localhost:8000/hello/world
you asked for /hello/world
```

Webmachine is not limited to specific path tokens; it can also dispatch on arbitrary paths while binding the interesting path tokens to identifiers for use in your resource's functions.

Parameterized Dispatch

Webmachine has a special path term that matches any number of arbitrary path terms: '*'. Note that this is the Erlang atom '*', not a string; atoms that don't start with lowercase letters must be surrounded in single quotes. This path term can only appear as the last term in a path specification. The parts of the path that match the star term can be retrieved by calling wrq:disp_path(ReqData). Create a new module, star_resource, that prints out the dispatch path, and play with it by adding a dispatch rule for ["hello", '*'] and by rebuilding and running dispatcher:

```
webmachine/dispatcher/src/star_resource.erl
-module(star_resource).
-export([init/1, to_html/2]).

-include_lib("webmachine/include/webmachine.hrl").

init([]) -> {ok, undefined}.

to_html(ReqData, State) ->
    {["you asked for ", wrq:path(ReqData), "\n",
      "star path was ", wrq:disp_path(ReqData), "\n"],
     ReqData, State}.
```

```
webmachine/dispatcher/priv/dispatch.conf
{["hello", '*'], star_resource, []}.
```

```
$ curl http://localhost:8000/hello/webmachine
you asked for /hello/webmachine
star path was webmachine
```

```
$ curl http://localhost:8000/hello
you asked for /hello
star path was
```

```
$ curl http://localhost:8000/hello/how/are/you
you asked for /hello/how/are/you
star path was how/are/you
```

Webmachine also lets you bind path terms to named atoms. A path specification of ["goodbye", who] matches any path with two parts where the first part is goodbye. In addition, wrq:path_info(who, ReqData) will return the second path term by its bound name. Let's add named_resource and an appropriate dispatch rule.

```
webmachine/dispatcher/src/named_resource.erl
-module(named_resource).
-export([init/1, to_html/2]).

-include_lib("webmachine/include/webmachine.hrl").

init([]) -> {ok, undefined}.

to_html(ReqData, State) ->
    {["goodbye, ", wrq:path_info(who, ReqData), "\n"],
     ReqData, State}.
```

```
webmachine/dispatcher/priv/dispatch.conf
{["goodbye", who], named_resource, []}.
```

```
$ curl http://localhost:8000/goodbye/world
goodbye, world
```

wrq:path_info(ReqData), without a specific name, will return the entire property list of named path terms.

What We Learned on Day 1

Not only is Webmachine unique in its approach to handling HTTP requests by modeling HTTP as a state machine, but it's also written in Erlang, a functional language that is quite different from most other things you've probably used before. Even though it might look unfamiliar, there is wisdom to be gained from the way of Webmachine.

Writing apps with Webmachine is like creating a Choose Your Own Adventure book for incoming HTTP requests. Webmachine asks simple questions, you provide simple answers, and Webmachine navigates the complex state machine of HTTP processing on your behalf. Its simple nature is deceiving and affords access to many parts of the HTTP protocol that other frameworks hide or make difficult to interact with.

Day 1 Self-Study

Find:

- Examples of Webmachine-based apps on the Internet
- The Webmachine wiki

Do:

- Find out how to deal with query string parameters in your resource functions. (Hint: Explore the functions available in the wrq module, known as the Request Data API in the wiki.)
- Read the Mechanics section of the Webmachine wiki to learn more about how it all works.

Day 2: Building Apps

Yesterday we saw most of the pieces we'll need to build a link shortener, and today we'll put those pieces together to build the first version of it, called Petite.

Today we'll also look at basic front-end tasks with Webmachine and related libraries as we build a web UI for Petite. You'll see how to integrate HTML templating into a Webmachine resource with mustache.erl,[3] a Mustache template implementation for Erlang.

Webmachine makes it easy to handle different types of incoming data to support both human and API use of the same resource. You'll discover that representations of incoming data and the resource itself are important parts of Webmachine.

Shortening Links

We'll apply what we learned yesterday to build the first iteration of Petite, our link shortener. This first version will be able to shorten links and redirect incoming visitors to the corresponding real URLs.

First, create a new Webmachine project called petite. Starting from this shell, we'll keep expanding Petite as we go along.

Compression and Storage

Before we can write our Webmachine resource for Petite's shortening API, we must have (1) a way to shorten the link and (2) a lookup table that associates shortened codes with their corresponding URLs. Erlang contains built-in tools to help with both of these problems.

If you want to make a string of digits shorter, one easy trick is to write it in a larger numeric base. For example, 10000000 in binary becomes 128 in decimal and 3K in base 36. Using this, we can attach a number to each real URL,

---

3. https://github.com/mojombo/mustache.erl

incrementing the number each time. The short code returned can just be the number represented in a high numeric base so that it's as compact as possible. Erlang can convert to different numeric bases up to base 36 with integer_to_list(Number, Base).

Storing the lookup table can be done a number of ways, but the easiest is to use an ETS (short for Erlang Term Storage) table. An ETS table is an in-memory key value store that is built into the Erlang standard library. You can store arbitrary Erlang tuples in it, and the first element becomes the key and the whole tuple is the value.

Putting these two pieces together, we can write a gen_server module, which is a self-contained Erlang service that produces codes given URLs and returns URLs given codes. There's not enough room to fully explain gen_servers here, which are part of Erlang's standard library; if you're interested, see *Erlang Programming [CT09]* by Francesco Cesarini and Simon Thompson or Joe Armstrong's book, *Programming Erlang [Arm13]*. Let's just look at the important bits:

webmachine/petite/day1/petite/src/petite_url_srv.erl
```erlang
-module(petite_url_srv).

%% public API
-export([start_link/0,
         get_url/1,
         put_url/1]).

-behaviour(gen_server).
-export([init/1,
         terminate/2,
         code_change/3,
         handle_call/3,
         handle_cast/2,
         handle_info/2]).

-define(SERVER, ?MODULE).
-define(TAB, petite_urls).

-record(st, {next}).

%% public API implementation

start_link() ->
    gen_server:start_link({local, ?SERVER}, ?MODULE, [], []).

get_url(Id) ->
    gen_server:call(?SERVER, {get_url, Id}).
```

```erlang
put_url(Url) ->
    gen_server:call(?SERVER, {put_url, Url}).

%% gen_server implementation

init(_) ->
    ets:new(?TAB, [set, named_table, protected]),
    {ok, #st{next=0}}.

terminate(_Reason, _State) ->
    ok.

code_change(_OldVsn, State, _Extra) ->
    {ok, State}.

handle_call({get_url, Id}, _From, State) ->
    Reply = case ets:lookup(?TAB, Id) of
                [] ->
                    {error, not_found};
                [{Id, Url}] ->
                    {ok, Url}
            end,
    {reply, Reply, State};

handle_call({put_url, Url}, _From, State = #st{next=N}) ->
    Id = b36_encode(N),
    ets:insert(?TAB, {Id, Url}),
    {reply, {ok, Id}, State#st{next=N+1}};

handle_call(_Request, _From, State) ->
    {stop, unknown_call, State}.

handle_cast(_Request, State) ->
    {stop, unknown_cast, State}.

handle_info(_Info, State) ->
    {stop, unknown_info, State}.

%% internal functions

b36_encode(N) ->
    integer_to_list(N, 36).
```

❶ The public API of this module simply delegates to the server process. This is common for gen_server implementations, since the server itself may later change the internal message formats.

❷ We initialize the server by creating a new ETS table to store the codes and their corresponding URLs, and we start the counter at 0.

Webmachine threads the State variable returned from a resource's init function through all the resource functions, and gen_server does the same. You can see where Webmachine got the idea.

❸ Retrieving a URL is a simple matter of looking it up in the ETS table.

❹ Putting a URL into the server creates a code and then inserts a corresponding entry. Notice that it increments the counter in the returned state.

❺ Creating a code is as easy as integer_to_list, at least if you don't need anything higher than base 36.

gen_servers are usually attached to a supervisor process that ensures they keep running and restarts them when they crash. In order to use petite_url_srv, we must add it to Petite's main supervisor, petite_sup. The following highlighted lines inside the init function show the modifications that are needed:

```
webmachine/petite/day1/petite/src/petite_sup.erl
Web = {webmachine_mochiweb,
        {webmachine_mochiweb, start, [WebConfig]},
        permanent, 5000, worker, [mochiweb_socket_server]},
➤ UrlServer = {petite_url_srv,
➤               {petite_url_srv, start_link, []},
➤               permanent, 5000, worker, []},
➤ Processes = [Web, UrlServer],
{ok, { {one_for_one, 10, 10}, Processes} }.
```

Compile and start Petite, and let's play with our new service at the Erlang shell. Note that if you don't see the 1> prompt after you start the app, hit Enter to make one appear.

```
$ ./start.sh
«omitted output»
=PROGRESS REPORT==== 15-May-2013::21:10:14 ===
        application: petite
         started_at: nonode@nohost
1> whereis(petite_url_srv).
<0.92.0>
2> petite_url_srv:put_url("https://pragprog.com/").
{ok,"0"}
3> petite_url_srv:put_url("https://github.com/basho/webmachine").
{ok,"1"}
4> petite_url_srv:get_url("1").
{ok,"https://github.com/basho/webmachine"}
5> petite_url_srv:get_url("3K").
{error,not_found}
```

Our service works, and it is ready for use by any Webmachine resources we create.

Redirection

You've already learned how to create Webmachine resources and how to use resource functions like resource_exists and moved_permanently to redirect HTTP requests. You also saw how to bind path tokens to atoms during dispatch and retrieve them with wrq:path_info. All that remains is to combine these with petite_url_srv, and Petite can shorten links.

First, create a rule in priv/dispatch.conf for your new resource:

```
webmachine/petite/day1/petite/priv/dispatch.conf
{[code], petite_fetch_resource, []}.
```

Then create the petite_fetch_resource module. Try modifying the redirection example in *Working with Resource Functions*, on page 161, to use petite_url_srv before peeking at the following implementation:

```
webmachine/petite/day1/petite/src/petite_fetch_resource.erl
-module(petite_fetch_resource).
-export([init/1,
         to_html/2,
         resource_exists/2,
         previously_existed/2,
         moved_permanently/2]).

-include_lib("webmachine/include/webmachine.hrl").

init([]) ->
    {ok, ""}.

to_html(ReqData, State) ->
    {"", ReqData, State}.

resource_exists(ReqData, State) ->
    {false, ReqData, State}.

previously_existed(ReqData, State) ->
    Code = wrq:path_info(code, ReqData),
    case petite_url_srv:get_url(Code) of
        {ok, Url} ->
            {true, ReqData, Url};
        {error, not_found} ->
            {false, ReqData, State}
    end.

moved_permanently(ReqData, State) ->
    {{true, State}, ReqData, State}.
```

Recompile Petite and add some links at the Erlang shell as before. Once it has shortened a few links, you can test the resource:

```
$ curl -i http://localhost:8000/1
HTTP/1.1 301 Moved Permanently
Server: MochiWeb/1.1 WebMachine/1.9.2
Location: https://github.com/basho/webmachine
Date: Thu, 16 May 2013 03:29:09 GMT
Content-Type: text/html
Content-Length: 0
```

Our link shortener is working but is still short a few features. We need an HTTP API to shorten new links. For that, we'll create a new resource, petite_shorten_resource.

Shortening API

The API to shorten a link is simple. HTTP POST requests will include form data with a url field set to the link to shorten. Petite will return the shortened link as text in the response.

Let's think about the first questions Webmachine asks our resource and how our resource should answer them. First, we'll need to answer allowed_methods by indicating support for HTTP POST. Next, since our response will be text, the resource must respond appropriately to content_types_provided and provide to_text. Webmachine requires we provide a body-generating function even in the case of POSTs where it's not strictly needed.

So far, these are resource functions that you've seen before when processing HTTP GET requests. For HTTP POST requests, Webmachine first calls post_is_create to determine if this request creates a new resource. If the answer is false, the Webmachine state machine delegates processing to process_post. If the answer is true, Webmachine follows a path of inquiry in the state machine that we don't have room to cover in this chapter. Since Petite is not creating new resources in this API call, it will follow the former path.

process_post must parse the form data in the request, shorten the link, and then generate a suitable response. Let's look at how this is done:

webmachine/petite/day1/petite/src/petite_shorten_resource.erl
```erlang
-module(petite_shorten_resource).
-export([init/1,
         allowed_methods/2,
         process_post/2,
         content_types_provided/2,
         to_text/2]).

-include_lib("webmachine/include/webmachine.hrl").

init([]) ->
    {ok, undefined}.
```

```erlang
allowed_methods(ReqData, State) ->
    {['POST'], ReqData, State}.

content_types_provided(ReqData, State) ->
    {[{"text/plain", to_text}], ReqData, State}.

process_post(ReqData, State) ->
    Host = wrq:get_req_header("host", ReqData),
    Params = mochiweb_util:parse_qs(wrq:req_body(ReqData)),
    Url = proplists:get_value("url", Params),
    {ok, Code} = petite_url_srv:put_url(Url),
    Shortened = "http://" ++ Host ++ "/" ++ Code ++ "\n",
    {true, wrq:set_resp_body(Shortened, ReqData), State}.

to_text(ReqData, State) ->
    {"", ReqData, State}.
```

wrq:get_req_header returns the value of a request header. Here it's used to retrieve the host and port the client is connected to so that we can use that information to build the final shortened link.

mochiweb_util:parse_qs is a function that parses query strings or form data. This is provided by MochiWeb, which is the HTTP processing library that Webmachine—and most other Erlang web libraries—are built on top of. We have provided it wrq:req_body(ReqData) as input, which is the extracted body of the incoming request.

mochiweb_util:parse_qs returns an Erlang property list, and process_post grabs the url property, sends it to the internal shortening service, and then builds a new, shortened link.

Finally, wrq:set_resp_body is used to set the body of the response to the shortened link. Since data in Erlang is immutable, wrq:set_resp_body returns an altered version of the ReqData structure that is passed along. Returning true from process_post indicates successful processing.

Petite will also need a new dispatch rule for this resource. Put this rule before the petite_fetch_resource rule:

webmachine/petite/day1/petite/priv/dispatch.conf
```
{["shorten"], petite_shorten_resource, []}.
```

You can now rebuild Petite and test it out:

```
$ curl -i -X POST http://localhost:8000/shorten \
> --data 'url=https%3A%2F%2Fpragprog.com%2F'
HTTP/1.1 200 OK
Server: MochiWeb/1.1 WebMachine/1.9.2
Date: Fri, 17 May 2013 04:56:25 GMT
```

```
Content-Type: text/plain
Content-Length: 24

http://localhost:8000/0
```

```
$ curl -i http://localhost:8000/0
HTTP/1.1 301 Moved Permanently
Server: MochiWeb/1.1 WebMachine/1.9.2
Location: https://pragprog.com/
Date: Fri, 17 May 2013 04:57:03 GMT
Content-Type: text/html
Content-Length: 0
```

Petite can now shorten long links and redirect shortened links to their original URLs. Developers have written link shorteners in many languages and frameworks, but it's hard to imagine a simpler implementation than this Webmachine version. By modeling HTTP as a state machine and separating decision logic from simple answers, Webmachine has made dealing with redirection almost as simple as "Hello, World."

Even with just this basic functionality, it could serve as an internal shortening service for your own web applications. Of course, you'd probably want to persist the lookup table in a production version.

While Petite is working, it doesn't yet have any front end for human users of the service. Let's look at how Webmachine handles front-end tasks so we can remedy this situation.

Templating with Mustache

Our goal is to create a resource that can output the latest links shortened by users of the service. Like most frameworks, we'll do this with a templating language, since generating HTML by hand can be quite tedious. Every language has dozens of templating libraries, but the declarative nature of Mustache makes it feel right at home in a functional language like Erlang.

You may have already seen Mustache in action in Chapter 2, *CanJS*, on page 35. Perhaps due to its simplicity, Mustache templating systems have appeared in nearly every language. Erlang is no exception, and mustache.erl is the implementation we'll be using with Webmachine.

Like most templating languages, we need to provide both the template itself, via a string or a file, and the template's *context*. The context is a dictionary of key-value pairs providing the variables that the template will have access to during rendering. The template will always be the same, but the context is always changing.

Let's see the simplest example. Create a new Webmachine project called template, and edit the rebar.config file to add the mustache.erl dependency to our app:

webmachine/template/rebar.config
```
{deps, [{webmachine, "1.10.1",
         {git, "git://github.com/basho/webmachine",
          {tag, "1.10.1"}}},
        {mustache, "0.1.0",
         {git, "git://github.com/mojombo/mustache.erl.git",
          {branch, "master"}}}]}.
```

Now make a new resource, template_basic_resource.erl, and an appropriate dispatch rule.

webmachine/template/priv/dispatch.conf
```
{["basic"], template_basic_resource, []}.
```

webmachine/template/src/template_basic_resource.erl
```
-module(template_basic_resource).
-export([init/1, to_html/2]).

-include_lib("webmachine/include/webmachine.hrl").

init([]) -> {ok, undefined}.

to_html(ReqData, State) ->
    Template = "<html><body>Visit {{ url }}</body></html>",
    Context = dict:from_list([{url, "https://pragprog.com/"}]),
    Response = mustache:render(Template, Context),
    {Response, ReqData, State}.
```

The context here is just the name url associated with the Pragmatic home page. The template contains a tag with the same name. Visiting http://localhost:8000/basic in your browser should show "Visit https://pragprog.com/."

Presenting a collection is very similar since Mustache templates are declarative. The value of a collection context variable should be a list, each item of which is a dictionary of new context variables that will be in scope during each iteration. This will be easy to see in an example:

webmachine/template/priv/dispatch.conf
```
{["list"], template_list_resource, []}.
```

webmachine/template/src/template_list_resource.erl
```
-module(template_list_resource).
-export([init/1, to_html/2]).

-include_lib("webmachine/include/webmachine.hrl").
```

```
init([]) -> {ok, undefined}.
to_html(ReqData, State) ->
    Template = "<html><body>" ++
        "<ul>" ++
        "{{#urls}}" ++
        "<li>{{ url }}</li>" ++
        "{{/urls}}" ++
        "</ul>" ++
        "</body></html>",
    Urls = [{url, "https://pragprog.com/"},
            {url, "https://github.com/basho/webmachine"},
            {url, "https://github.com/mojombo/mustache.erl"}],
    Dicts = [dict:from_list([U]) || U <- Urls],
    Context = dict:from_list([{urls, Dicts}]),
    Response = mustache:render(Template, Context),
    {Response, ReqData, State}.
```

❶ We create an intermediate representation of the data as a list of tuples. In Erlang parlance, these are property lists.

❷ We transform the list with a list comprehension into a list of dictionaries.

❸ We create the top-level context by associating the variable urls with the list of dictionaries.

Using string templates is a bit tedious. We can improve things by loading templates from files:

webmachine/template/priv/dispatch.conf
```
{["file"], template_file_resource, []}.
```

webmachine/template/src/template_file_resource.erl
```
-module(template_file_resource).
-export([init/1, to_html/2]).
-include_lib("webmachine/include/webmachine.hrl").

init([]) -> {ok, undefined}.
to_html(ReqData, State) ->
    {ok, TemplateBin} = file:read_file(
                            code:priv_dir(template) ++ "/simple.mustache"),
    TemplateStr = binary_to_list(TemplateBin),
    Context = dict:from_list([{message, "Hello from a file"}]),
    Response = mustache:render(TemplateStr, Context),
    {Response, ReqData, State}.
```

webmachine/template/priv/simple.mustache
```
<html>
<body>
  {{ message }}
</body>
</html>
```

code:priv_dir returns the location of the Erlang application's priv directory, which is where we've chosen to store the template. Erlang applications often store application-specific data under priv. The template name is added to this path, and then file:read_file returns a binary of the file's content. After turning this into a string, which in Erlang is just a list, we can call render just as before.

Templating in Petite

With templating basics under our belt, we can now add a cool new feature to Petite, a list of the most recently shortened links. When users visit http://localhost:8000/latest, they'll see the most recent twenty links that have been shortened. To do this we'll need to create a template, build up the context with the latest links, and then render it to the page.

First, we'll need a template:

```
webmachine/petite/day2/petite/priv/latest.html.mustache
<!DOCTYPE html>
<html>
  <head>
    <link href="/css/bootstrap.min.css" rel="stylesheet" type="text/css">
    <link href="/css/petite.css" rel="stylesheet" type="text/css">

    <title>Latest Links</title>
  </head>
  <body>
    <div class="navbar navbar-inverse">
      <div class="navbar-inner">
        <a class="brand" href="/">Petite</a>
      </div>
    </div>

    <div class="container">
      <p>
        The latest shortened links are:
        <ul>
          {{#links}}
          <li>
            <a href="{{ short_link }}">{{ short_link }}</a>
            =>
            <a href="{{ long_link }}">{{ long_link }}</a>
          </li>
          {{/links}}
        </ul>
      </p>
    </div>
  </body>
</html>
```

The interesting bit of the template is highlighted and shows a simple list tag enumerating the latest links.

Next, petite_url_srv will need a new function to return a list of the latest shortened links:

```
webmachine/petite/day2/petite/src/petite_url_srv.erl
get_latest(Count) ->
    gen_server:call(?SERVER, {get_latest, Count}).
```

Just like the other public functions, this one delegates to a remote procedure call:

```
webmachine/petite/day2/petite/src/petite_url_srv.erl
handle_call({get_latest, Count}, _From, State = #st{next=N}) ->
    Start = N - 1,
    End = max(N - Count, 0),
❶  Ids = [b36_encode(I) || I <- lists:seq(Start, End, -1)],
    Result = lists:map(
                fun(Id) ->
❷                       [Record] = ets:lookup(?TAB, Id),
                        Record
                end, Ids),
    {reply, {ok, Result}, State};
```

❶ Starting from the last N value, we generate codes for the values we're interested in until we have the number asked for.

❷ For each of the codes, we find the corresponding link in the lookup table.

With a new dispatch rule and a new resource, everything will be in place:

```
webmachine/petite/day2/petite/priv/dispatch.conf
{["latest"], petite_latest_resource, []}.
```

```
webmachine/petite/day2/petite/src/petite_latest_resource.erl
-module(petite_latest_resource).
-export([init/1, to_html/2]).
-include_lib("webmachine/include/webmachine.hrl").

init([]) ->
    {ok, undefined}.

to_html(ReqData, State) ->
    {ok, TemplateBin} = file:read_file(
                        code:priv_dir(petite) ++ "/latest.html.mustache"),
    TemplateStr = binary_to_list(TemplateBin),

    Host = wrq:get_req_header("host", ReqData),
    BaseUrl = "http://" ++ Host ++ "/",
```

```
➤       {ok, LatestLinks} = petite_url_srv:get_latest(20),
        LatestDicts = [dict:from_list([{short_link, BaseUrl ++ ShortLink},
                                       {long_link, LongLink}])
                       || {ShortLink, LongLink} <- LatestLinks],
        Context = dict:from_list([{links, LatestDicts}]),

        Response = mustache:render(TemplateStr, Context),
        {Response, ReqData, State}.
```

The resource is very similar to the list example. The highlighted line shows where the resource gets its data—from the new petite_url_srv:get_latest function instead of from a hard-coded list.

Handling Multiple Content Types

Having a pretty page is great for humans, but these days services need to support humans and machines accessing the same data. Each consumer of your resource prefers a different representation, and in the case of machines using your API, multiple representations are often desired. For example, some clients might prefer JSON and some XML.

Yesterday we saw how to provide multiple representations from the same resource, responding with "Hello, World!" in both plain text and HTML. Today we'll elaborate on that example to provide plain text and JSON versions of the latest links.

First, let's add a content_types_provided function to add to_text and to_json:

webmachine/petite/day2/petite/src/petite_latest_resource.erl
```
-export([content_types_provided/2, to_text/2, to_json/2]).

content_types_provided(ReqData, State) ->
    {[{"text/html", to_html},
      {"text/plain", to_text},
      {"application/json", to_json}], ReqData, State}.
```

We'll look at to_text first:

webmachine/petite/day2/petite/src/petite_latest_resource.erl
```
to_text(ReqData, State) ->
    {ok, LatestLinks} = petite_url_srv:get_latest(20),
    Result = lists:map(
               fun({Code, Link}) ->
❶                      [base_url(ReqData), Code, " ", Link, "\n"]
               end,
               LatestLinks),
    {Result, ReqData, State}.
❷ base_url(ReqData) ->
    Host = wrq:get_req_header("host", ReqData),
    "http://" ++ Host ++ "/".
```

❶ Each shortened link and its original URL are listed on a line together.

❷ The base_url helper function uses the Host value in the HTTP headers to determine the server's hostname and port so they don't have to be hard-coded in the source.

Here's the JSON version:

```
webmachine/petite/day2/petite/src/petite_latest_resource.erl
to_json(ReqData, State) ->
    {ok, LatestLinks} = petite_url_srv:get_latest(20),
    LinkList = lists:map(
                  fun({Code, Link}) ->
                      ShortLink = base_url(ReqData) ++ Code,
                      {struct, [{<<"short_link">>, list_to_binary(ShortLink)},
                                {<<"long_link">>, list_to_binary(Link)}]}
                  end,
                  LatestLinks),
    Result = mochijson2:encode({struct, [{latest, LinkList}]}),
    {[Result, "\n"], ReqData, State}.
```

❶ A JSON list is represented as a regular Erlang list, but a JSON object is a special tuple starting with struct and containing a property list of keys and values.

❷ mochijson2 is a JSON library provided as part of MochiWeb, which is the HTTP server Webmachine is built upon.

Each representation is self-contained and knows nothing about the other ones. Let's test out these new representations:

```
$ curl --header 'accept: text/plain' http://localhost:8000/latest
http://localhost:8000/2 http://erlang.org/
http://localhost:8000/1 https://github.com/basho/webmachine
http://localhost:8000/0 https://pragprog.com/

$ curl --header 'accept: application/json' http://localhost:8000/latest
{"latest":[{"short_link":"http://localhost:8000/2","long_link":"http://erlang.
org/"},{"short_link":"http://localhost:8000/1","long_link":"https://github.com
/basho/webmachine"},{"short_link":"http://localhost:8000/0","long_link":"https
://pragprog.com/"}]}
```

If a new representation is needed in the future, it can be added easily without touching any of the other representation's code. Just add a new content type to content_types_provided and a new representation function to go with it.

What We Learned on Day 2

Today you learned how to integrate HTML templates into Webmachine and how to easily provide multiple representations for a resource. Perhaps you are starting to see why Webmachine is so useful for powering APIs.

Tomorrow we'll finish by looking at two pieces that are normally quite difficult in other frameworks—caching and authorization. Webmachine's simple, inquisitive nature will make these tasks easy too.

Day 2 Self-Study

Find:

- Investigate some of the other templating options for Erlang. erlydtl is another popular choice with a quite different flavor.

- Study src/petite_static_resource.erl, which was not covered in the text. Look up any Webmachine functions you haven't seen before in the documentation.

Do:

- Add persistence to Petite. (Hint: DETS is a disk-backed version of ETS, with a very similar API.)

- Add support for custom short codes. For example, a user might want the shortened version of https://pragprog.com/ to be http://localhost:8000/prag.

- Create another front-end resource to let users shorten links without going through the API.

Day 3: Illuminating HTTP's Dark Corners

Webmachine has a unique way of modeling HTTP requests as a state machine, but so far you've seen it handling things you've likely seen in most web libraries and frameworks. Let's look at some things that Webmachine enables that aren't usually found in its peers.

First, we'll take a look at caching. The HTTP protocol has a lot of support for caching, including expiry and versioning. Webmachine exposes these features in resource functions, just like the other parts of HTTP you've already seen.

After caching, we'll look at HTTP authorization. While some frameworks support authorization, most don't support HTTP-based authorization and many don't support any kind at all out of the box. For Webmachine, it's just another piece of the HTTP protocol—one that is particularly well suited to the state machine treatment—exposed for your application to control.

Making Things Cacheable

Modern web applications are expected to be lightning fast and accessible from a wide range of devices and networks. They often support many more simultaneous users than other types of software. One way to make applications faster and scale better is caching of resources.

In most frameworks, caching is an afterthought or, at best, an advanced feature. Webmachine has built-in support for caching, and it's so easy to use that your app is much more likely to leverage it and give your users an optimized and fast experience.

HTTP provides several types of caching information to web browsers. We're going to look at last modified headers, ETags, expire headers, and cache control directives. With this small set of tools, you can add the right kind of caching behavior to each resource for almost any kind of use case.

Last Modified Headers

The last modified header does what it describes—it tells the client when the last modification to the resource occurred. For example, if a user's profile hasn't changed since last Thursday, the last modified header will have last Thursday as the date in the header. Web browsers and other HTTP clients, after they've seen a resource with a last modified header, can conditionally request the resource in the future by using the If-Modified-Since header. Clients will only get a new copy of the resource if it has been changed since the time indicated.

All of this logic is already implemented in clients, so the only thing you must do is generate a date and time for the last modified header and return it when resources are requested. In Webmachine, this can be done by implementing the last_modified resource function. Webmachine and the HTTP clients take care of all the rest.

Create a new Webmachine application called cache to start experimenting with caching. Next, modify the cache_resource to add last modified headers:

```
webmachine/cache/src/cache_resource.erl
-module(cache_resource).
-export([init/1,
         to_html/2,
         last_modified/2]).
-include_lib("webmachine/include/webmachine.hrl").
init([]) -> {ok, undefined}.

last_modified(ReqData, State) ->
    {{{2013, 6, 12}, {22, 42, 00}}, ReqData, State}.
to_html(ReqData, State) ->
    {"<html><body>Hello, new world</body></html>\n", ReqData, State}.
```

The last_modified function returns a date of June 12, 2013, at 10:42 p.m. GMT. Dates and times in last modified must always be GMT. Webmachine uses a two-tuple of three-tuples to represent the date (the first tuple) and the time (the second tuple).

Compile and start the server, and then we can see how everything works from the command line:

```
$ curl -i http://localhost:8000/
HTTP/1.1 200 OK
Server: MochiWeb/1.1 WebMachine/1.10.0
Last-Modified: Wed, 12 Jun 2013 22:42:00 GMT
Date: Thu, 13 Jun 2013 04:47:25 GMT
Content-Type: text/html
Content-Length: 43

<html><body>Hello, new world</body></html>

$ curl -i --header 'if-modified-since: Wed, 12 Jun 2013 22:42:00 GMT' \
> http://localhost:8000/
HTTP/1.1 304 Not Modified
Server: MochiWeb/1.1 WebMachine/1.10.0
Date: Thu, 13 Jun 2013 04:47:30 GMT
```

First, we ask for the resource normally, and Webmachine returns it along with a Last-Modified header. The next time we request the resource, we provide the If-Modified-Since header to do a conditional GET, and since the resource has not been modified, an empty 304 Not Modified response is returned.

This example seems a bit silly since it's such a small resource, but imagine if this were returning a long chat history or a detailed configuration information about a service. Also, often the information about whether a resource has changed is much cheaper to get than the resource itself. If the resource hasn't been modified, Webmachine won't run your to_html function or anything after last_modified, meaning that any expensive representation generation logic is skipped.

ETags

Last-Modified headers are great if you have modification times or can compute them, but there are plenty of situations where they can be a chore. Also, Last-Modified headers require servers be time synchronized or else things can get out of whack. Instead of using modification times to influence caching, ETags use arbitrary strings that represent the version of a resource.

As a concrete example, we're going to add ETags support to petite_latest_resource, which lists the latest shortened links on the service. To use Last-Modified headers, we'd need to store the timestamp of when the last link was shortened. This is certainly possible, but Petite already has enough data to generate a suitable version string—the last value of the counter that was used to shorten a link.

Let's modify Petite to return an appropriate ETag to the HTTP client. Once this is done, just as in the Last-Modified case, HTTP clients can use conditional GET requests with the If-None-Match header to check for updated resources.

First, we'll need to add a new API call for petite_url_srv to return the last value of the counter and its corresponding handler. Don't forget to add the new API call to the list of exported functions at the top!

```
webmachine/petite/day3/petite/src/petite_url_srv.erl
get_last_id() ->
    gen_server:call(?SERVER, get_last_id).
```

```
webmachine/petite/day3/petite/src/petite_url_srv.erl
handle_call(get_last_id, _From, State=#st{next=N}) ->
    {reply, {ok, N - 1}, State};
```

Note that this piece of information is essentially free to compute, as it is stored directly in the service's internal state.

Now that we have a way to get the counter value, which we'll be using as the ETag value to represent the resource's version, we just need to implement the generate_etag resource function in Webmachine and it will handle the rest:

```
webmachine/petite/day3/petite/src/petite_latest_resource.erl
-export([generate_etag/2]).
```

```
webmachine/petite/day3/petite/src/petite_latest_resource.erl
generate_etag(ReqData, State) ->
    {ok, N} = petite_url_srv:get_last_id(),
    {integer_to_list(N), ReqData, State}.
```

As you can see from the code, it's not really any more complicated than the last modified case we saw earlier. The two approaches are basically identical except for how the resource's cachability is represented.

After adding ETag support to Petite, recompile and let's see how its responses change:

```
$ curl -I http://localhost:8000/latest
HTTP/1.1 200 OK
Vary: Accept
Server: MochiWeb/1.1 WebMachine/1.9.2
ETag: "1"
Date: Thu, 13 Jun 2013 05:39:26 GMT
Content-Type: text/html
Content-Length: 925
```

```
$ curl -i --header 'if-none-match: "1"' http://localhost:8000/latest
HTTP/1.1 304 Not Modified
Vary: Accept
Server: MochiWeb/1.1 WebMachine/1.9.2
ETag: "1"
Date: Thu, 13 Jun 2013 05:44:40 GMT
```

First, the resource is requested normally. Webmachine inserts a new ETag header with the version string that was returned in generate_etag. Next, a new request for the same resource is made along with a If-None-Match header containing the same ETag value. Nothing has changed, so the now familiar 304 Not Modified response is generated.

Let's add a new link and ask for the latest links using the same ETag again:

```
$ curl -X POST http://localhost:8000/shorten \
> --data 'url=https%3A%2F%2Fgithub.com%2Ferlang%2Fotp'
http://localhost:8000/2
```

```
$ curl -I --header 'if-none-match: "1"' http://localhost:8000/latest
HTTP/1.1 200 OK
Vary: Accept
Server: MochiWeb/1.1 WebMachine/1.9.2
ETag: "2"
Date: Thu, 13 Jun 2013 05:46:46 GMT
Content-Type: text/html
Content-Length: 1132
```

Because the supplied ETag value did not match the current ETag on the server, Webmachine generates a new response. This new response contains a new ETag. That's really all there is to it.

Both Last-Modified headers and ETags allow browsers to conditionally request resources they have already seen before. Another caching pattern is to unconditionally cache a resource for a given period of time, and this can be accomplished with the next two caching methods we'll see: expires and cache control headers.

Expires

Imagine a resource that both changes often and is requested quite often but isn't so important that it always needs to be fully up-to-date. In those cases, you might want to tell clients that they can use the data for a given amount of time, after which they should request it again. Expires headers accomplish this by using dates and times to indicate when the returned resource data expires.

Let's add a new expire_resource to the cache example application created earlier:

webmachine/cache/priv/dispatch.conf

```
{["expire"], expire_resource, []}.
```

webmachine/cache/src/expire_resource.erl

```
-module(expire_resource).
-export([init/1,
         to_html/2,
         expires/2]).

-include_lib("webmachine/include/webmachine.hrl").

init([]) -> {ok, undefined}.

expires(ReqData, State) ->
    {{{2013, 6, 15}, {05, 11, 00}}, ReqData, State}.

to_html(ReqData, State) ->
    {"<html><body>Hello, new world</body></html>\n", ReqData, State}.
```

In the new resource we've implemented expires, which is another of Webmachine's resource functions. Like last_modified, it needs to return a tuple of tuples representing the expiry date and time. The particular date and time in the example should be updated to something in your own near future, but remember that it must be in GMT.

Expires logic is a little harder to test because there is no conditional GET operation one can use; its value is purely informational. Browsers keep track of the expiry times on resources they download; and when requested, they grab the cached data if the expiry time is still in the future. If you want to test expire_resource, open your browser's network panel in a new tab and request http://localhost:8000/expire. You should see the browser make a normal HTTP request. If you then request the same URL again, you should see nothing happen because it reuses the cached data. Note that hitting refresh in the browser will request a new copy regardless of the expiry time, so retype the URL in the same tab instead to simulate what would happen if you clicked a link back to the same resource.

Cache Control

The last caching mechanism we'll look at is the Cache-Control header. Like the Last-Modified header, the Expires header operates on date and time values, but these may not always be convenient to provide. Cache-Control operates more like ETag in that it can more directly provide the relevant information. For example, instead of saying the resource expires on Saturday at 2:43 p.m., Webmachine can just say that it expires after five minutes.

Webmachine does not currently have a cache_control resource function, but we can piggyback on the expires function to add cache control support. Instead of returning the normal date and time tuple response, undefined—Webmachine's default answer for expires—is returned and the wrq module is used to modify the response headers appropriately.

Add a new control_resource to the cache example application:

```
webmachine/cache/priv/dispatch.conf
{["control"], control_resource, []}.
```

```
webmachine/cache/src/control_resource.erl
-module(control_resource).
-export([init/1,
         to_html/2,
         expires/2]).

-include_lib("webmachine/include/webmachine.hrl").

init([]) -> {ok, undefined}.

expires(ReqData, State) ->
    ReqData2 = wrq:set_resp_header("Cache-Control", "max-age=30", ReqData),
    {undefined, ReqData2, State}.

to_html(ReqData, State) ->
    {"<html><body>Hello, new world</body></html>\n", ReqData, State}.
```

Now the expires function sets the Cache-Control header and specifies a max-age property of thirty seconds. This lets the browser know it is free to cache the resource for up to thirty seconds before checking if a newer version is available.

You can test control_resource the same way as expire_resource using your browser's network inspector. It should not request the resource again for thirty seconds, even though you continue to browse to it repeatedly.

Cache-Control headers are much easier to use, because you often know how long the representation is valid. It saves the steps of computing the current time, adding in the age offset, and then returning a date and time to the client. It has a lot of other attributes that you can manipulate for even more complex caching behavior.

You can certainly add caching headers in other frameworks, but usually only by manually manipulating the HTTP headers yourself. Some frameworks have middleware that can add caching support, but this is usually configured per application and not per resource. Webmachine exposes HTTP's caching features as another part of its state machine model and makes it extremely easy to add custom caching behavior to any resource.

Authorization

Authorization is another HTTP feature that is often hard to use, if it is exposed at all. It is common these days for frameworks to leave authorization and similar details up to a real web server that sits in front of the application. While this makes the framework developers' jobs easier, it can make it complicated to integrate any authorization beyond the most basic into an application. Since it's just another HTTP feature, Webmachine makes it easy.

Here's a simplified diagram of the authorization part of Webmachine's state machine model.

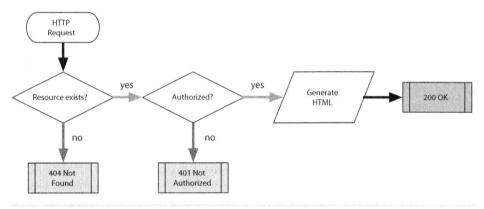

Figure 23— Authorization state machine

Webmachine resources can provide the is_authorized function to check if the current request is authorized and return either true, which allows the request to continue to the rest of the resource functions, or an authorization header, which will be returned to the client as the value of the WWW-Authenticate header in a 401 Not Authorized response.

The default is_authorized implementation always returns true. To observe more interesting behavior, we can create an is_authorized function that always returns an authentication header. First, create a new Webmachine project called auth, and add an auth_never_resource:

```
webmachine/auth/priv/dispatch.conf
{["never"], auth_never_resource, []}.
```

```
webmachine/auth/src/auth_never_resource.erl
-module(auth_never_resource).
-export([init/1,
         is_authorized/2,
         to_html/2]).
```

```
-include_lib("webmachine/include/webmachine.hrl").
init([]) -> {ok, undefined}.

is_authorized(ReqData, State) ->
    {"Basic realm=testing", ReqData, State}.

to_html(ReqData, State) ->
    {"<html><body>Hello, new world</body></html>\n", ReqData, State}.
```

There's not much to this resource, but poking at it with curl reveals a new behavior:

```
$ curl -i http://localhost:8000/never
HTTP/1.1 401 Unauthorized
WWW-Authenticate: Basic realm=testing
Server: MochiWeb/1.1 WebMachine/1.10.0
Date: Tue, 18 Jun 2013 03:13:17 GMT
Content-Type: text/html
Content-Length: 159

<html><head><title>401 Unauthorized</title></head><body><h1>Unauthorized
</h1>Unauthorized<p><hr><address>mochiweb+webmachineweb server</address>
</body></html>
```

Instead of a friendly "hello," we've gotten 401 Unauthorized. If you open http://localhost:8000/never in a web browser, you'll see a password dialog box. It doesn't matter what you input here, it will always return 401 Unauthorized.

Adding support for usernames and passwords is pretty easy. When an web browser gets an initial 401 Unauthorized error along with a WWW-Authenticate header including an authorization method and realm, it will prompt the user for a username and password and then attempt to request the resource again with an Authorization header.

The Authorization value the client sends is the authorization method—in this case Basic—and a base 64–encoded authorization string. For HTTP basic authentication, this string is just the base 64–encoded version of a string containing the username, a colon, and then the password.

Let's implement basic authentication by creating an auth_basic_resource:

webmachine/auth/priv/dispatch.conf
```
{["basic"], auth_basic_resource, []}.
```

webmachine/auth/src/auth_basic_resource.erl
```
-module(auth_basic_resource).
-export([init/1,
         is_authorized/2,
         to_html/2]).
```

```
    -include_lib("webmachine/include/webmachine.hrl").
    init([]) -> {ok, undefined}.
    is_authorized(ReqData, State) ->
        AuthHead = "Basic realm=Identify yourself!",
❶      Result = case wrq:get_req_header("authorization", ReqData) of
                    "Basic " ++ EncodedAuthStr ->
❷                      AuthStr = base64:decode_to_string(EncodedAuthStr),
                        [User, Pass] = string:tokens(AuthStr, ":"),
❸                      case authorized(User, Pass) of
                            true ->
                                true;
                            false ->
                                AuthHead
                        end;
                    _ ->
                        AuthHead
                end,
        {Result, ReqData, State}.

❹  authorized(User, Pass) ->
        User =:= "test" andalso Pass =:= "12345".

    to_html(ReqData, State) ->
        {"<html><body>Hello, new world</body></html>\n", ReqData, State}.
```

❶ We inspect the HTTP headers to see if an Authorization header is provided by the client.

❷ If an Authorization header is provided, it should have the form Basic AUTH_STRING, and we must decode the base 64–encoded authorization string.

❸ We call authorized with the username and password to see if the user is indeed authorized.

❹ Our authorization function tests against hardcoded values, but you can imagine that it could look up the username in a database.

Let's see how this resource responds to requests from the command line:

```
$ curl -v -u test:12345 http://localhost:8000/basic
«omitted output»
> GET /basic HTTP/1.1
> Authorization: Basic dGVzdDoxMjM0NQ==
> User-Agent: curl/7.24.0 (x86_64-apple-darwin12.0) libcurl/7.24
.0 OpenSSL/0.9.8x zlib/1.2.5
> Host: localhost:8000
> Accept: */*
>
< HTTP/1.1 200 OK
< Server: MochiWeb/1.1 WebMachine/1.10.0
< Date: Tue, 18 Jun 2013 03:25:10 GMT
```

```
< Content-Type: text/html
< Content-Length: 43
<
<html><body>Hello, new world</body></html>
* Connection #0 to host localhost left intact
* Closing connection #0
```

You can see the base 64–encoded authorization string in the client's request. The server happily responds with a 200 OK when given the magic words.

What We Learned on Day 3

Webmachine exposes much more of the HTTP protocol than other libraries and frameworks, and this can easily be seen in its support for caching and authorization. Where these are advanced or missing features in other frameworks, Webmachine includes them in its state machine model and makes them just as easy to implement as returning "Hello, World."

To show off the ease with which Webmachine handles caching logic, we looked at four caching strategies and how to implement them—Last-Modified headers, ETags, Expires headers, and cache control directives. With these four tools, almost any caching logic you might want is at your fingertips and a single resource function away.

Last-Modified headers and ETags allow browsers to conditionally request resources based on whether it has changed since the last request. While they differ in how the change is represented, they are both useful, and Webmachine makes them equally easy to use.

Expires headers and cache control directives inform browsers how long data is valid for and are often used to control how often data is requested regardless of how often it actually changes.

Finally we looked at HTTP authorization, which is often delegated to a real web server. Webmachine can handle it directly, making it much easier to integrate with your application.

Day 3 Self-Study

Find:

- More Cache-Control attributes you can use in your application

Do:

- If you've implemented caching in an application before, compare it with how easy it is to do in Webmachine.

- Modify petite_latest_resource to use Expires or Cache-Control headers in addition to ETags.

- Add authorization support to Petite so that only authorized users can shorten links.

Interview with Justin Sheehy

Justin Sheehy is the CTO of Basho, where he works on distributed systems such as the Riak distributed database system. He honed his distributed computing skills as an architect at Akamai and by working on research projects for the intelligence community at MITRE. Webmachine is just one of the many open source projects he's worked on.

Us: *Where did the inspiration for Webmachine's unique view on web applications come from?*

Justin: *A few of us at Basho (including but not limited to myself and Andy Gross) did the very first version of Webmachine together after being frustrated by the backward approach to HTTP that we thought most frameworks imposed. We wanted something that would allow us to think about exposing resource transfer to and from underlying systems, not something that would help create yet another cookie-cutter CRUD application. A flowchart written by Alan Dean was definitely also a primary inspiration; that flowchart is a direct predecessor of the one that now makes up the visual description of Webmachine's execution flow. A bit later, the decision flow chart inspired the amazing visual debugger that Bryan Fink added. That was probably the inflection point for the system, when it became something that really "clicked" for developers. I'd say that Webmachine wouldn't have become what it is without any of those people.*

Us: *What are the most interesting things you've seen built with the help of Webmachine?*

Justin: *Since one of our goals with Webmachine was to enable infrastructure to be part of the Web in a well-behaved way, it shouldn't be surprising that one of my favorites is even more deep infrastructure than we imagined. Caleb Tennis used Webmachine to build a web interface to the physical management of a datacenter! That is, he exposed resources that let administrators do things like examining and changing the motor speed on a cooled water pump. That's interesting work, I think, and Webmachine's clear resource model lends itself well to developing such things.*

Most of the things I find interesting that people build with Webmachine, though, are not very visible. This is because it lends itself so well to "middleware," or infrastructure systems, and is used less often for directly browser-facing Web apps.

Us: *What benefits do developers receive from building web applications on top of Webmachine and, more generally, Erlang?*

Justin: *I think that one of the benefits is that Webmachine makes it somewhat harder to accidentally do HTTP wrong. We certainly can't make anyone do everything right, even in the cases where there are objective criteria (when clear and explicit in standards, for instance) for correctness. But many Web frameworks place abstractions around HTTP that are shaped so very differently from HTTP itself that a user can't tell what will or won't be interoperable with other systems built from the same specifications. With Webmachine, you are more likely to build well-behaved and thus highly interoperable systems. As developers want to take advantage of more of HTTP's interesting features over time, Webmachine generally lets them do so very easily, without having to "break out" of a framework.*

The advantages of Erlang would make for a whole other interview and would also depend a great deal on the problem domain. It should suffice for here to say that we saw advantages in Erlang for web development or else we wouldn't have written Webmachine in it in the first place.

Us: *Webmachine has been widely imitated in many different languages. What have other communities learned from Webmachine, and what has Webmachine learned from them?*

Justin: *That is absolutely the highest form of flattery! We knew that Webmachine was really starting to have an impact when we started seeing clones pop up for Ruby, Clojure, Agda(!), Node.js, and other languages. Hopefully, the core simple ideas behind Webmachine have helped many more programmers as a result of those reimplementations. One of the nice benefits of these for Webmachine itself is that different communities have different expectations and so raise different questions. We've absolutely had some of the better ideas for Webmachine improvements come out of some of those satellite Webmachine communities.*

Wrapping Up

Webmachine does things a bit differently, but its unique design modeling HTTP as a state machine makes advanced HTTP processing a mundane matter. There's no need to guess what HTTP status codes to return or a need to create complicated views; Webmachine requires only a series of simple answers to specific questions, and it takes care of all the complex decisions. Instead of Choose Your Own Adventure, using Webmachine is like Choose Your Own Application.

Throughout this chapter, we explored many features of Webmachine in small examples and in the context of Petite, a small link-shortening app. We implemented resource functions for returning multiple representations of resources, managing existence and redirects, caching, and authorization. In Webmachine, these features are enabled by writing functions just a few lines long, but in most other frameworks, these features are considered advanced if they're available at all, and often it's up to you to write the messy decision logic.

Webmachine's Strengths

Back-end systems are where Webmachine is really in its element. It often gets used for exposing existing systems as HTTP endpoints, whether they are search engines, databases, or data analysis systems. Webmachine makes it easy to create robust HTTP APIs since it handles all the messy details of HTTP and lets you concentrate on your application.

Webmachine is also built on Erlang, which has a reputation for high availability and for handling large-scale problems. These are exactly the sorts of features that heavily used back-end systems must possess.

Erlang's lightweight process model gives Webmachine a much more concurrent architecture than other frameworks, which makes it ideal for implementing proxies between services or aggregations of services even when the services are in a variety of protocols.

We didn't cover it in this chapter, but Webmachine has built-in support for handling streaming responses, which comes in quite handy when dealing with data that is large and unwieldy.

Webmachine's Weaknesses

While templating systems and other front-end-focused features exist and can be integrated with Webmachine, it is does not come out of the box with the kinds of features wanted for typical CRUD applications. It doesn't take much to add form processing and database management, but people generally only use Webmachine for these tasks when they are part of a larger application, where Webmachine provides lots of back-end value.

For most people, Erlang is a strange language, both by its functional semantics as well as its nonmainstream syntax. Some people have difficulty thinking functionally, such as forgoing the familiar looping constructs and dealing with immutable data.

Final Thoughts

Webmachine is one of the most unique tools around for programming web apps. Its state machine model allows you to harness the full power and beauty of the HTTP protocol in a surprisingly simple way. To this, Webmachine adds all the concurrency, robustness, and scalability of Erlang. And just like a Choose Your Own Adventure book, it's a lot of fun.

CHAPTER 6

Yesod

Yesod may be one of the fastest web frameworks in existence,[1] but that's not the only reason it's worth learning. Yesod is written in Haskell, a language that is as expressive as many dynamic languages but which has a static type system that makes Java's or C++'s look like a toy. This rich type system is used over and over again in Yesod to create safe code that is resilient to programmer error and hostile attack.

If you've heard of Haskell before, you might think that a web framework in Haskell would be like the game Magic the Gathering,[2] full of complexity and arcane rules that take many hours to master. Don't let the mystique intimidate you. Yesod is Set,[3] a fast-paced card game that is inspired by weighty concepts but easy and fun to learn and understand.

Yesod brings its own unique ideas to web development, remixing and building on ideas from strongly typed languages. With Sinatra or Clojure you discover many of your application's bugs when you test it, but with Yesod, the compiler will find many kinds of bugs for you before the application is ever run. Yesod leverages the type system of Haskell to encode domain concepts into the types themselves, forcing the compiler—instead of the programmer—to do the hard work of reasoning about correctness.

Introducing Yesod

Yesod is the Hebrew word for foundation, and the framework strives to provide a robust and strong foundation for your apps. Some of the frameworks in this book attempt to explore new ways of building apps, but Yesod instead

---

1.   http://www.yesodweb.com/blog/2011/03/preliminary-warp-cross-language-benchmarks
2.   http://en.wikipedia.org/wiki/Magic_the_gathering
3.   http://en.wikipedia.org/wiki/Set_%28game%29

takes the traditional architecture and tries to leverage the strengths of Haskell to make it incredibly solid.

The Pieces

Yesod has models, views, and controllers like most modern frameworks, but its strong, static type system gives them a unique flavor. The keys for querying models have distinct types, ensuring that you can never confuse user ID 123 with invoice 123. View templates are compiled and enforce easily neglected security invariants. Controllers deal with URLs that cannot become outdated.

Yesod has all the same pieces as many other frameworks, but programming with Yesod feels like nothing else. Haskell is a pure functional, lazy language that is likely to be quite foreign to you, and programming web apps with a rich type system at hand is also unusual. In some ways, Yesod is a framework that could be from a strangely familiar, parallel universe.

The Plan

Over the next three days, you'll see how Haskell's type system prevents common errors, ensures your app is robust to attack, and is still expressive enough to feel like most dynamic languages.

First, on Day 1, we'll see the basics of routing and models, and we'll start to build the database portions of the chapter's app, Rumble.

On Day 2 we'll explore Yesod's templating languages—Hamlet and Lucius—and its widget abstraction, which enables you to build reusable components for your app. We'll also play with Yesod's declarative forms and finish the day with authentication and authorization.

Day 3 is all about integrating what we've learned into a real application. We'll combine everything from the first two days to build a social news aggregation site where users can share and comment on posts.

This week is going to be both fun and challenging, so let's dive right in.

Day 1: Data You Can't Get Wrong

This week we'll be building a social news aggregation site called Rumble. Sites focused on user-generated content, like Rumble, have a history of being vulnerable to attack, because they combine dynamic page generation with untrusted, user-submitted content. Developers have combatted these attacks by sanitizing and restricting user input, but dynamic languages offer little help or assurance that every possible case is covered.

Today we'll get a sample app up and running and we'll start to see how Yesod uses Haskell's type system to alleviate these problems. At the end of the day we'll build the models of Rumble, and hopefully you'll start to get a sense of how much work the compiler is doing to keep your code correct and your app safe.

Getting Started

The easiest way to start experimenting with Yesod is to install the Haskell Platform.[4] The Haskell Platform is available for Windows, Mac, and Linux and is probably included in your package manager of choice as well.

Cabal is the build tool that most Haskell developers use, and it comes with the Haskell Platform. Once the Haskell Platform is installed, you can use Cabal to update its package database and install Yesod:

```
$ cabal update
$ cabal install yesod-platform yesod-bin persistent-sqlite
```

This will install the Yesod framework, the yesod command-line tool, and the SQLite back end of Yesod's database library, respectively. These packages have quite a few dependencies that Cabal will download, compile, and install for you. Compiling all this took about fifteen minutes on our relatively fast machines; your mileage may vary.

You can check that everything is working properly by running yesod version. It should print the version of Yesod that is installed. This chapter requires at least version 1.2.

```
$ yesod version
yesod-bin version: 1.2.1
```

With Yesod installed, we're ready to create our first application.

Hello, World

The yesod command-line tool is used both to create a new application and to compile and run applications during development. While Yesod apps can be created by hand, it's much easier to let the tool do the work for us. You can create a new application using yesod init; when prompted, type hello for the application name and type s to choose the SQLite database when prompted:

```
$ yesod init
Welcome to the Yesod scaffolder.
I'm going to be creating a skeleton Yesod project for you.

What do you want to call your project? We'll use this for the cabal name.
```

---

4.   http://www.haskell.org/platform/

```
Project name: hello
Yesod uses Persistent for its (you guessed it) persistence layer.
This tool will build in either SQLite or PostgreSQL or MongoDB support for you.
We recommend starting with SQLite: it has no dependencies.

    s      = sqlite
    p      = postgresql
    pf     = postgresql + Fay (experimental)
    mongo  = mongodb
    mysql  = MySQL
    simple = no database, no auth
    url    = Let me specify URL containing a site (advanced)

So, what'll it be? s
That's it! I'm creating your files now...
«omitted output»
```

This will create a new directory called hello and fill it with your new project. We can compile and run the application with yesod devel from within the application directory.

```
$ cd hello
$ yesod devel
Yesod devel server. Press ENTER to quit
«omitted output»
```

The yesod devel command will watch for changes to your application and recompile the app as necessary. You can leave it running as you work, but if you need to quit, just hit Enter.

When it first starts up, you'll notice that it creates the application's database tables. It will also print out logging information as you access the application from your browser. Go ahead and visit http://localhost:3000/ to see the default Yesod scaffolding.

Let's modify the default app to add a "Hello, World" route and handler. The yesod command-line tool has a subcommand called add-handler that can add a new route and handler module to your application. Let's use that to add a route for /hello:

```
$ yesod add-handler
Name of route (without trailing R): Hello
Enter route pattern (ex: /entry/#EntryId): /hello
Enter space-separated list of methods (ex: GET POST): GET
```

This will create a new entry in hello/config/routes:

```
yesod/hello/config/routes
/static StaticR Static getStatic
/auth   AuthR   Auth   getAuth
```

```
/favicon.ico FaviconR GET
/robots.txt RobotsR GET

/ HomeR GET POST
/hello HelloR GET
```

The last line is the one that was just added by yesod add-handler. As you can probably guess from looking at the file, each route is listed on its own line and consists of a path, a handler name, and a list of accepted methods. Our new route points to a new handler called HelloR, which can be found in hello/Handler/Hello.hs:

```
yesod/hello/Handler/Hello.hs
module Handler.Hello where
import Import
getHelloR :: Handler Html
getHelloR = return "Hello, world!"
```

❶ Handler functions are named like methodHandlerR, where method is the HTTP method like GET or POST and Handler is the name of the handler's module. The functions contain the R suffix by convention to make it clear they handle routes.

The type signature of Handler Html tells what kind of representation the function will generate. Here, HTML is generated, but other representations are possible, as is switching representations based on the request information.

❷ This is almost the simplest possible implementation, returning unprocessed HTML as a string.

If yesod devel is still running, it will see your new handler and recompile and load your application automatically. If you visit http://localhost:3000/hello in your browser, you should see your friendly greeting.

Describing Data with DSLs

The config/routes file was a list of routes written in plain text. It is written in a very simple DSL that Yesod turns into Haskell and compiles into your application. Yesod is full of DSLs, and we'll be exploring several more of them throughout this chapter. The next one we'll investigate is the data modeling DSL.

Yesod's database library is called Persistent. It supports both SQL and noSQL databases and includes its own DSL for defining models. While not as sophisticated as an object-relational mapper (ORM), it's quite flexible and it's completely type-safe, as we'll see.

Our social news aggregator, Rumble, needs only a simple data model. Users submit posts, and all users can comment on these posts. Models are stored in config/models in a simple format. Let's look at Rumble's models file:

yesod/rumble/v1/rumble/config/models

```
❶ User
❷     ident Text
❸     password Text Maybe
❹     UniqueUser ident
❺     deriving Typeable Show

  Post
      title String
      url String
      author UserId
❻     score Int default=0
      created UTCTime default=now
      deriving Typeable Show

  Comment
❼     post PostId
      author UserId
      created UTCTime default=now
      body Text
      deriving Typeable Show
```

❶ A model is defined by writing its name, followed by an indented list of its fields. Here the User model is created.

Each model defines a Haskell type. Types in Haskell are distinguished from variables and functions by starting with a capital letter. Types and other identifiers are typically written in camel case.

❷ A field is specified with its name in lowercase, followed by its type. The type Text is a single string. Other common types are Int, Bool, and UTCTime.

❸ After the type come the options. Here we add Maybe, which wraps the value in Haskell's Maybe type, which will be either Just Text or Nothing. This is how database columns that can be NULL are represented.

❹ This is a uniqueness constraint since it starts with an uppercase letter. A list of fields is given, and the combination of these fields must be unique for this model. Here we require that idents be unique.

❺ We use Haskell's deriving syntax to tell the compiler to automatically generate implementations for the Typeable and Show type classes. Typeable allows this model to be stored in Yesod's caches, and Show allows us to print a representation of the model that is useful for debugging. All our models will use this.

❻ The default option allows an initial value to be set. This is used primarily in migrations.

❼ post and author are foreign key relationships. The PostId and UserId types are generated by the Post and User models and represent the primary keys of those models. Notice that the ID and the model are tied together. You won't be able to use a PostId to query for a user accidentally. The type system will prevent you from doing the wrong thing.

We need to tell Haskell's package manager, Cabal, that we'll need the time package, because the UTCTime type is not included in the scaffolding by default. First, add the package to the list of packages in rumble.cabal. The next listing shows a small part of the scaffolded rumble.cabal to show you where the new dependency line goes:

```
yesod/rumble/v1/rumble/rumble.cabal
    , warp                      >= 1.3          && < 1.4
    , data-default
    , aeson
    , conduit                   >= 1.0
    , monad-logger              >= 0.3
    , fast-logger               >= 0.3
➤   , time                      >= 1.4
```

Next, we'll need to import Data.Time in Model.hs to make the UTCTime available to our models:

```
yesod/rumble/v1/rumble/Model.hs
module Model where

import Prelude
import Yesod
import Data.Text (Text)
import Database.Persist.Quasi
import Data.Typeable (Typeable)
➤ import Data.Time

share [mkPersist sqlOnlySettings, mkMigrate "migrateAll"]
    $(persistFileWith lowerCaseSettings "config/models")
```

After adding the highlighted line, our models are ready to go.

Working with Models

Inside our project's directory, we can run ghci and start playing with our models. Constructing model objects is easy; each model has a constructor function of the same name.

```
$ ghci Model
GHCi, version 7.6.3: http://www.haskell.org/ghc/   :? for help
```

❶ *Model> **User "foo" Nothing**
```
User {userIdent = "foo", userPassword = Nothing}
```

```
*Model> let bar = User "bar" (Just "12345")
```
❷ *Model> **userPassword bar**
```
Just "12345"
```

❶ Constructing a User requires values for the two fields. Since the password field is a Maybe field, it can have values Nothing for NULL and Just "some string" when it has a value.

❷ Every model has accessor functions defined automatically for each field. Here userPassword is used to retrieve the password field. These functions are all named modelField. For example, to get the ident field value, you'd use userIdent.

Now that we can construct model objects, we need to insert them into the database. We'll need to use the runSqlite function to run database actions on our database and the insert function to insert new data:

❶ *Model> **import Database.Persist.Sqlite**
《*omitted output*》

❷ *Model> **id <- runSqlite "rumble.sqlite3" $ insert (User "foo" Nothing)**
```
*Model> id
```
❸ Key {unKey = PersistInt64 1}

```
    *Model> :type id
id :: Key User
```

❶ runSqlite is provided by Database.Persist.Sqlite, which we need to import.

❷ The final argument to runSqlite is the set of actions to run. The only action here is the call to insert, which creates a new row in the database for the given model object and returns its key.

❸ At first glance, it looks like the Key that is returned is generic, but inspecting the type shows that it is tied to the User model.

Retrieving data from the database is easy. First, let's look at two functions that return a single object, get and getBy. get takes Key m, where m is the model and returns a Maybe m. getBy takes a uniqueness constraint and associated values and tries to look up an object. It also returns a Maybe value, but of type Entity m, which we'll see shortly.

❶ *Model> let withDB a = runSqlite "rumble.sqlite3" a

❷ *Model> withDB $ get id
Just (User {userIdent = "foo", userPassword = Nothing})

*Model> e <- withDB $ getBy (UniqueUser "foo")
*Model> :type e
❸ e :: Maybe (Entity User)

*Model> e
❹ Just (Entity {entityKey = Key {unKey = PersistInt64 1},
                entityVal = User {userIdent = "foo",
                                  userPassword = Nothing}})

*Model> import Data.Maybe
❺ *Model> userIdent (entityVal (fromJust e))
"foo"

*Model> withDB $ getBy (UniqueUser "missing")
Nothing

❶ First, we define a helper function to save some typing.

❷ The variable id is the user we created in the previous example. The result is wrapped in Just when returned, since it's possible that the lookup will fail if the key is not in the database.

❸ You might expect getBy to return Maybe User just like get, but instead it returns an Entity User wrapped in a Maybe. The reason for this is that since we queried by a uniqueness constraint, we probably don't know the key for the object; and since the key is not part of the model, an entity is returned that combines a model object with its key.

❹ Entity User has two pieces: the key, which is a Key User, and the value, which is just a User. The accessor functions for the two pieces are entityKey and entityVal.

❺ The user ident field can be pulled out of the entity. fromJust is the accessor for Maybe types.

Constructing models and inserting them into the database is only part of the story. To build our social news site, we'll need to be able to query them too. For that task, Persistent provides selectList.

selectList takes two list parameters, a set of filters and a set of options, and returns a list of matching entities. In order to play with these, let's add more users and a few posts for each:

```
*Model> fred <- withDB $ insert $ User "fred" Nothing
*Model> jack <- withDB $ insert $ User "jack" Nothing
*Model> now <- getCurrentTime
*Model> withDB $ insert $ Post "Yesod" "http://www.yesodweb.com/"
  fred 17 now
*Model> withDB $ insert $ Post "Haskell" "http://www.haskell.org/"
  jack 103 now
*Model> withDB $ insert $ Post "Yesod @ Hackage"
 "http://hackage.haskell.org/package/yesod" fred 11 now
*Model> withDB $ insert $ Post "Persistent @ Hackage"
 "http://hackage.haskell.org/package/persistent" jack 5 now
```

Let's ask for all posts that were posted by jack:

```
*Model> posts <- withDB $ selectList [PostAuthor ==. jack] []
*Model> length posts
2
*Model> map (postTitle . entityVal) posts
["Haskell","Persistent @ Hackage"]
```

The filters use the familiar operators except with a . suffix. If there are multiple filters in the list, all must match for a record to match:

```
*Model> posts <- withDB $ selectList [PostScore >=. 15, PostAuthor ==. fred] []
*Model> map (postTitle . entityVal) posts
["Yesod"]
```

If you would like records where any of a set of filters match, use ||. between filter sets:

```
*Model> posts <- withDB $ selectList ([PostAuthor ==. fred] ||.
  [PostScore >. 100]) []
*Model> map (postTitle . entityVal) posts
["Yesod","Haskell","Yesod @ Hackage"]
```

We can use the options list to sort the results by using Asc for ascending or Desc for descending and by providing the field to sort by:

```
*Model> posts <- withDB $ selectList [] [Desc PostScore]
*Model> map (postTitle . entityVal) posts
["Haskell","Yesod","Yesod @ Hackage","Persistent @ Hackage"]
*Model> map (postScore . entityVal) posts
[103,17,11,5]
```

That takes care of half of the CRUD operations. Next we'll see how to update and delete data.

Modifying and Deleting Models

Updating and deleting your data with Persistent can be done in a few different ways. These are easiest to see with some examples:

```
❶ *Model> withDB $ update jack [UserPassword =. Just "asdf"]
  *Model> withDB $ get jack
  Just (User {userIdent = "jack", userPassword = Just "asdf"})

❷ *Model> withDB $ updateWhere [PostAuthor ==. fred] [PostScore +=. 10]
  *Model> posts <- withDB $ selectList [PostAuthor ==. fred] []
  *Model> map (postScore . entityVal) posts
  [27,21]

  *Model> let post = (entityKey . head) posts
❸ *Model> withDB $ delete post
  *Model> posts <- withDB $ selectList [PostAuthor ==. fred] []
  *Model> map (postScore . entityVal) posts
  [21]

❹ *Model> withDB $ deleteWhere [PostAuthor ==. jack]
  *Model> posts <- withDB $ selectList [] [Desc PostScore]
  *Model> map (postTitle . entityVal) posts
  ["Yesod @ Hackage"]

❺ *Model> withDB $ deleteBy (UniqueUser "jack")
  *Model> withDB $ selectList [] [Asc UserIdent]
  [Entity {entityKey = Key {unKey = PersistInt64 1},
           entityVal = User {userIdent = "fred",
                             userPassword = Nothing}}]
```

❶ update takes a key and a list of changes and makes the changes to that
key. Notice that these use the same operator plus dot syntax as the filters,
but the operators are assignments. Here we set a password for Jack.

❷ If you need to update multiple records at a time, updateWhere takes a list
of filters and a list of changes. In this example we increment the score of
all Fred's posts by ten.

❸ To delete a specific model object, delete just needs the key. After deleting
the top post by Fred, only one is left.

❹ deleteWhere takes a list of filters and removes all the matching model objects.
All Jack's posts are deleted.

❺ If you don't have a key for the model object you wish to delete, deleteBy
takes a uniqueness constraint. Jack's user is deleted.

These are all the tools we'll need to create and manipulate our data for
Rumble. Most of these things are common to other frameworks, but Yesod
puts a little bit of a twist on things.

In Yesod, we never used plain numbers for keys or strings for matching unique
records. Keys are strongly typed, and you can't accidentally use the key for

a post when you query for a user. Even though the database uses primitive types and can't tell one number from another, Yesod makes sure you always do the right thing.

What We Learned on Day 1

Today we started, as always, with "Hello, World!" and learned how to use the yesod tool to create projects and add new handlers. We also got a preview of how to generate output to the browser.

Our next stop was learning about the models and Yesod's database library, Persistent. We defined a simple structure for our social news aggregator, Rumble, and explored creating, querying, modifying, and deleting model objects.

Along the way, you saw a few of the ways that Yesod uses Haskell's strong, static type system to ensure that your code is correct before it is ever run. This is one of Yesod's biggest strengths, and you can bet we'll be seeing more of this during the week.

Tomorrow we'll look at Yesod's Shakespearian templating systems and its widget models, which help organize your views.

Day 1 Self-Study

Find:

- The Yesod book, and specifically the chapter on Persistent
- The "powered by Yesod" page in the Yesod wiki

Do:

- Use ghci to add some Comment model data to the database.

- Add a description field to the Post model.

- Try giving a sequence of actions to runSqlite or withDB. What happens to the other actions when one fails?

- See if you can figure out a way to subvert the type system and forge keys or convert keys from one model to another. Could you? How much work did it take?

Day 2: Views, Forms, and Auth

Web frameworks rely heavily on HTML templating systems to make adding dynamic output convenient. Unfortunately, most templating systems are thin veneers on string substitution, and as a result, it is very easy to introduce bugs and security vulnerabilities into your web app. For example, you might include incorrect links in a view or allow untrusted user-generated content to control a user's browser.

Yesod includes several templating systems, but while they appear similar to ones you've no doubt seen before, they work very hard to prevent the kinds of bugs that are common in those other systems. In Yesod, URLs and inserted document content are type-safe, which means you don't have to worry about updating views when routes change or whether you have accidentally enabled a cross-site scripting attack. This requires using a special syntax for referencing URLs, but the template syntax is very similar to other systems, so it is a small price to pay.

Today we'll explore Hamlet and Lucius, which are the templating languages for HTML and CSS in Yesod. There is a third language, called Julius, for templating JavaScript, but it's very similar to the other two, so we won't be covering it here. We'll also see Yesod's form-handling abilities while we build the front end for Rumble.

Ye Olde Templating Languages

The first of Yesod's templating languages is Hamlet, which generates HTML. Hamlet is inspired to some extent by Ruby's Haml,[5] in that it is whitespace sensitive and attempts to be as minimal as possible.

To see Hamlet in action, let's create a new Yesod app. Run yesod init and follow the prompts just as we did before, choosing wellmet for the project name and SQLite as the database. Then we'll create a new handler, GreetR.

```
$ yesod init
«omitted output»
$ cd wellmet
$ yesod add-handler
Name of route (without trailing R): Greet
Enter route pattern (ex: /entry/#EntryId): /greet/#Text
Enter space-separated list of methods (ex: GET POST): GET
```

Notice the #Text in the route pattern. This parameterizes the pattern and will call our getGreetR, which handles the route with an argument of type Text. We'll need to import the Text data type so that our handlers can use it.

We do this in Foundation.hs, which is where the main app's data type is defined:

---

5.   http://haml.info/

yesod/wellmet/Foundation.hs

```
import Model
import Text.Jasmine (minifym)
import Text.Hamlet (hamletFile)
import System.Log.FastLogger (Logger)
➤ import Data.Text (Text)
```

The Foundation

Yesod means "foundation" in Hebrew, so you can bet a file called Foundation.hs in a Yesod project must be important. The foundation module defines the application's main data types and basic configuration.

It defines the App data type that binds together the settings, the database configuration, static resources, and other app-specific things. It then creates instances of the Yesod type class—and several others—that control the application's high-level behavior.

Now we can use Hamlet to implement getGreetR:

yesod/wellmet/Handler/Greet.hs

```
module Handler.Greet where

import Import

getGreetR :: Text -> Handler Html
getGreetR name = defaultLayout [whamlet|<p>Well met, #{name}! #{after}|]
    where after = "Good day!" :: Text
```

Yesod's templating languages are implemented in Template Haskell, just like the routes and models we saw earlier. To generate Template Haskell in regular code, we use the quasi-quote syntax [name|template|], where name is the quasi-quoting function and template is the template code. In this example, whamlet is used to turn a Hamlet template into HTML.

Hamlet tags don't need to be explicitly closed because the templating language is whitespace sensitive. Variables and functions in the handler's scope can be referenced in the template by using #{expression}. Because Yesod is statically typed, it ensures that the expression you provide returns something that can be turned into HTML.

If you run yesod devel and visit http://localhost:3000/greet/developer, you should see the expected greeting.

Try visiting http://localhost:3000/greet/%3Cscript%3Ealert%28%27uh%20oh%27%29%3C/script%3E, which attempts to inject the JavaScript alert('uh oh') into the page. Yesod automatically escapes Text that you convert to HTML. Many other frameworks contain similar features, but in Yesod correct escaping is enforced at compile time by the type system. One enormous benefit of doing it this way is that you can't forget.

The defaultLayout function takes a *widget* as input and embeds it in the site's default template, which is found in templates/default-layout-wrapper.hamlet. A widget is a collection of data that represents some arbitrary content on a web page. For example, a single widget might contain the HTML for a self-contained component in your app along with the component's CSS and JavaScript.

This is a powerful unit of abstraction, and it means that you don't have to remember which resources are needed for a given page; everything is kept conveniently together. Let's see a widget in action. First use yesod add-handler to create a handler called Greet2 with the route /greet2/#Text. Then modify getGreet2R to match the following code:

```
yesod/wellmet/Handler/Greet2.hs
getGreet2R :: Text -> Handler Html
getGreet2R name = defaultLayout $ do
                      color <- return ("blue" :: Text)
❶                     setTitle "Greetings"
❷                     toWidget [lucius|
                              .greet { font-weight: bold; color: #{color}; }|]
❸                     toWidget [whamlet|<p .greet>Well met, #{name}!|]
```

❶ setTitle sets the page title.

❷ toWidget adds content to a widget. First, we add a Lucius template, which produces CSS output. Note that variable interpolation works the same way as with Hamlet.

❸ Hamlet is used to produce the HTML. The syntax .greet expands into class="greet". If we had used #greet instead, it would expand to id="greet".

You can visit http://localhost:3000/greet2/developer to view your handiwork.

Building widgets programmatically can be a little tedious, so Yesod provides the $(widgetFile "foo") syntax, which looks for appropriate templates named foo.hamlet, foo.lucius, and foo.julius. It combines all the templates it finds into the widget, and in development mode it will recompile them automatically when they change. Here's a Greet3 handler using this new syntax, along with its templates:

```
yesod/wellmet/Handler/Greet3.hs
getGreet3R :: Text -> Handler Html
getGreet3R name = defaultLayout $(widgetFile "greet3")
    where color = "blue" :: Text
```

```
yesod/wellmet/templates/greet3.hamlet
<p .greet>
  Well met, #{name}!
```

```
yesod/wellmet/templates/greet3.lucius
.greet {
  font-weight: bold;
  color: #{color};
}
```

This code does the same thing as the Greet2 handler, but it's organized nicely in separate files. Perhaps you can already imagine how useful this is for organizing the building blocks of views. You just combine the widgets you want in a page, and Yesod figures out what style sheets and code is needed.

There's a lot more to the templating languages themselves, and we'll see that later today. For now, let's create some forms so that we can get some data into our database.

Functional Forms

In order to collect data from the user, we need to include forms in our views and process those forms when they are submitted. Thankfully, Yesod includes a helpful set of tools for creating, validating, and processing forms.

We're going to explore the basics of Yesod forms by building a very simple user management interface for Rumble. We'll be able to see the list of users and add and delete them.

First, change back into the project directory for Rumble, and add a new handler called Users with a route of /users and responding to both GET and POST. Start the server with yesod devel and keep it running while we write some code.

We'll define a form-generating function by adding the following code to our new Users handler:

```
yesod/rumble/v2/rumble/Handler/Users.hs
❶ userForm :: Form User
❷ userForm = renderDivs $ User
❸          <$> areq textField "ID" Nothing
❹          <*> aopt textField "Password" Nothing
```

❶ The type signature indicates a form wrapping a User model object.

❷ renderDivs will generate the HTML for the form.

❸ This form is an *applicative* form, which means that it uses Haskell's Control.Applicative module to construct it. You can think of applicative as meaning that you can sequence operations (appending form fields) but not do any variable bindings like we've seen in database queries or widget construction. The <$> and <*> are operators defined by Control.Applicative. The end result is a nice internal DSL.

The areq function defines a required field; its arguments define the type of the field, the label for the field, and its default value.

❹ You might have guessed that aopt defines an optional field, and you'd be right. By combining areq and aopt you can build most any kind of form.

Our form generator won't do much by itself, so it's time to create a template for the Users page, where the form will be displayed after the list of users. Create a new Hamlet template in the templates directory called users.hamlet:

```
<h1>Users

❶ $if null users
    <p>There are no users.
  $else
    <ul>
❷      $forall Entity _ user <- users
          <li>#{userIdent user}
  <hr>

<form method="post" enctype="#{enctype}">
❸  ^{userFormWidget}
    <input type="submit" value="Add User">
```

❶ Hamlet uses $if .. $else ... to do conditional output. Here we test if the users variable is empty.

❷ $forall is Hamlet's version of a for loop. It iterates over users, matching each element to the pattern on the left side of the <-. This binds user to an Entity value, which can then be used to print the user's ID.

❸ Like #{...}, which renders Haskell expressions to HTML, ^{...} renders the expression to a widget. Here the userFormWidget will be embedded as the content of the form.

Now that we have a template, we can use it in our handler's getUsersR function. We'll need to query the database for a list of users and then process the template we just created:

```
yesod/rumble/v2/rumble/Handler/Users.hs
getUsersR :: Handler Html
getUsersR = do
❶  users <- runDB $ selectList [] [Asc UserIdent]
❷  (userFormWidget, enctype) <- generateFormPost userForm
❸  defaultLayout $(widgetFile "users")
```

❶ Yesod handlers can use runDB to execute database queries. runDB knows what kind of database to use because that information is encoded in the handler's type. We saw this query yesterday; it returns all the users sorted alphabetically by their IDs.

❷ generateFormPost creates a blank form of the given kind, and it returns the form's generated widget and the encoding type that will be used in the <form> tag. These variables are then available inside our template.

❸ All that's left to do is render our widget with defaultLayout.

Visit http://localhost:3000/users in your browser to see the results. You should see the users we added to the database yesterday. If you try to submit the form, you will get an error, because we've not yet implemented postUsersR.

The last piece of this handler is to process form submissions by adding users to the database and then redirect back to the Users handler:

```
yesod/rumble/v2/rumble/Handler/Users.hs
postUsersR :: Handler Html
postUsersR = do
  ((result, _), _) <- runFormPost userForm
  case result of
    FormSuccess user -> do
                    _ <- runDB $ insert user
                    redirect UsersR
    _ -> defaultLayout [whamlet|whoops|]
```

❶ runFormPost takes a form and processes it, filling in the fields with the submitted data. It returns the result, a widget, and the encoding type used, only the first of which we need here. Behind the scenes generateForm-Post and runFormPost are inserting and validating security tokens to prevent cross-site request forgery (CSRF) attacks.

❷ If the form processing is successful, it includes a user model object that we can use.

❸ The user gets inserted into the database, and runDB returns the new database ID for it.

❹ We redirect the user back to the Users handler. Note that we don't use the URL directly but use the name of the handler, which provides a safe reference to the route. If the route used for the Users handler ever changes, this redirect will still work. Even better, Yesod requires that we pass it a route type here; it will fail to compile if we attempt to give it a raw string. The type system prevents a possible bug potentially caused by a future change to a different piece of your application's code.

Although we've just processed the most basic kind of form, it has shown off a lot of Yesod's unique features. There's a lot of work going on even though we only wrote a few lines of code. We constructed a form declaratively, used Hamlet to embed widgets within widgets, and prevented routing changes from breaking our app's URLs. Best of all, we didn't have to test the app to see if we made a mistake; the compiler finds many errors before the code is ever run.

We have almost all the pieces we'll need for Rumble, but we still need to handle authentication and authorization.

A Tale of Two Auths

Authentication is the determination of the identity of a user. Whether a user provides a secret password or uses some third-party service to vouch for the user, the goal is to be confident that the user is who he or she claims to be. Authorization is concerned with what users can do. Are they allowed to create resources or delete them? Can they view a particular item? Many frameworks intertwine these two "auths," but in Yesod, they are treated separately.

By keeping them separate you keep everything simple. Your controllers aren't concerned with the mechanics of authentication, only what kind of authorization is needed. Most of the time, as you will see, authorization can be done declaratively outside of the controllers, keeping them focused on their true purpose.

Both of these features are controlled in an application's Foundation.hs file, which sets up the main data structures for the app.

Authentication

Let's look at the settings available in Foundation.hs:

```
yesod/authme/Foundation.hs
instance YesodAuth App where
❶    type AuthId App = UserId
❷    loginDest _ = HomeR
     logoutDest _ = HomeR

❸    getAuthId creds = runDB $ do
         x <- getBy $ UniqueUser $ credsIdent creds
         case x of
             Just (Entity uid _) -> return $ Just uid
             Nothing -> do
                 fmap Just $ insert $ User (credsIdent creds) Nothing
❹    authPlugins _ = [authBrowserId def, authGoogleEmail]
     authHttpManager = httpManager
```

❶ The AuthId associated type tells Yesod which model ID will be used to represent an authenticated user.

❷ loginDest and logoutDest control the default redirect location after logging in and out. Here we set both destinations to the home page.

❸ Yesod uses getAuthId to look up the AuthId for a given set of credentials. When using third-party authentication services, the only thing needed is to create a User if one doesn't already exist for those credentials.

❹ By default, Yesod turns on the Persona and Google authentication plugins.

These defaults are great for many cases and are a safer default than the built-in password authentication of most frameworks. It's easy to get password storage or transmission wrong, and doing so can have dire consequences.

Let's create a simple example site to play with authentication. Use yesod init to create a new project called authme and select SQLite as the database. Modify the config/routes file to only have a GET route for HomeR, and replace the Home handler with the following code:

yesod/authme/Handler/Home.hs
```
{-# LANGUAGE TupleSections, OverloadedStrings #-}
module Handler.Home where
import Import
import Yesod.Auth

getHomeR :: Handler Html
getHomeR = do
❶  user <- maybeAuth
   defaultLayout $ do
           setTitle "AuthMe"
           $(widgetFile "homepage")
```

❶ maybeAuth returns the authenticated Entity wrapped in a Maybe. There is also a maybeAuthId that returns only the AuthId. If you want to force users to be authenticated or be redirected to the login page, you can use requireAuth and requireAuthId.

We'll also need to replace the homepage template. Be sure to delete or empty templates/homepage.julius and homepage.lucius if you are following along.

```
❶ $maybe (Entity _ u) <- user
    <p>Logged in as #{userIdent u}
    <p>
❷     <a href=@{AuthR LogoutR}>Logout
  $nothing
      <a href=@{AuthR LoginR}>Login
```

❶ We try to match on the user. maybeAuth gives us an Entity UserId User if the user is authenticated. If we get a match, we print out the user's ident value.

❷ Yesod provides an AuthR route that takes a parameter LoginR or LogoutR, depending on whether you wish the user to log in or log out.

After running yesod devel you can visit http://localhost:3000/ and try to log in with Persona or Google. Once you're logged in, you should see your email address printed and you can log out.

We can make this a bit nicer by skipping the login page and putting a direct link to the Persona login system right on the page. Here's another handler and template that do just that:

```
yesod/authme/Handler/Direct.hs
module Handler.Direct where

import Import
import Yesod.Auth
import Yesod.Auth.BrowserId

authLinkWidget :: Widget
authLinkWidget = do
❶   onclick <- createOnClick def AuthR
❷   loginIcon <- return $ PluginR "browserid" ["static", "sign-in.png"]
❸   [whamlet|<a href="javascript:#{onclick}()"><img src=@{AuthR loginIcon}></a>|]

getDirectR :: Handler Html
getDirectR = do
  user <- maybeAuth
  defaultLayout $ do
            setTitle "AuthMe Direct"
            $(widgetFile "direct")
```

❶ createOnClick is a helper function of Yesod.Auth.BrowserId that creates the JavaScript code to execute when you want to trigger a Persona login (Browser ID is the old name for Persona).

❷ PluginR is the type-safe way to access plugin resource URLs.

❸ Our widget just becomes a link to trigger the JavaScript we created along with a pretty image.

```
$maybe (Entity _ u) <- user
  <p>Logged in as #{userIdent u}
  <p>
    <a href=@{AuthR LogoutR}>Logout
$nothing
  ^{authLinkWidget}
```

The only difference from our previous template is that we insert the authLinkWidget widget instead of a link to the login page.

Now that users are authenticated, we still need to control what they are allowed to do.

Authorization

The main control point for authorization is the isAuthorized function in your application's foundation type in Foundation.hs.

isAuthorized takes a route and a boolean indicating whether the request is a write request—a PUT or a POST for example. It can return Authorized, which allows the request; Unauthorized, which prevents the request; and AuthenticationRequired, which redirects the user to the login page.

This makes it very easy, and declarative, to design authentication for your routes. The default isAuthorized implementation simply returns Authorized for everything.

Let's see a quick example. Create a Secret handler using yesod add-handler at /secret. Then add the highlighted lines to Foundation.hs:

```
yesod/authme/Foundation.hs
authRoute _ = Just $ AuthR LoginR

isAuthorized SecretR _ = do
                maybeUserId <- maybeAuthId
                return $ case maybeUserId of
                        Just _  -> Authorized
                        Nothing -> AuthenticationRequired

isAuthorized _ _ = return Authorized
```

With that change made, try visiting http://localhost:3000/secret when logged both in and out. With these simple tools, authorization can be as simple or as complex as your app requires without getting in the way of any of the rest of your code.

What We Learned on Day 2

We covered a lot of stuff today. First, we saw Yesod's Shakespearian templating languages and learned about its widget abstraction. Unlike most templating systems, Yesod templates are type-safe and compiled before your app ever runs. Widgets combine one or more templates into a single, reusable unit, which allows you to keep the styles and markup for a component separate from other components.

This widget abstraction doesn't cost anything to use, because Yesod will compile your widgets into your pages just as if they had been combined in the first place. The benefit is that each widget stays simple, and all the hard work of figuring out what pieces are needed for which pages is taken care of by the compiler, not you.

Next, we looked at Yesod's declarative forms and used them to build a basic user creation page.

Finally, we explored authentication and authorization and saw how Yesod has built-in support for several well-known authentication systems and keeps authorization separate from the handlers.

Tomorrow we'll put everything together to build a working version of Rumble.

Day 2 Self-Study

Find:

- Some examples of Cassius, Yesod's other CSS templating system

- The special syntax for optional attributes in Hamlet

- The difference between applicative, monadic, and input forms

Do:

- Change wellmet's Greet3 handler to use a unique class name that is generated on the fly instead of a hardcoded class name. (Hint: You can create a unique name with name <- lift newIdent in your widget.)

- Experiment with some different isAuthorized functions. Try refactoring the final example so that the user check doesn't have to be repeated in every clause.

Day 3: Rumbling Along

Today we'll put everything together to build our social news aggregator. We'll use the Shakespearian templates to generate views and Yesod's declarative forms to handle new content. We'll also see how to modify the default layout.

We'll start top-down by building Rumble's front page list of posts and then move to displaying single posts. This will make a lot of use of Hamlet templates and widgets. Then we'll add forms for new posts and comments using Yesod's declarative forms. By the end of the day, Rumble will be ready for beta testers and should look similar to this screenshot.

Figure 24— Rumble: A social news site

Creating the Front Page

Yesod's defaultLayout function takes page content, usually a widget, and includes it in the site's default layout template for rendering. The generated scaffolding code uses templates/default-layout-wrapper.hamlet as the default template. We'll need to replace that with something more appropriate and then modify the Home handler to create Rumble's list of posts.

Let's start by creating all the routes we'll need. By creating them now, we'll be able to use them to generate type-safe URLs in our templates, even if their handlers aren't fully implemented. Use yesod add-handler to make the following routes and handlers:

- Create a Post handler with the route /post/#PostId responding to GET. This will be used to show individual posts.

- Create a PostNew handler with the route /new responding to both GET and POST. This will be used to show the new post form and to process new posts.

- Create a Comments handler with the route /post/#PostId/comments responding to POST. This will process new comments on a particular post.

If everything has gone according to plan, you should see the following new routes:

```
yesod/rumble/v2/rumble/config/routes
/post/#PostId PostR GET
/new PostNewR GET POST
/post/#PostId/comments CommentsR POST
```

Let's build a new default layout template. Replace the code in templates/default-layout-wrapper.hamlet with the following template:

❶ ```
$doctype 5
<html>
  <head>
    <meta charset="UTF-8">

    <title>#{pageTitle pc}

    ^{pageHead pc}

  <body>
    <div .navbar .navbar-inverse>
      <div .navbar-inner>

        <div .container>
```
❷ ```
          <a .brand href=@{HomeR}>Rumble

          <ul .nav>
            <li>
              <a href=@{PostNewR}>submit
          <ul .nav .pull-right>
            <li>
```
❸ ```
              ^{pageBody authLinkContent}

    <div .container>
```
❹ ```
      ^{pageBody pc}
```

❶ The $doctype 5 directive tells Hamlet to generate an HTML5 <!DOCTYPE>
tag.

❷ Our nav bar contains a link to the main page and a link to the new post
form. Notice that we used the @{...} syntax with the names of our routes.
These are Yesod's type-safe URLs. If the URLs for these routes ever change,
these links will still work, and Yesod will throw an error during compilation
if we try using something in a @{...} construct that isn't a route type.

❸ Here we include the Persona login button. The default template is run
slightly differently, so we cannot include a widget directly. Our authLinkWidget
from yesterday has been transformed into PageContent similar to the normal
embedded content.

❹ The pc variable is the page content that is passed to defaultLayout. Here the
body widget is included in the content area of the page.

We'll need to set up the authLinkContent by modifying defaultLayout. Add the
following line to defaultLayout, and add the definition of authLinkWidget from
Authentication, on page 215, to the definition of defaultLayout in Foundation.hs:

```
yesod/rumble/v2/rumble/Foundation.hs
defaultLayout widget = do
    master <- getYesod
    mmsg <- getMessage
    pc <- widgetToPageContent $ do
        $(combineStylesheets 'StaticR
            [ css_normalize_css
            , css_bootstrap_css
            ])
        $(widgetFile "default-layout")
➤   authLinkContent <- widgetToPageContent authLinkWidget
    giveUrlRenderer $(hamletFile "templates/default-layout-wrapper.hamlet")
```

If you wish to see the results so far, take a look at the user management page, http://localhost:3000/users, that you built earlier. You should see it in prettier surroundings now. The front page should contain a list of posts that users have submitted and commented on. Since each post will look the same, we'll use a widget to handle their rendering. The following code should replace the scaffolding in the Home handler:

```
yesod/rumble/v2/rumble/Handler/Home.hs
getHomeR :: Handler Html
❶ getHomeR = do
    posts <- runDB $ selectList [] [Desc PostScore]
    defaultLayout $ do
                setTitle "Rumble"
                $(widgetFile "home")
❷ generatePostWidget :: Entity Post -> Widget
generatePostWidget (Entity postId post) = do
❸   (author, comments) <- handlerToWidget $ runDB $ do
                        comments <- selectList [CommentPost ==. postId]
                                               [Asc CommentCreated]
❹                       author <- get404 $ postAuthor post
                        return (author, comments)
    $(widgetFile "post")
```

❶ Grab a list of posts sorted by score and hand them off to a widget for display. It doesn't get much easier than this.

❷ To render each post, we'll need to transform an Entity Post model object into a widget. In addition to the post data, we'll also need the author and comments information.

❸ runDB is a function that normally runs inside a handler. If you want to use it in a widget, handlerToWidget is needed to make it work.

❹ get404 is a convenience function to return a model object or cause the handler to return a 404 Not Found HTTP error.

The handler itself doesn't contain much; it is mostly responsible for setting up the context for the template. Let's look at the templates:

```
yesod/rumble/v2/rumble/templates/home.hamlet
$if null posts
  <p>Nothing here yet.
$else
  $forall post <- posts
    ^{generatePostWidget post}

<article>
  <header>
    <h1>
      <span .score>#{postScore post}
      <a href=@{PostR postId}>#{postTitle post} #
      <small>#{postUrl post}
    <p>added by #{userIdent author}
    <p>#{length comments} comments
```

❶ Notice another use of type-safe URLs with @{...}. Since the PostR route takes a parameter, we must supply one to generate a safe URL.

There's not much to the templates beyond variable interpolation. The handlers set up the context and then delegate the rendering to the templates. In a few dozen lines, we've accomplished a lot. You can visit http://localhost:3000/, but there isn't much there yet since there aren't any posts. Let's build the new post form now.

Building a Post Form

Our forms for Rumble are going to be slightly more complicated than the user form we saw yesterday. The renderDivs function that generates the form takes a constructor function as one of its arguments, and when the form is run, it uses this function along with the form data to construct an object. In the user form, we use the User model constructor: Rumble's forms need something a little different.

One of the parts of a Post is the post's creation time. This is not something that the user will provide in a form; the server should generate the time stamp at the instant it adds the post to the database. This means we can't use the Post constructor with renderDivs, but must make our own constructor function. Our form then contains the pieces of data the user will input, and our constructor function will combine those with the rest of the data needed to generate an actual Post value.

An example will illustrate. Here is the GET portion of the new post handler:

```
yesod/rumble/v2/rumble/Handler/PostNew.hs
module Handler.PostNew where
import Import
import Data.Time
import Yesod.Auth
```
❶ `postForm :: Form (UserId -> Int -> UTCTime -> Post)`
❷ `postForm = renderDivs $ Post`
```
              <$> areq textField "Title" Nothing
              <*> areq textField "URL" Nothing
getPostNewR :: Handler Html
```
❸ `getPostNewR = do`
```
  _ <- requireAuthId
  (postFormWidget, enctype) <- generateFormPost postForm
  defaultLayout $(widgetFile "post-new")
```

❶ postForm doesn't directly return a form that creates a Post; it returns a form that creates a function that takes a UserId, an integer, and a UTCTime and then returns a Post.

❷ We use the Post constructor here, but because it will only receive the first two of its five arguments, it's partially applied. This means that it will return a function expecting the final three arguments.

❸ The GET handler is simple. It just generates the blank form and renders the post-new widget. Note the call to requireAuthId, which will redirect users if they are not logged in.

There's not much to the post-new template. It just wraps the post form widget:

```
yesod/rumble/v2/rumble/templates/post-new.hamlet
<h1>New Post

<form method="post" enctype="#{enctype}">
  ^{postFormWidget}
  <input type="submit" value="Post">
```

The final piece of the new post handler is to process the forms when they are submitted. Here's postPostNewR:

```
yesod/rumble/v2/rumble/Handler/PostNew.hs
postPostNewR :: Handler Html
postPostNewR = do
  authorId <- requireAuthId
  ((result, _), _) <- runFormPost postForm
  case result of
```
❶ `    FormSuccess makePost -> do`
❷ `                  time <- liftIO getCurrentTime`
❸ `                  post <- runDB $ insert $ makePost authorId 0 time`
❹ `                  redirect $ PostR post`
```
    _ -> defaultLayout [whamlet|whoops|]
```

❶ Remember that the result of form processing is a constructor function, not a Post value.

❷ We need the three extra pieces of Post to create it—the time, the score, and the author. Since getCurrentTime is an IO action, we must use liftIO to call it.

❸ With all the information obtained, we can use makePost to generate a Post value and insert it into the database.

❹ Our task is done, and we redirect the user to the post's page. We again make use of Yesod's safe URLs to generate a link that won't get out of date if the routes change later.

You can now visit http://localhost:3000/new to add new posts to Rumble, although the redirect will take you to an unimplemented view. Once you add a post, just manually go back to the home page to see the results in the list.

Our final tasks today are to create the post handler and add the ability to comment on posts.

Viewing Posts and Making Comments

Implementation of the post and comment handlers follows the same patterns you've seen with the home and new post handlers. Let's look at the post handler:

```
yesod/rumble/v2/rumble/Handler/Post.hs
module Handler.Post where
import Import
import Data.Maybe
import Yesod.Auth
import Handler.Comments (commentForm)
getPostR :: PostId -> Handler Html
getPostR postId = do
  authId <- maybeAuthId
  (post, author, comments, commentsWithAuthors) <- runDB $ do
          post <- get404 postId
          author <- get404 $ postAuthor post
          comments <- selectList [CommentPost ==. postId] [Asc CommentCreated]
          authors <- mapM (get . commentAuthor . entityVal) comments
          return (post, author, comments,
                  zip (map entityVal comments) (map fromJust authors))
  (commentFormWidget, enctype) <- generateFormPost $ commentForm postId
  defaultLayout $ do
    setTitle $ toHtml $ (postTitle post) <> " - Rumble"
    $(widgetFile "post-full")
generateCommentWidget :: Comment -> User -> Widget
generateCommentWidget comment author = $(widgetFile "comment")
```

❶ The main job of the handler is to retrieve all the necessary info from the database. It might seem strange that we must fetch the related data by hand; this is because Persistent is not limited to relational databases and doesn't enforce relational representations. It does mean some common tasks are a bit more work.

❷ mapM works like map, except it maps a monadic function over a list. This is needed, as get operates in the database monad.

❸ The comments and authors are "zipped" together. zip takes two lists and produces a list of tuples, where each tuple contains one element from each list.

❹ Notice that we can't directly pass raw strings to setTitle because this could be unsafe. Yesod requires that they be properly transformed to HTML, which will ensure they are safely escaped.

❺ Like generatePostWidget, which we saw previously, generateCommentWidget is just a helper to turn Comment values into widgets. We must also pass the author, as the Comment value only contains the UserId foreign key, not the User value.

The post-full template is quite similar to the post template, except that it includes all the comments. If the user is logged in, the new comment form is also displayed. There's nothing in it that you haven't seen before in some form:

```
yesod/rumble/v2/rumble/templates/post-full.hamlet
<article>
  <header>
    <h1>
      <span .score>#{postScore post}
      <a href=@{PostR postId}>#{postTitle post}
      <small>#{postUrl post}
    <p>added by #{userIdent author}
    <p>#{length comments} comments

$maybe _ <- authId
  <hr>
  <form method="post" enctype="#{enctype}" action="@{CommentsR postId}">
    ^{commentFormWidget}
    <input type="submit" value="Post Comment">
<hr>

$forall (comment, author) <- commentsWithAuthors
  ^{generateCommentWidget comment author}
```

The comment widget contains two templates, one for the HTML and one for the CSS:

```
yesod/rumble/v2/rumble/templates/comment.hamlet
<article .comment>
  <header>
    <span .author>comment by #{userIdent author}
    <span .time>on #{show (commentCreated comment)}
  #{commentBody comment}
```

```
yesod/rumble/v2/rumble/templates/comment.lucius
.comment {
  background-color: #eee;
  padding: 10px;
  margin-bottom: 10px;
}

.comment header {
  color: #aaa;
  text-align: right;
}
```

Finally, we need to create the comments handler with its comment form. The comments handler must process the submitted forms from the post's page and add the new comments to the post in the database:

```
yesod/rumble/v2/rumble/Handler/Comments.hs
module Handler.Comments where
import Import
import Data.Time
import Yesod.Auth

❶ makeComment :: PostId -> Textarea -> UserId -> UTCTime -> Comment
  makeComment post body = \author time -> Comment post author time body

❷ commentForm :: PostId -> Form (UserId -> UTCTime -> Comment)
  commentForm post = renderDivs $ makeComment post
                         <$> areq textareaField "Comment" Nothing
❸ postCommentsR :: PostId -> Handler Html
  postCommentsR post = do
    authorId <- requireAuthId
    ((result, _), _) <- runFormPost $ commentForm post
    case result of
      FormSuccess mkComment -> do
                       time <- liftIO getCurrentTime
                       _ <- runDB $ insert $ mkComment authorId time
                       redirect $ PostR post
      _ -> defaultLayout [whamlet|whoops|]
```

❶ makeComment is a helper function to make a constructor function for a Comment. Unlike Post, whose first two fields were user-filled and whose remaining fields were filled in during processing, Comment's fields are more scattered. This means we can't use a partially applied Comment as the constructor function. This helper just takes the fields that will be filled out by the user and returns a function that takes the remaining fields and returns the constructed Comment.

❷ With the helper in place, the comment form becomes quite simple.

❸ Finally, the POST handler mirrors the one for new posts. We fetch the remaining pieces of data needed to complete the Comment value and then call the returned constructor. The final Comment value is inserted into the database.

Rumble should now be ready for use at http://localhost:3000/. You can create new posts and comment on ones that are there.

What We Learned on Day 3

Today we put all our knowledge to use building the rest of Rumble, our social news app. Templates and widgets, forms and models all mixed cohesively to bring Rumble to the world. Best of all, the end result is safe from many forms of attack and is robust against future changes thanks to Yesod's leverage of Haskell's type system.

You're happy because your app is fast and small, reaping the benefits of a compiled language while not giving up many benefits of dynamic languages. Your users are happy because their favorite app won't throw strange errors; most errors will be discovered and fixed before the app is ever run.

Day 3 Self-Study

Find:

- A few interesting projects on GitHub using Yesod

- The Yesod blog and the Yesod cookbook—they are both full of interesting examples of how to use Yesod.

Do:

- The login link is always present, even when logged in. Have it switch to the user's email address when that person is logged in.

- Rumble is missing the ability to vote on posts. Add a new handler that can process submitted votes and add them to a post's score. Modify the templates to include voting links on the home and post pages.

- Create a profile page that collects a user's posts and comments. Link the username in each post and the comment to the corresponding profile page.

Interview with Michael Snoyman

Michael Snoyman is the creator of Yesod and the lead software engineer at FP Complete, a company dedicated to bringing Haskell into the mainstream. His desire to improve his own development led him to Haskell and to creating Yesod.

Us: *Haskell's excellent type system makes Yesod quite unique among web frameworks. How has strong, static typing influenced the web apps you've developed?*

Michael: *In order to fully leverage a strong type system, you have to spend a bit more time up front designing your type system. The goal is to express as many invariants in the types as you can so that the compiler can enforce them for you. Based on experience with weaker type systems (like Java), people often come away with the idea that a type system cannot express much information. My experience with Haskell has been quite different. Some simple examples would be:*

- *protection against cross-site scripting attacks by labeling all user data as untrusted,*

- *distinguishing numerical database identifiers based on table type, and*

- *encoding business logic invariants, such as "a user must enter an email address, a phone number, or both, but may not omit both fields."*

Once this initial work has been done, the benefits are huge. Any invariant you've successfully encoded can be relied upon fully to be enforced by the compiler. This is far more powerful than unit tests. While testing can ensure specific properties in certain circumstances, a type-level requirement is enforced through every piece of your software.

Refactoring becomes a much easier exercise as well. Oftentimes, when I get a change in specifications, my first task is to change the data types. Once that has been done appropriately, I embark on compiler-guided coding: I let the compiler tell me what needs to be updated, and I fix that. And in many cases, once the code compiles again, the software works correctly.

Us: *Yesod seems to be setting the bar high for performance. Why is performance important for web apps?*

Michael: *It's a funny question. It's certainly true that Yesod scores very well on benchmarks, and some people have spent a lot of effort optimizing various pieces of the Yesod infrastructure, from the Warp web server to our cryptographic client session cookie code. All of this contributes to a great user experience. But my real opinion is that most of the time, there's essentially some minimum bar for reasonable performance. This depends on various factors, such as user expectations and the nature of the program. Once you get beyond that minimum level, we're really talking about a savings in hardware costs, which, while nice, is not the most important factor.*

What I consider more important is scalability. The ability to write a program that easily scales out to multiple cores, and ultimately multiple machines, means that you'll be able to meet the needs of large increases in users. The web architecture lends itself very well to this with its stateless approach, but that's not enough. Using a language like Haskell, which encourages immutable data structures and referential transparency, simplifies scalability drastically. And having powerful concurrency and parallelism tools, like software transactional memory and data parallel Haskell, are significant boons as well.

Us: *Do you find that Yesod enables new kinds of web apps or makes existing types of apps much easier to develop?*

Michael: *For the most part, Yesod is not about any radical new approaches. Yesod follows a very standard model-view-controller web framework design and tries to leverage Haskell to provide reliability, correctness, and performance. My philosophy has been to be revolutionary in one aspect only, and that aspect was using Haskell. So to answer the question more directly, I wouldn't say that we've enabled any new kinds of web apps. As for making development easier, I've found that Yesod greatly eases the debugging and maintenance of any large projects while taking about the same amount of time for initial development as other popular frameworks from other languages.*

Some related projects are attempting to be more revolutionary than Yesod. Functional reactive programming and continuation-based frameworks are two interesting areas being developed in the Haskell community right now and that do have the potential to enable new kinds of web apps.

Us: *What are the most interesting things you've seen people do with Yesod?*

Michael: *For the most part, I've seen people writing very exciting web projects using Yesod, without any outward visibility that Yesod is being used behind the scenes (besides perhaps the "server" HTTP response header).*

One interesting phenomenon has been using Yesod to create user interfaces that would normally be desktop applications. Since Yesod can embed static resources and a web server into a single executable, it's quite possible to create a program that launches a background server process and then opens up a web browser to view the user interface. We even provide a library (wai-handler-launch) designed around making this kind of usage trivial. This makes it much easier to create cross-platform graphical applications. Some such applications include git-annex assistant, some Wiki platforms, a complete personal finance management system, and Git history viewers.

And then of course there's the usual range of "standard" web sites written using Yesod, everywhere from personal blogs to a full-blown Haskell integrated development environment in the cloud (FP Haskell Center).

Us: *What plans do you have for the future of Yesod?*

Michael: *At this point, Yesod is a mature web framework that meets the initial problem domain I had for it (and then some). My goal for that core is to continue to* *improve quality and performance and update with any necessary bug and security fixes. But I'm quite happy with where the API is right now, and the goal is to try to maintain long release cycles between backwards-incompatible changes. I've heard lots of feedback from the community and commercial users, and I strongly believe stability is something we must provide to our users.*

That said, there are many new domains that we are expanding into on the periphery. Haskell to Javascript compilers, better client-side coding abstractions, more integration with newer web technologies (like WebSockets), and more powerful server-side abstractions for features such as autoscaling and clustering are all on the radar and to one extent or another being worked on right now. Yesod's development strategy encourages having rapid iterations on experimental features and, after a design has been converged on, encourages including deeper integration with the core Yesod technologies. I intend to continue that process.

And, of course, encouraging wider adoption is something we're actively working on. More comprehensive documentation, whether it be the Yesod book, various online tutorials, cookbook recipes, or screencasts, is vital to helping new users get started. At FP Complete, we're working on many of these issues not just for Yesod but for the Haskell language in general. I strongly believe that Haskell and Yesod have the potential to help software developers write better, more robust software, and hope others are able to reap these benefits.

Wrapping Up

Yesod is a traditional framework built out of a very nontraditional language. Yesod has models, views, and controllers, but it is also compiled, lazily evaluated, and has static typing. Far from being a burden, Haskell adds much to the traditional web stack—safety, speed, and robustness against programmer error.

Many errors you'd normally find while testing your app will be found by the compiler. You can't accidentally forget to escape content when including it in an HTML template because in Yesod, strings and HTML are different types and you can't substitute one for the other. You won't be surprised by null pointer exceptions or undefined results; the compiler forces you to handle all cases of a Maybe value.

In this chapter, we've taken a short tour of what Yesod has to offer and built an app that is often hard to get right. With Yesod, we can rest easier knowing that the compiler is double-checking that our code does what we wanted and preventing much of our human tendency to make errors.

Yesod's Strengths

Yesod makes heavy use of Haskell's type system to prevent programmer error. This is important on the Web not just to avoid unhappy users, but also to prevent malicious actors from harming your business or your users. It's not a silver bullet that negates the need for testing, but you'll find that it catches a large class of errors you previously had to find via testing.

Yesod is also extremely fast. In the crowded space of web frameworks, it is leaps and bounds ahead of almost all its competition with regard to raw speed. Better still, you don't have to give up what you're used to in dynamic languages in order to take advantage of this.

Many of Yesod's libraries are very rich. The templating languages cover a wide range of functionality without giving up type safety; the authentication plugins come out of the box with support for Persona, Google login, and more; and Yesod can easily make use of both SQL and noSQL databases.

Yesod's Weaknesses

There's no denying that Haskell is a strange language to most programmers, and its combination of laziness, pure functions, and strong types requires a bit of a learning curve.

Yesod's persistence library is a bit underdeveloped compared to most other frameworks. In particular, the lack of joins makes some things clumsy, even while it makes handling noSQL databases easier.

Final Thoughts

Type systems are wonderful things, and if you've been scarred by less-capable type systems, it's easy to dismiss their utility. Yesod leverages Haskell's types everywhere it can and does so without seeming clever. This is a feature that can't be matched by frameworks in other languages and is a hard tool to give up once you're used to it.

Programming with Yesod is both liberating and frustrating. It frees you from many worries about security issues or worries about lingering bugs, but since it finds most bugs before you run the app, you get most of your debugging pain in a single lump. However, a few more frowns during development are a small price to pay for happy users.

CHAPTER 7

Immutant

Dwarf Fortress is a computer game renowned for its depth and complexity as well as its user-hostile interface and steep learning curve.[1] Hours of training videos exist to help you get started, but most people give up before they get very far. Those that persevere are rewarded with rich gameplay but are frustrated by the poor interface.

Contrast this to Minecraft,[2] a game heavily inspired by Dwarf Fortress. It has a simple user interface and interesting graphics but retains many of the creative gameplay elements that people love from Dwarf Fortress.

Enterprise Java web development has a lot to offer, but it's been wrapped up in a form that is complicated, painful to use, and difficult to learn. Immutant takes those same elements and mixes them together with Clojure to make things simple, pleasant to use, and much easier to get started with. Just as Minecraft has brought elements of the creative gameplay of Dwarf Fortress to the masses, Immutant aims to make the sophisticated tools of the enterprise developer easy and accessible to all.

Introducing Immutant

Web frameworks typically build on top of a lower level of the stack that handles dealing with HTTP. This lower level often contains little else, and this design drives the simple architectures of most frameworks, where all code happens in the context of some web request. Immutant expands on this lower level, providing many more primitives like message queues, daemons, distributed caching, and scheduled jobs.

---

1.   http://www.bay12games.com/dwarves/
2.   http://minecraft.net/

Immutant's Features

Immutant is based on JBoss AS7, which is a Java Enterprise Edition application server with a long history. With this richer underpinning, Immutant enables much more sophisticated architectures and applications. While Rails apps must resort to external services like memcached and RabbitMQ, Immutant not only provides those same services, but integrates them fully. This makes them significantly easier to use and deploy.

Immutant can also be clustered across many machines, and its components will do the right thing. By default, scheduled jobs will only run once within the cluster; cache data will be replicated and sharded. All of these features are just as useful to startups as they are to the enterprise, but in Immutant, you don't have to deal with the ceremony of Java or spend your days in XML configuration files.

Because Immutant apps are written in Clojure and Immutant's web component is based on Ring, which is covered in Chapter 4, *Ring*, on page 115, we'll be concentrating on the other pieces—message queues, jobs, and caching. We'll be building an app that monitors a set of URLs and tests whether the links on those pages are valid. This will require asynchronous processing and scheduled work and will need caching to keep things efficient.

The Plan

On the first day, we'll see how to install the Immutant app container and deploy our own applications to it. Next, we'll learn how to use the distributed cache and how to schedule jobs. We'll use the cache to store the results of fetching web pages.

Day 2 will involve message queues and pipelines. Message queues are important for getting work done asynchronously outside the confines of a web request. Pipelines are an abstraction over message queues that allow work to be decomposed into separate steps, each of which can run in parallel and which are connected by queues.

On our last day, we'll look at overlays, which allow you to mix languages in Immutant to enable polyglot programming. You'll see that Ruby and Clojure apps can be deployed together and interact seamlessly. We'll also look at clustering, which spreads your app across several nodes and allows it to handle more data and fail more gracefully.

Immutant has a lot to offer, so let's get started.

Day 1: Beyond the Web Basics

Modern web apps continue to push the boundaries of what is possible with software, especially when it comes to operating at scale. To cope with increasing complexity and growing demand, developers rely not just on databases but on memory-backed, distributed caches, message queues, and asynchronous processing. Unfortunately, the full stack frameworks that were designed for last year's apps haven't quite caught up to today's needs. Immutant closes the gap.

Today we'll cover Immutant's basics—just enough to get us started building Overwatch, a link-monitoring app that needs these more modern architectural features. After we get Immutant up and running, we'll build the piece that fetches pages and caches the results.

Getting Started

To use Immutant, you will need a Java Virtual Machine (JVM) as well as the Leiningen build tool. You can find more information about these in *Getting Started*, on page 117.

Once you have Leiningen, you'll need to add the lein-immutant plugin to your Leiningen user profile. Add the plugin to the list in your ~/.lein/profiles.clj, or create that file and directory if it doesn't exist and fill it with the following configuration:

immutant/profiles.clj
```
{:user {:plugins [[lein-immutant "1.0.1"]]}}
```

We've used version 1.0.1 here—the current version at the time of writing—but you can probably use the latest version available (refer to the Immutant install page for more information[3]).

You can test that everything is working by running lein immutant, which should produce output similar to this:

```
$ lein immutant
Manage the deployment lifecycle of an Immutant application.

Subtasks available:
undeploy   Undeploys a project from the current Immutant
archive    Creates an Immutant archive from a project
deploy     Deploys a project to the current Immutant
run        Starts up the current Immutant, displaying its console output
env        Displays paths to the Immutant that the plugin is currently using
overlay    Overlays a feature set onto the current Immutant
test       Runs a project's tests inside the current Immutant
```

---

3.   http://immutant.org/install/

```
version    Prints version info for the current Immutant
install    Downloads and installs an Immutant version
list       Lists deployments or Immutant installs
```

```
Run `lein help immutant $SUBTASK` for subtask details.
```

```
Arguments: ([subtask] [project-or-nil subtask & args])
```

The final step is to install the Immutant app server and start it up:

```
$ lein immutant install
«ommitted output»
```

```
$ lein immutant run
Starting Immutant: /Users/jack/.immutant/current/jboss/bin/standalone.sh
===========================================================================
«omitted output»
```

The first command downloads and installs the latest stable Immutant release. The second starts up the app server. You should see a lot of logging output as the server starts. If you wish to stop the server, just hit Ctrl-C. Now we're ready to create and deploy our first Immutant app.

Hello, World

We can create a simple scaffold app by using lein new as we did in the Ring chapter (see *Hello, World!*, on page 118). We'll also create an extra file, immutant/init.clj, that is needed for Immutant apps. Let's create hello:

```
$ lein new hello
Generating a project called hello based on the 'default' template.
```

The two important files lein new creates are project.clj, the Leiningen project description, and src/hello/core.clj, the core namespace for our app. First, let's update project.clj to add Compojure as a dependency:

immutant/hello/project.clj
```
(defproject hello "0.1.0-SNAPSHOT"
  :dependencies [[org.clojure/clojure "1.5.1"]
                 [compojure "1.1.5"]])
```

Then, we'll use the same code from the Ring chapter's "Hello, World" app in src/hello/core.clj:

immutant/hello/src/hello/core.clj
```
(ns hello.core
  (:use compojure.core))
(defroutes app
  (GET "/" []
    "Hello, World!"))
```

Finally, we'll need to tell Immutant to start a web service using the Ring handler we created with Compojure's defroutes. Create src/immutant/init.clj, the initialization code for our Immutant app and add the following code to it:

immutant/hello/src/immutant/init.clj
```
(ns immutant.init
  (:require [immutant.web :as web]
            hello.core))
```

➤ `(web/start "/" hello.core/app)`

The highlighted line shows how to start a web service in an Immutant app. We provide the root path and the Ring handler, and Immutant will do the rest. In the Ring chapter, we accomplished this same task by adding special metadata to project.clj, which the lein-ring plugin used to find the main Ring handler. Immutant just does the same thing a bit differently.

As we'll see later today, the immutant.init can start more than just web services; it's these other services—caching, scheduled jobs, messaging, and more—that give Immutant apps much of their power.

To deploy the app to the running Immutant server, you can use lein immutant deploy. You should see a short message when the deploy is done, and a few seconds later, the Immutant app server should start up the hello app. You can see your handiwork at http://localhost:8080/hello/.

Distributed Caching

Retrieving data can be quite expensive, especially when the data is stored on spinning metal. Even solid-state disks (SSDs) are not nearly as fast as RAM. Web apps with large audiences can easily place unsatisfiable demands on databases, and these apps must adapt by caching most data in memory. Since datasets are large and growing and the amount of memory one machine can address is relatively small, services like Memcached enable memory caches distributed over many computers.[4]

Immutant contains a distributed memory caching system in the immutant.cache namespace. It is automatically spread over the entire Immutant cluster, and it can even support transactions. In this section we'll look at how to store and retrieve data in the cache. We'll also look at memoization, which is a technique for caching the results of functions that is common in functional programming.

Immutant is built on Clojure and enjoys much of the same interactive development capability available to other Clojure apps. Let's create a new app to

---

4. http://memcached.org/

explore caching that has a REPL we can connect to. First, create a new app
called overwatch:

```
$ lein new overwatch
Generating a project called overwatch based on the 'default' template.
```

Next, we'll need to enable the REPL. This can be done by adding the :nrepl-port
property to the :immutant options in the project.clj. We'll also need a few extra
dependencies for later:

immutant/overwatch/project.clj
```
(defproject overwatch "0.1.0-SNAPSHOT"
  :dependencies [[org.clojure/clojure "1.5.1"]
                 [org.clojure/tools.logging "0.2.6"]
                 [clj-http "0.7.6"]
                 [enlive "1.1.4"]]
  :immutant {:nrepl-port 0})
```

A port value of 0 indicates that Immutant should choose a random free port.
Go ahead and run lein immutant deploy to deploy the app to the Immutant server.
When the app is deployed, Immutant will write the port it chose to a file called
.nrepl-port alongside each deployed project's project.clj file.

Everything else we need to do—add dependencies, start services, or reload
the project—we can do from inside the REPL. To start a REPL client, you can
use the lein repl command:

```
$ lein repl :connect `cat .nrepl-port`
Connecting to nREPL at 127.0.0.1:55432
REPL-y 0.2.1
Clojure 1.5.1
    Docs: (doc function-name-here)
          (find-doc "part-of-name-here")
  Source: (source function-name-here)
 Javadoc: (javadoc java-object-or-class-here)
    Exit: Control+D or (exit) or (quit)

user=>
```

Our REPL is ready to go.

Caching Basics

Immutant doesn't have just one cache but as many as you like. Each cache
has a name, and multiple caches work a bit like namespaces, segregating
your data. They can also have different configurations such as expiry time
and durability.

We can create a new cache with create:

```
user=> (require '[immutant.cache :as cache])
user=> (def c (cache/create "testing" :ttl [1 :minute]))
{}
```

The parameter here controls the default time to live (TTL), given as a vector of a value and a keyword describing the units. Anything we add to the cache will expire and disappear after its TTL has elapsed.

We can write data to the cache with put. Reading data from the cache is the same as reading data from any Clojure map. With these operations we can add a new entry to the cache and watch it expire:

❶
```
user=> (cache/put c :url "http://pragprog.com/")
nil
```

❷
```
user=> (:url c) "http://pragprog.com/"
;; wait more than a minute
```
❸
```
user=> (:url c)
nil
```

> ❶ Using put we add key and value pairs to the cache. Note that put returns the previous value that was stored.

> ❷ Accessing the value immediately returns it.

> ❸ After the value expires, accessing it returns nil.

There are several other ways to add entries to a cache. put-all takes a map and puts all the key and value pairs into the cache. put-if-absent only puts the key and value into the cache if no value for that key is already present. put-if-present only changes the cache if the key already exists in the cache. put-if-replace takes a key and value as well as a previous value and only changes the value in the cache if the previous value equals the one supplied; this is a compare and swap operation. All of these conditional put functions are atomic.

It's easier to see how these conditional put functions work at the REPL:

❶
```
user=> (cache/put c :foo "foo" {:ttl -1})
nil
```

❷
```
user=> (cache/put-if-absent c :foo "bar")
"foo"
user=> (:foo c)
"foo"
```

❸
```
user=> (cache/put-if-absent c :bar "bar")
nil
user=> (:bar c)
"bar"
```

```
❹ user=> (cache/put-if-present c :foo "bar")
"foo"
user=> (:foo c)
"bar"
❺ user=> (cache/put-if-present c :baz "baz")
nil
user=> (:baz c)
nil

❻ user=> (cache/put-if-replace c :foo "foo" "quux")
false
user=> (:foo c)
"bar"
❼ user=> (cache/put-if-replace c :foo "bar" "quux")
true
user=> (:foo c)
"quux"
```

❶ We create a new entry in the cache, overriding the default TTL with a new one. Negative values disable expiry.

❷ Since :foo already has a value in the cache, put-if-absent returns its value and doesn't make any changes.

❸ There is no :bar entry, so put-if-absent creates one.

❹ put-if-present checks if :foo is in the cache, finds it, and updates its value.

❺ :baz is not in the cache, so put-if-present makes no changes.

❻ put-if-replace checks if the current value of :foo in the cache is equal to "foo". Since it's actually "bar", it returns false and doesn't change the value.

❼ When the value matches, put-if-replace returns true and updates the value in the cache.

You can use delete to remove things from the cache. It returns the value that was stored in the cache.

```
user=> (cache/delete c :foo)
"quux"
```

You can also pass a value to delete, and the key will only be removed if the value matches:

```
user=> (cache/put c :foo "foo" {:ttl -1})
user=> nil
user=> (cache/delete c :foo "bar")
false
user=> (:foo c)
"foo"
```

These basic operations cover pretty much anything you'd ever want to do with cached data. Also, you can put any Clojure data directly in the cache. Immutant's distributed cache is extremely versatile and convenient, but it gets even better.

Memoization

One nice thing about working with functional languages and immutable data structures is *referential transparency*. Referential transparency means that given the same inputs, a function will produce the same outputs. This implies there is no global state being used to produce the output or side effects caused by the function.

Functions in mathematics are referentially transparent. The square root of 4 is always 2. An example of a function that isn't referentially transparent is (java.util.Date.), which takes no arguments but produces a different value almost every time it is called.

If we know that a function is referentially transparent, we can cache its result since we know it will never change given the same inputs. The cached value is just as good as running the function again. Caching the results of functions and using the cached values the next time the function is used is called *memoization*. Memoization is such a common use case that Immutant provides the memo function to make it easy to use.

You could probably write memo yourself: build a key from the inputs; look up the key in the cache; if found, return the cache value; otherwise, run the real function with the inputs and store the result in the cache and return it. Let's see an example:

❶
```
user=> (defn slow-double [x]
  #_=>    (Thread/sleep 5000)
  #_=>    (+ x x))
```

❷
```
user=> (slow-double 10)
;; wait 5 seconds
20
user=> (slow-double 10)
;; wait 5 seconds
20
```

❸
```
user=> (def cached-double (cache/memo slow-double "slow-double"))
```
❹
```
user=> (cached-double 10) ;; wait 5 seconds
20
user=> (cached-double 10)
20
```

❶ First, we define slow-double, which sleeps for five seconds before it produces an answer.

❷ Calling slow-double is indeed slow. Every answer takes a long time.

❸ We use memo to memoize the function. memo returns a new function that wraps the slow function and takes care of checking and populating the cache. memo takes the function to memoize, a cache name, and the same parameters as create. Here we just use the default cache parameters.

❹ The first call to cached-double takes five seconds since the input is not yet in the cache. However, calling it again with the same input returns immediately.

Memoization is a great way to speed up your apps. Combining memoization with TTL specifications allows you to control how long the answers are good for when the functions aren't fully referentially transparent as well. For example, it might be fine for computed statistics to be slightly out-of-date on highly trafficked pages, and caching them for even a few minutes might make a significant difference to server load.

Memoizing Web Pages

Fetching web pages is a slow operation since it involves traversing networks. Since most web pages don't change that often and since Overwatch is concerned with basic health, not content, we can easily memoize fetching web pages to speed up our app.

The nice thing about this is that the rest of the application does not need to know that any optimizations have been done, nor does it need to know any of the caching details. The other pieces of the app can just call a function to fetch a web page, and most of the time it will be lightning fast.

Let's create an overwatch.link namespace and create our fetch function:

immutant/overwatch/src/overwatch/link.clj
```
(ns overwatch.link
  (:require [immutant.cache :as cache]
            [clj-http.client :as http]))
(defn fetch-slow [url]
  (http/get url))
(def fetch (cache/memo fetch-slow "fetch" :ttl 1 :units :days))
```

The web pages will be cached for a single day. All calls beyond the first to fetch during that day will return immediately with the cached results. We'll be using this fast fetch function as a building block for the rest of Overwatch tomorrow.

Scheduled Jobs

Some work needs to happen at specific times. A cleanup task may need to run every night, a reminder might need to be sent to a user after a few days, or reports might need to be generated every week. Our app, Overwatch, will need to monitor URLs at regular intervals, not just in response to user requests.

Scheduled jobs are integrated into the rest of the system. Your app can create jobs at any time, and when your app is undeployed, its jobs will be unscheduled. If you are running jobs in a cluster, Immutant will make sure only one instance of the job runs in the cluster.

To create a scheduled job, Immutant provides the schedule function found in the immutant.jobs namespace. Let's see a few examples:

```
user=> (require '[immutant.jobs :as jobs])

❶ user=> (jobs/schedule "say.hello" #(println "Hello!") :in 3000)

❷ user=> (jobs/schedule "repeat.hello" #(println "Hello!")
   #_=>   :in 5000 :every 2000 :repeat 4)

❸ user=> (jobs/schedule "weekly.hello" #(println "Hello!") "0 15 8 ? * 2")
```

❶ schedule takes the name of the job, a function to run whenever the job executes, and keyword arguments describing when the job should run. Here we print "Hello!" once after three seconds have elapsed.

❷ Here's a slightly more complicated set of arguments. This runs the job every two seconds, repeating it four times. The first run will begin in five seconds. You can check the results in the Immutant app server console.

❸ Instead of passing a variety of arguments, you can also use cron specifications.[5] This job is run every Monday (the second day of the week, which is provided in the sixth field) at 8:15:00 a.m.

Unscheduling jobs can be done by passing the name of the job supplied to schedule to unschedule. For example, to remove the last job in the previous example, just call (jobs/unschedule "weekly.hello").

There's not much else to say about jobs. They are extremely simple but quite indispensable. Once you have scheduling functionality in your app server, it's hard to live without. Sure you can use cron and other similar tools, but it's much more convenient to let Immutant handle the grunt work of synchronizing multiple

---

5. http://en.wikipedia.org/wiki/Cron

machines' cron configurations and the hairy edge cases around making sure the right code is always running and not running more than once.

What We Learned on Day 1

Today we got Immutant up and running. We installed and launched an Immutant app server and deployed several apps to it as we explored Immutant's capabilities.

First, we built a basic "Hello, World" app to see how to use Immutant's web services. Since Immutant uses Ring to power its web services, all the tools and tricks from Chapter 4, *Ring*, on page 115, can be used to build powerful apps.

Next, we looked at Immutant's distributed caching features, which are one of the many enterprise features that Immutant integrates for use by your apps. Caching is widely used by most production web apps these days, but the tight integration with the app server makes it a joy to use.

Finally, we learned how to create jobs that run at specific times or repeat indefinitely.

By now you're probably noticing that Immutant is full of these extra services that most web apps eventually need but few frameworks provide out of the box. With Immutant, you need far fewer external services to make your app work so that you can concentrate on business logic instead of service glue.

Day 1 Self-Study

Find:

- The Immutant tutorials for caching and jobs

- The Immutant documentation for caching and jobs

Do:

- Play with the other caching parameters you find in the documentation. Use the REPL to explore :idle and :persist.

- Scheduling is quite dynamic; you can even schedule new jobs from within jobs. Create a job that runs after one day, one week, and one month. Such a job might be useful to send reminders at increasing intervals.

- Immutant can run any Ring app. Port Zap from the Ring chapter to Immutant. Think about where you could tie in the services Immutant offers.

Day 2: Building Data Pipelines

Modern web apps often use third-party message queue services to handle asynchronous and horizontally scalable processing of data. Whether sending images off to be resized and transformed or just sending email, queues have all sorts of uses and are very useful for decoupling components of your application from each other.

Immutant has messaging built right in to the app server. There's no separate system to maintain, and data doesn't need to be transformed to other protocols and back. Because the toolchain is integrated and able to process most Clojure data, using it couldn't be easier.

Today we'll learn about Immutant's message queues and the abstractions built on top of them.

Message Queues

Message queues are simple things with an enormous number of uses in modern apps. They are often employed to schedule work asynchronously or to tackle processing jobs in parallel. For example, sending email from a web app generally involves putting the message in a queue; if you are sending a large amount of mail you might have multiple machines grabbing work from the queue and dispatching the messages to their remote destinations.

Normally items added to a queue are removed by some worker function or process. Only one worker will get any particular item. There is another common mode of operation called publish-subscribe, where items put in a queue are received by every worker watching the queue. In Immutant, these are called topics.

Create a new app called messaging with lein new messaging, and edit the project.clj to add REPL support:

immutant/messaging/project.clj
```
(defproject messaging "0.1.0-SNAPSHOT"
  :dependencies [[org.clojure/clojure "1.5.1"]
                 [compojure "1.1.5"]]
  :immutant {:nrepl-port 0})
```

Alternatively you could add the :immutant {:nrepl-port 0} map entry to your user profile in ~/.lein/profiles.clj, which would add nREPL support to all your Immutant projects and prevent you from inadvertently deploying to production with a REPL enabled, assuming you don't deploy with the :user profile. The following is a sample profiles.clj you could use:

```
{:user {:immutant {:nprel-port 0}}}
```

Deploy the app with lein immutant deploy, and use lein repl :connect `cat .nrepl-port` to connect to the REPL.

Queues

Let's create our first queue:

```
user=> (require '[immutant.messaging :as msg])
❶ user=> (msg/start "queue.test")
❷ user=> (msg/start "queue.test")
```

❶ The start function declares a queue or a topic. If the name contains "queue," it is a queue; if it contains "topic," it's a topic.

❷ Calls to start are idempotent. Declaring the queue a second time does nothing if it already exists. Every app on the Immutant server can declare the queues it uses and doesn't have to worry whether some other app already did so.

Publishing and receiving messages is done with publish and receive. We can pass any Clojure data to publish and get it back on the other side:

```
❶ user=> (msg/publish "queue.test" "http://pragprog.com/")
  user=> (msg/publish "queue.test" ["http://immutant.org" "http://clojure.org"])

❷ user=> (msg/receive "queue.test")
  "http://pragprog.com"

  user=> (msg/receive "queue.test")
  ["http://immutant.org" "http://clojure.org"]

❸ user=> (msg/receive "queue.test" :timeout 5000)
  nil
```

❶ publish takes the name of the queue and the message and adds it to the queue. Most Clojure data can be published as a message; here we publish a string and a vector of strings. Another common choice is to publish maps.

❷ You can receive a message, waiting until one arrives if none are in the queue, by calling receive and passing the queue name. We get back exactly what we put in, in the same order.

❸ We pass the :timeout option to receive, which will return nil if no message arrives before the timeout expires. Here we wait five seconds for a message.

Our examples have published and then immediately received messages. In real apps there would be multiple receivers all waiting for messages from the queue, and the queue would act as a distribution mechanism for the work.

Immutant also provides a convenient function for handling all messages from a queue called listen. It takes a function that will process the message and can process messages in parallel:

```
user=> (msg/start "queue.listen")
user=> (msg/listen "queue.listen" #(println "i heard:" %))
user=> (msg/publish "queue.listen" [1 2 3])
user=> (msg/publish "queue.listen" #{:a :b :c})
```

We create a new queue and set up a listener that prints whatever it hears. After publishing two messages, you can inspect the running Immutant server's console output to see the results. It should look something like the following:

```
22:13:26,581 INFO  [stdout] (Thread-16 (HornetQ-client-...)) i heard: [1 2 3]
22:16:48,023 INFO  [stdout] (Thread-16 (HornetQ-client-...)) i heard: #{:a :c :b}
```

Queues are quite simple: some group of tasks publishes messages to the queue, and another group of tasks receives those messages and does some work. Any message is only ever received by a single task. The message publishers don't need to know anything about the receivers, not who they are or how many there are or even whether they come and go. Everybody just needs to know the queue name and be able to understand the messages. It creates a very loose coupling between components.

Topics are a little different, and we'll look at those next.

Topics

Topics are a broadcast mechanism. Messages are sent to the topic, and every listener receives a copy of the message. If you have a few dozen tasks handling work and you need to coordinate some action among them, like setting a new configuration or shutting down, then topics are perfect.

In Immutant, topics and queues have exactly the same API; the difference is that all parties receiving or listening for a message to a topic will receive it, not just one of them. We can easily see the difference by creating both a topic and a queue, attaching several listeners, and then publishing several messages to them. Let's start with the queue:

```
❶ user=> (msg/start "queue.multi")
❷ user=> (defn worker [m]
   #_=>   (let [id (.getId (Thread/currentThread))]
   #_=>     (println "worker" id ":" m)
   #_=>     (Thread/sleep 5000)))

❸ user=> (msg/listen "queue.multi" worker :concurrency 5)

❹ user=> (dotimes [i 3] (msg/publish "queue.multi" (str "hello " i)))
```

❶ First, we create a new queue.

❷ We create a simple worker that prints out the message along with its thread ID and then sleeps for a while, simulating doing some lengthy task.

❸ We attach a listener to the queue with a concurrency of 5, which allows up to five threads to process the messages.

❹ Three distinct messages are published to the queue.

You can check the Immutant server console for the results of this test. It should look similar to the following:

```
23:14:59,247 INFO  [stdout] (Thread-25 (HornetQ-client-...)) worker 241 : hello 0
23:14:59,252 INFO  [stdout] (Thread-20 (HornetQ-client-...)) worker 225 : hello 1
23:14:59,260 INFO  [stdout] (Thread-26 (HornetQ-client-...)) worker 242 : hello 2
```

Three different threads handled messages, but each message was only handled once. Let's try the same experiment with a topic:

```
user=> (msg/start "topic.multi")
user=> (msg/listen "topic.multi" worker :concurrency 5)
user=> (dotimes [i 3] (msg/publish "topic.multi" (str "hello " i)))
```

Looking at the output now, you should see something quite different:

```
... worker 250 : hello 0
... workerworker  worker 254249  :251:    : workerhello 0hello 0
...
...   248 hello 0: hello 0
...
... worker 249worker  :254  : hello 1hello 1
...
... worker worker251  worker250:   :hello 1 248
...   hello 1
... : hello 1
... worker 249 : hello 2
... worker 250 : hello 2
... workerworker  254 248:  hello 2:
...   workerhello 2
... 251 : hello 2
```

The output is interleaved from all the threads, but you can see that each message was processed five times, once per concurrent listener.

With queues and topics, many interesting architectures are possible, and these architectures can often be scaled to very large workloads, all while reducing coupling between different components.

Pipelines

Some tasks involve multiple steps, each stage taking some input, performing a computation, and then generating some results for the next stage. Many computations may need to run in parallel to keep up with the rate of input.

To solve these kinds of problems, you might have each stage read its input from a queue, do its computation, and publish its results to a new queue. Since this is a common pattern, Immutant provides pipelines, which wrap this architecture into a more convenient form.

Pipelines make these kinds of distributed and parallelized data flows look much like data flow in Clojure itself. Consider this normal Clojure code that handles sending an email:

immutant/messaging/src/messaging/email.clj
```
(def send-email [username]
  (-> username
      get-email
      make-msg
      send-msg))
```

This code fetches the user's email address from somewhere, perhaps a database, creates an email message, and then sends it, assuming that the functions get-email, make-msg, and send-msg already exist.

It is often the case that functions that need to access other systems, like get-email and send-msg, take a nontrivial amount of time to complete. The rest of the web page your app is generating probably doesn't depend on the outcome of this task, and so you'd like to do this work asynchronously.

With Immutant, you can turn this same code into a pipeline with the pipeline function:

immutant/messaging/src/messaging/email.clj
```
(require '[immutant.pipeline :as pl])

(def send-email-pipe
  (pl/pipeline "email"
               get-email
               make-msg
               send-msg
               :concurrency 5))
```
❶
❷

❸

❶ The pipeline function takes the name of the pipeline, the steps, and optional parameters. It returns a function that places data on the first step of the pipeline, which we've assigned to send-email-pipe.

❷ The same functions are listed here as in the normal Clojure example with ->. For each function, pipeline will create a step in the pipeline. Many copies of each step will run simultaneously depending on the setting of the :concurrency parameter.

Remember, between each of the steps, the result of the step is being published as a message to a queue, and a pool of workers waiting to execute the next step is listening for those messages.

❸ The parameters supplied at the end of pipeline apply to all steps in the pipeline. Here we set the concurrency to 5, which means that each step will have five concurrent workers processing messages at that step.

Sending data to a pipeline is as easy as invoking the pipeline function. For example, (send-email-pipe "someone") will get everything going. Pipelines return a delay, which is a reference to a future value. You can get the actual value, potentially blocking until it is available, by calling deref on it or prefixing it with @. For this particular pipeline, the return value is not particularly useful, and you can pass a :result-ttl parameter value of -1 to disable storing the return values. By default, they are stored for an hour.

We can change parameters on a per-step basis as well with the step function:

```
immutant/messaging/src/messaging/email.clj
(def send-email-pipe2
  (pl/pipeline "email2"
               (pl/step get-email :concurrency 10)
               make-msg
               send-msg
               :concurrency 5))
```

❶ The step function allows us to override the :concurrency parameter at this particular step. Perhaps get-email is particularly slow and needs more workers to keep up with demand.

That covers pipeline basics. Pipelines can call other pipelines, and input can be sent to any step of a pipeline. We'll see some of these more advanced uses as we build a pipeline for processing URLs for Overwatch.

Overwatch's Pipeline

Let's imagine how Overwatch might process URLs for monitoring. We can publish the URL to a queue. A set of parallel workers can listen to this queue and fetch the content of the URL, publishing the result to a new queue. Another set of workers can take the content and parse the URLs it contains. These new URLs can be fed to another set of workers to fetch the contents, and then a final set of workers can store the results in a database. This pipeline is shown in the following figure.

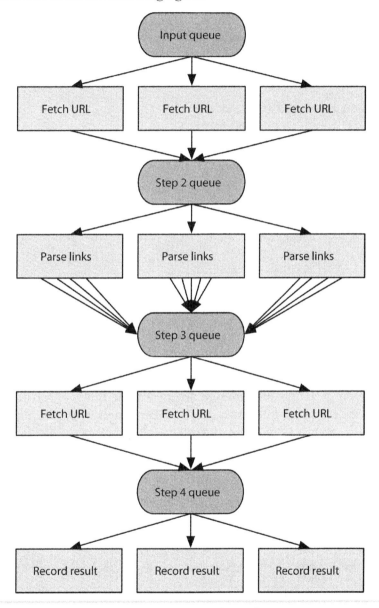

Figure 25—Overwatch pipeline

At each step of the pipeline, results are collected and placed on a queue for the next step. You might notice that the link-parsing step looks a little different. Web pages contain many links, and each of the links here gets placed on the next queue as its own job. This fanning out of the result distributes the workload more evenly.

It's easy to create such a pipeline with Immutant. Here's the start of the overwatch.check namespace where we'll build our pipeline:

immutant/overwatch/src/overwatch/check.clj

```
(ns overwatch.check
❶  (:require [immutant.pipeline :as pl]
            [immutant.cache :as cache]
            [clj-http.client :as http]
            [net.cgrand.enlive-html :as html]
            [clojure.tools.logging :as log])
   (:import [java.io StringReader]
            [java.net URL]))

❷ (def check-url
   (pl/pipeline :check-url
                fetch-url
                parse-links
❸               fetch-url
                record-result
                :concurrency 5
                :result-ttl -1))
```

❶ We'll need these imports later on when we implement the steps of the pipeline.

❷ Each step in the pipeline tries to do one simple thing. By stringing them together and using Immutant to parallelize each step, this pipeline will be able to do a large volume of work.

❸ fetch-url appears a second time in the pipeline because after parsing a page for links, we want to fetch all the new links we found.

Let's implement the first function of the pipeline, fetch-url, which appears in the first and third steps. This code, as well as the rest of the example code here, should go after the ns block and before the check-url definition in check.clj:

immutant/overwatch/src/overwatch/check.clj

```
(defn fetch-url [url]
  {:url url
   :response (http/get url {:throw-exceptions false})})
```

fetch-url simply returns a dictionary storing the URL and the content retrieved. Normally clj-http throws exceptions for 400- and 500-level status codes, but we have turned that feature off and get the normal response map instead.

The next step is parse-links, which must take the body of the response and pull out any <a> tags and send those along to be fetched. This step is the most complicated, as we must normalize the links since they will appear in the page in a number of different forms, such as http://example.com/foo, /foo, and ../bar:

immutant/overwatch/src/overwatch/check.clj
```
❶ (defn normalize-url [base-url url]
    (cond
❷    (.startsWith url "http") url
❸    (.startsWith url "/")
     (let [base-url (URL. base-url)
           new-url (URL. (.getProtocol base-url)
                         (.getHost base-url)
                         (.getPort base-url)
                         url)]
       (str new-url))
❹    :else
     (let [base (re-find #".*/?" base-url)
           base (if (.endsWith "/" base) base (str base "/"))]
       (str base url)))))
```

❶ normalize-url takes the base URL and the value of the href attribute of some <a> tag. There are three cases to handle: full URLs with a protocol, absolute paths, and relative paths.

❷ If the URL starts with http, then we assume it's a full URL and no transformation is necessary.

❸ For absolute paths, we construct a new URL using the protocol, host, and port of the base URL and the new path.

❹ Relative paths are slightly harder. We chop off everything after the last slash in the base URL with a regular expression and then concatenate the given path.

Now that we can normalize all the href attributes, we can build parse-links:

immutant/overwatch/src/overwatch/check.clj
```
❶ (def fetch-cache
    (cache/cache "fetch" :ttl 1 :units :days))
❷ (def link-cache
    (cache/cache "links" :ttl 2 :units :days))

  (defn parse-links [data]
    (let [url (:url data)
          response (:response data)
❸         nodes (html/html-resource (StringReader. (:body response)))
❹         links (->> (html/select nodes [[:a (html/attr? :href)]])
❺                   (map (comp #(normalize-url url %) :href :attrs))
❻                   (apply hash-set url))]
```

```
        (log/info "URL:" url links)
⑦       (cache/put fetch-cache url response)
        (cache/put link-cache url links)
⑧       (pl/fanout links)))
```

❶ The fetch-cache will store the responses from fetching URLs. You may have noticed it has the same name as the memoized fetch function from yesterday; this means it uses the same cache. Responses we store here will be available to fetch.

❷ The link-cache will store a URL together with all the links we discover for it. This sets up a relation between a URL and the pages it links to.

❸ To parse the links, we use Enlive (see *Enlive*, on page 145, for more details). First, we turn the body of the response into a list of nodes we can manipulate. Remember that ->>, the thread-last operator in Clojure, takes the result of each step and inserts it as the last argument to the function in the next step.

❹ Within the nodes, we select those that are <a> tags and have an href attribute.

❺ This is a concise bit of functional programming that normalizes all the links we just selected. For each node, map uses the function created by comp to transform the node. This function is the composition of selecting the attributes (:attrs), returning the href attribute (:href), and then normalizing the value.

❻ Running hash-set on all the links will turn the list of possibly duplicate links into a set with no duplicates.

❼ With our task done, we store the response for the main URL in the fetch-cache and the list of links in the link-cache for other pieces of code to use later.

❽ fanout takes each item of a list and sends it to the queue for the next step in our pipeline. This means each input URL will generate potentially many outputs for the next step. Note that if we put these links into the first step of the pipeline, we would create a web crawler.

The last step in our pipeline is to record the results:

immutant/overwatch/src/overwatch/check.clj
```
(defn record-result [data]
  (let [url (:url data)
        response (:response data)]
    (log/info "Link:" url (:status response))
    (cache/put fetch-cache url response)))
```

This function just writes the responses into the fetch-cache for other code to use.

Now that we've built our pipeline, we can deploy our app with lein immutant deploy and connect to it via the REPL to test it out. It should print something like the output below:

```
user=> (require '[overwatch.check :as check])
nil
user=> (check/check-url "https://pragprog.com/")
#<Delay@574b02: :pending>
user=> URL: https://pragprog.com/ #{...}
Link: https://pragprog.com/terms-of-use 200
Link: https://pragprog.com/about 200
Link: http://www.defectivebydesign.org/drm-free 200
Link: http://pragprog.com/news/test-ios-apps-with-ui-auto... 200
Link: https://forums.pragprog.com 200
Link: https://pragprog.com/frequently-asked-questions/returns 200
Link: http://pragprog.com/news/no-batteries-required-book-sale... 200
Link: https://pragprog.com/resources/credits 200
Link: https://pragprog.com/my_profile 200
Link: http://pragmaticstudio.com 200
«omitted output»
```

With just a few small functions and Immutant's pipelines, we've created a highly parallel data flow that can scale horizontally across many machines and cores in a cluster. Not only did we leverage Immutant's built-in message queues, but it took care of all the plumbing for us.

What We Learned on Day 2

Messaging is a very important piece of many modern apps, so much so that many startups exist just to provide easier messaging capabilities for developers. Today we spent the whole day exploring Immutant's built-in messaging support.

We began by looking at queues. Data is published to a queue and then received by only one of potentially many receivers. These are great for farming out work to a large number of workers or for decoupling to parts of your app that don't really need to know about each other.

We also looked at topics, which are like queues in that you can publish messages to them, but unlike queues because the messages are received by all subscribers, not just one. Topics are great for publishing systemwide state or for building things shaped like chat systems. Topics are an example of a publish-subscribe system, and these are enormously useful tools to build with.

Finally, we built the basis of Overwatch's link checker with Immutant's pipelines. Pipelines are a convenient abstraction over queues, which create data flows organized into steps with queues between each step. Each step processes its input from one queue and sends its result automatically to another queue, and each step can be parallelized easily to create pipelines that can handle massive amounts of data.

Day 2 Self-Study

Find:

- The Immutant tutorials for messaging

- Documentation for messaging configuration parameters such as :priority and :error-handler

Do:

- Topics are a really good abstraction for building chat-like things. Think about how you'd design something like Twitter using topics. Can you build a simple chat system at the REPL?

- You can insert data at any step in a pipeline, even from within another step in the same pipeline. Try experimenting with inserting URLs directly into the second fetch-url stage from the REPL.

Day 3: Polyglot Apps

Different tools have different strengths and weaknesses, and everyone would prefer to use the right tool for every job. Many developers build applications with a mixture of languages—polyglot development. The Java Virtual Machine has made polyglot programming easier than ever, and Immutant supports this development style with overlays. For example, you could write your main web app in Ruby, which submits data for processing and receives results from Immutant pipelines. Or perhaps your web app needs to use a rule engine; there are several in the Java ecosystem, just a function call away.

Overlays

Immutant overlays allow you to mix different languages on the same app server. Currently, Immutant supports overlaying TorqueBox on top of Immutant, which allows you to mix and match Clojure and Ruby applications.[6]

---

6.   http://torquebox.org/

TorqueBox and Immutant apps share the same access to and capabilities of the underlying JBoss platform, including caching, messaging, and jobs. Immutant apps can publish messages to queues that TorqueBox apps listen to, and TorqueBox can cache data that is then available to Immutant.

Creating an Overlay

In order to set up a TorqueBox overlay, you need to run lein immutant overlay, which will download and install TorqueBox alongside our Immutant server. Once that is finished, you need to shut down the running app server, if it's still running, by pressing Ctrl-C and then starting it again:

When Immutant starts up, it will print the versions of Immutant and TorqueBox that it is running. You should see something similar to the following output if everything is working:

```
$ lein immutant overlay
No feature set provided, assuming 'torquebox'
Downloading http://downloads.immutant.org/.../torquebox-dist-bin.zip
«omitted output»
$ lein immutant run
Starting Immutant: /Users/jack/.immutant/current/jboss/bin/standalone.sh
========================================================================
«omitted output»
22:07:30,922 INFO  ... Welcome to TorqueBox AS - http://torquebox.org/
22:07:30,922 INFO  ...    version.......... 3.x.incremental.1728
«omitted output»
22:07:30,923 INFO  ... Welcome to Immutant AS - http://immutant.org/
22:07:30,923 INFO  ...    version.......... 1.0.1 (PuntoBueno)
«omitted output»
```

Now that you have both a Ruby- and a Clojure-capable app server, let's see what it can do.

Sinatra in a TorqueBox

First, we'll create a TorqueBox app using Sinatra, which is covered in detail in Chapter 1, *Sinatra*, on page 1. Create a new project directory called rubypoly:

```
$ mkdir rubypoly
$ cd rubypoly
```

Next, we'll create a "Hello, World" app by creating config.ru, hello.rb, Gemfile, and the TorqueBox configuration file, config/torquebox.rb:

immutant/rubypoly/config.ru
```
require 'torquebox'
require './hello'

run Sinatra::Application
```

immutant/rubypoly/hello.rb
```ruby
require 'sinatra'

get '/' do
  "Hello, world!"
end
```

immutant/rubypoly/Gemfile
```ruby
source 'https://rubygems.org'
gem 'torquebox'
gem 'sinatra'
```

immutant/rubypoly/config/torquebox.rb
```ruby
❶ TorqueBox.configure do
❷   web do
      context "/rubypoly"
    end
  end
```

❶ The TorqueBox.configure block configures various TorqueBox services in our application. It is equivalent to an Immutant app's immutant/init.clj.

❷ For the web service configuration, we set the context to our app name. TorqueBox sets this to "/" by default, unlike Immutant.

With our app created, we need to set up the environment, install our dependencies, and deploy it. While Immutant apps get deployed with Leiningen, TorqueBox apps get deployed with the torquebox command:

```
$ export TORQUEBOX_HOME=$HOME/.immutant/current
$ export PATH=$TORQUEBOX_HOME/jruby/bin:$PATH
❶ $ bundle install
Using rake (10.0.3)
Using blankslate (2.1.2.4)
Using parslet (1.4.0)
Using edn (1.0.0)
«omitted output»
❷ $ torquebox deploy
Deployed: rubypoly-knob.yml
    into: /Users/jack/.immutant/current/jboss/standalone/deployments
```

❶ We use the JRuby bundle command to install our dependencies that are listed in the Gemfile. This will download and install any missing Ruby gems.

❷ torquebox deploy will deploy the app to the TorqueBox app server overlaid on Immutant. This is equivalent to lein immutant deploy for Clojure apps.

With the app deployed, you should see a familiar "Hello, World" message at http://localhost:8080/rubypoly/.

Polyglot Messaging

Message queues and topics are resources available to all apps running in the app server. We can easily consume messages in a TorqueBox app that are published from an Immutant app. Not only do the messaging services decouple one piece of our app code from another, but the implementations of each piece of code can be in different apps and even in different languages.

Let's add a message handler to rubypoly to see how this works. First, add the following to config/torquebox.rb after the web section inside the configure block:

immutant/rubypoly/config/torquebox.rb
```
❶ options_for :messaging, :default_message_encoding => :edn

❷ topic "topic.poly" do
❸   processor PrintProcessor
   end
```

❶ By default, TorqueBox expects messages to be serialized Ruby objects, but Immutant uses extensible data notation (EDN). This sets our TorqueBox app to use EDN as well. You could also configure both the Immutant app and the TorqueBox app using a queue or a topic to use JSON instead, but as we'll see a bit later, EDN provides some unique advantages.

❷ This configures a topic and is roughly equivalent to Immutant's immutant.messaging/start function. Any configuration for the topic will go in this block.

❸ Instead of listeners being simple functions, in TorqueBox listeners are instances of a MessageProcessor subclass. The processor directive tells TorqueBox which subclass to use.

We'll also need to implement the PrintProcessor class:

immutant/rubypoly/print_processor.rb
```
❶ class PrintProcessor < TorqueBox::Messaging::MessageProcessor
❷   def on_message(msg)
     puts "ruby says: " + msg.to_s
   end
 end
```

❶ Processors subclass MessageProcessor. The work gets done in on_message.

❷ on_message receives the message and can do any processing required. When using EDN encoding, the incoming message will be transformed into an appropriate Ruby object. Our handler just prints out the message as a string, with a note mentioning that it's from the Ruby app.

Our rubypoly app is ready to be redeployed. Run torquebox deploy, and let's create a Clojure app to interact with.

Run lein new clojurepoly to create a new Immutant project for testing, and edit the project.clj to match the following:

immutant/clojurepoly/project.clj
```
(defproject clojurepoly "0.1.0-SNAPSHOT"
  :dependencies [[org.clojure/clojure "1.5.1"]]
  :immutant {:nrepl-port 0})
```

Use lein immutant deploy to deploy the app, and check the app server's output for the nREPL port number. Use lein repl :connect `cat .nrepl-port` to connect a REPL to the clojurepoly app.

Create a topic and attach a simple listener to it:

```
user=> (require '[immutant.messaging :as msg])
user=> (msg/start "topic.poly")
user=> (msg/listen "topic.poly" #(println "clojure says: " %))
```

Both the Ruby and Clojure apps are now listening to the same topic, topic.poly. Watch the app server output as we publish a message to the topic:

```
user=> (msg/publish "topic.poly" "polyhello")

23:37:51,375 INFO  [stdout] (...) clojure says:  polyhello
23:37:51,390 INFO  [stdout] (...) ruby says: polyhello
```

Since we used a topic instead of a queue, all listeners received and processed the message and both the Ruby and Clojure apps printed to the log.

Since the EDN encoding is used on both sides, we can pass maps, arrays, and even dates in messages, and both sides will see them as native objects:

```
user=> (msg/publish "topic.poly" [:a 1 "foo"])

23:42:41,443 INFO  [stdout] (...) clojure says:  [:a 1 foo]
23:42:41,470 INFO  [stdout] (...) ruby says: [:a, 1, "foo"]

user=> (msg/publish "topic.poly" {:a 1 :b 2})

23:44:29,321 INFO  [stdout] (...) clojure says:  {:a 1, :b 2}
23:44:29,345 INFO  [stdout] (...) ruby says: {:a=>1, :b=>2}

user=> (msg/publish "topic.poly" (java.util.Date.))

23:45:37,183 INFO  ... clojure says:  #inst "2013-09-23T05:45:37.166-00:00"
23:45:37,207 INFO  ... ruby says: 2013-09-23T05:45:37+00:00
```

The EDN encoding makes sending data between Clojure and Ruby very convenient; all the serialization and deserialization is taken care of for you, and the inputs and outputs are just native objects on each side.

This polyglot cooperation doesn't stop here either. The distributed caches are also accessible from different apps in different languages too. A Ruby app running in an overlaid TorqueBox could easily access the results of our Overwatch pipeline from the cache, or make modifications of its own.

Clustering

Multiple Immutant nodes can be connected together to form a cluster, expanding the amount of resources available to the deployed applications. Caches, jobs, messaging, and the other Immutant services are available across the cluster.

You can start Immutant as part of a cluster by running lein immutant run --clustered. However, simulating a real cluster on a single machine for demonstration purposes is a little bit more work.

First, shut down your app server (if it's running) by pressing Ctrl-C. Then, copy the Immutant app server to a second location and launch a cluster. In one shell window, execute the following commands:

```
$ cp -R ~/.immutant/current/ /tmp/immutant-node2
$ lein immutant run --clustered
```

This will start up the first node in the cluster. Now we can use a second shell window to start the second node:

```
$ rm -rf /tmp/immutant-node2/jboss/standalone/data
$ IMMUTANT_HOME=/tmp/immutant-node2 \
    lein immutant run --clustered \
      -Djboss.node.name=two \
      -Djboss.socket.binding.port-offset=100
```

The extra arguments set a manual node name and tell Immutant to use different ports so they don't conflict with the first node.

Now that we have a small cluster running, let's create a new project with REPL support and deploy it to both nodes in the cluster. Run lein new cluster and edit the project.clj to look like the following:

immutant/cluster/project.clj
```
(defproject cluster "0.1.0-SNAPSHOT"
  :dependencies [[org.clojure/clojure "1.5.1"]]
  :immutant {:nrepl-port 0})
```

Deploy the app to both nodes:

```
$ lein immutant deploy
«omitted output»
$ IMMUTANT_HOME=/tmp/immutant-node2 lein immutant deploy
«omitted output»
```

The last step of preparing our cluster is to connect a pair of REPLs to it, one to each node. Find the nREPL port numbers for each node in their log output and start a REPL session with each in its own terminal.

Clustered Caches

Immutant supports several modes for clustering the caches, but the default is to have them distributed. In this mode, each entry is copied to two nodes in the cluster. Because of this replication, the loss of a single node means the cache entries on that node will survive the failure.

When you ask for a cache entry, it doesn't matter whether that data is local or remote; if it's found in the cluster it will be returned to you. You can easily play with it in the REPL. In the first node's REPL, run the following:

```
user=> (require '[immutant.cache :as cache])
user=> (def c (cache/cache "cluster" :ttl [1 :day]))

user=> (cache/put c :immutant "http://immutant.org")
```

Now in the second REPL, do this:

```
user=> (require '[immutant.cache :as cache])
user=> (def c (cache/cache "cluster" :ttl [1 :day]))

user=> (:immutant c)
"http://immutant.org"
```

There's not much else to it; it just works. All the other caching functions we saw on the first day also work across the cluster.

Clustered Messaging

Messaging also operates as you would expect on a cluster. Messages are load-balanced across receivers in the cluster; a publish on one node might be received on a different node or on all nodes in the case of a topic. There's nothing extra to configure or call because the messaging system transparently handles things when the app server is clustered.

Let's create a queue on both nodes and attach some listeners. Once we have the queue and listeners set up, we can publish some messages to the queue and see what happens.

At the first node's REPL, run the following:

```
user=> (require '[immutant.messaging :as msg])
user=> (msg/start "queue.cluster")
user=> (msg/listen "queue.cluster" #(println "one:" %) :concurrency 2)
```

Now run the same thing, changing the println argument to read two, at the second node's REPL:

```
user=> (require '[immutant.messaging :as msg])
user=> (msg/start "queue.cluster")
user=> (msg/listen "queue.cluster" #(println "two:" %) :concurrency 2)
```

Now at either REPL, publish some messages:

```
user=> (msg/publish "queue.cluster" "first")
user=> (msg/publish "queue.cluster" "second")
user=> (msg/publish "queue.cluster" "third")
user=> (msg/publish "queue.cluster" "fourth")
```

Check the logs of your two nodes to see which nodes handled which messages. It should look something like the following:

```
# on node 1
«omitted output»
01:07:43,115 INFO  [stdout] ... one: first
01:07:49,935 INFO  [stdout] ... one: third
«omitted output»
# on node 2
«omitted output»
01:07:45,934 INFO  [stdout] ... two: second
01:07:53,198 INFO  [stdout] ... two: fourth
«omitted output»
```

As you can see, the Immutant cluster distributed the messages in a round-robin fashion, alternating between our two nodes. If you are farming out work to a queue, it's really easy to use every core on a machine by setting the :concurrency parameter appropriately and also to use every machine in your cluster. It could hardly be easier to scale a workload.

Clustered Jobs

The final stop on our tour of Immutant clusters is clustered jobs. Jobs in Immutant clusters are, by default, singletons; they run only on a single machine in the cluster. If a cluster node fails, the job will run somewhere on the remaining nodes.

Unlike caches and messages, jobs take a bit more setup. While the cluster makes sure that a given job only runs on a single node, jobs must be scheduled to run on all nodes.

This is not a big deal for jobs you create during initialization, as the same initialization is run on every node where your app is deployed. However, jobs that are scheduled at the REPL or dynamically by your application will need some method to schedule them throughout the cluster. Luckily, we already have the tool we need to do this: topics.

In order to show off clustered jobs, we'll create a topic and some listeners that can schedule jobs throughout our cluster. Then we'll schedule some jobs and watch how they operate on the cluster.

In both REPLs, run the following code:

```
user=> (require '[immutant.jobs :as jobs])
❶ user=> (def sched [{:keys [name code interval]}]
   #_=>    (jobs/schedule name (eval code) :every interval))

#'user/sched
❷ user=> (msg/start "topic.jobs")
user=> (msg/listen "topic.jobs" sched)
```

❶ The sched function is a helper that will destructure an incoming message and then schedule a corresponding job. Note the use of eval here, which turns data into code dynamically, allowing us to ship functions around the cluster inside messages.

❷ Here we create a topic and attach a listener, which just passes the message directly to sched. Because we are using a topic, every listener will get a copy of the message and will schedule the job.

Now, on one of the nodes, run the following code to schedule a new job:

```
user=> (msg/publish "topic.jobs"
   #_=>    {:name "the-job"
   #_=>     :code '(fn [] (println "doing a good job")
   #_=>     :interval 5000})
```

This will send the job description to the topic, which will be received on every node. The listener on each node will pass the message to sched, which will schedule the job on its own node.

Somewhere in the cluster, a node will start executing the job. You can look at each node's logs to figure out which one is repeating the job's message every five seconds:

```
«omitted output»
01:32:02,619 INFO  [stdout] (JobScheduler$cluster.clj_Worker-1) doing a job
01:32:07,620 INFO  [stdout] (JobScheduler$cluster.clj_Worker-2) doing a job
01:32:12,620 INFO  [stdout] (JobScheduler$cluster.clj_Worker-3) doing a job
«omitted output»
```

The other nodes in the cluster should not be running the job since Immutant ensures that job execution only happens on a single node in the cluster.

We can now simulate a node failure on the node that is running the job in order to see how the Immutant cluster reacts. Just hit Ctrl-C on the node that is printing the job messages repeatedly to shut it down, and then watch the log output of the remaining node. You should see the job start running and continue chugging along. You can even restart the missing node, and the job will keep running on the old one.

Clustering in Immutant is quite easy to do and quite powerful. All the services you use on a single machine work nearly transparently across the entire cluster, allowing your apps to scale to larger workloads and to more robustly handle failures.

What We Learned on Day 3

Today we wrapped up our exploration of Immutant by looking at two pretty remarkable features: polyglot programming with Immutant overlays and running many nodes as a single Immutant cluster.

By overlaying the TorqueBox app server on top of Immutant, we were able to mix and match Ruby and Clojure code that communicated over Immutant services like caches and messaging. This is an extremely useful feature, allowing you to use the best tool for the job or to make use of existing libraries in another language.

Clustering allowed us to pool resources across multiple nodes. Caches get larger because adding nodes increases the size of available memory in the cluster. Messages are distributed so that work can be spread across many nodes. And jobs are run on a single node but gracefully fail over to other nodes if something goes wrong.

Best of all, this is all built into Immutant and completely integrated with the rest of the system.

Day 3 Self-Study

Find:

- The TorqueBox tutorials and documentation
- The tutorials for the other Immutant services, such as distributed transactions and daemons, that we didn't have space to cover

Do:

- Try to use Immutant's other services, such as caching and jobs from Ruby. Check the TorqueBox documentation for hints.

- Create a topic and a listener to schedule Overwatch check-url jobs across a cluster.

- Complete Overwatch by adding a web front end that submits jobs to the cluster and lets users browse a table of results.

Interview with Jim Crossley

Jim Crossley is a core contributor to Immutant and TorqueBox and is a principle software engineer at Red Hat.

Us: *How did the Immutant project start and where did the idea of making a beautiful wrapper around JBoss come from?*

Jim: *The first "beautiful wrapper around JBoss" was TorqueBox, which was born in 2008 after Bob McWhirter took a sabbatical from JBoss to study Ruby on Rails. When he returned, he realized that JRuby enabled him to combine his newfound love for Ruby with his employer's flagship product, thereby not only justifying his employment but also simplifying Ruby application deployment. In 2010, he formed the "Project Odd" team, including myself and Toby Crawley to help him fulfill that vision.[7] As TorqueBox matured, we looked for other opportunities to extend the JBoss polyglot reach. Both Toby and I were excited by Clojure, and Toby built a proof of concept AS7 deployer for Ring apps in September of 2011. Immutant evolved from there.*

Us: *Messaging and caching seem absolutely essential features for many modern web applications, but Immutant is pretty unique in offering these features. What other things does Immutant bring to the table that developers are probably missing out on?*

Jim: *Immutant is an integrated stack of commodity services that most nontrivial web applications will require as they evolve. In addition to messaging and caching, Immutant provides built-in scheduling, daemons, transactions, and clustering, among other things—pretty much everything modern apps need except a database, though you could use a durable cache if your query needs are minimal. Because it's an integrated platform, the incidental complexity associated with the deployment of your applications is greatly reduced. An integrated stack also enables you to scale services uniformly; for example, automatic load balancing of your messaging, expansion of your caching data grid, and high availability of your scheduled jobs and daemons is achieved by merely adding more nodes to your Immutant cluster.*

---

7.   http://projectodd.org

Us: Is the Immutant team working on integration of other languages besides Ruby to expand its polyglot palette?

Jim: Red Hat/JBoss is "all in" on JVM polyglot. In addition to Immutant for Clojure and TorqueBox for Ruby, there is Escalante for Scala, and we have a few JavaScript efforts underway as well. We have the Overlay project that enables the creation of a single app server capable of hosting both Ruby and Clojure apps, but we think we can do even better. We're currently evaluating Vert.x as a means to unify our "polyglot palette" into something developers might be able to embed in their apps, similar to how many Clojure developers embed Jetty today. This would allow you to embed any commodity service in your application regardless of its JVM-based language.

Us: Interactive development is a big part of Lisps, and Immutant seems to embrace this wholeheartedly. Is this changing how you and your users create web apps?

Jim: Truthfully, the thing that excites me most about Immutant is the REPL. I love building my apps incrementally at a REPL while they're deployed and running on Immutant. I love interacting with the integrated services in real time, writing tests against those services, and running them immediately, without any mocking or packaging or deployment steps required. It's an intimate, frictionless, flow-rich development experience. Ruby developers can get close to it with something like Pry, but I'm not sure most Java developers appreciate it. Of course, their IDEs compensate in ways that are difficult to implement in dynamic languages like Clojure or Ruby, so I guess it's a trade-off, but I wouldn't trade the REPL for anything. :)

Wrapping Up

Immutant is a very different kind of framework compared to the others in this book. It goes well beyond what web frameworks typically offer and is packed with enterprise features like distributed caching, message queues, scheduled jobs, and clustering. It also has a few unique features, such as its support for polyglot programming with overlays and its leverage of Clojure's dynamic interactivity.

Modern web apps often make use of caching and messaging, but they resort to third-party services or gluing together several tools to get them. Immutant drastically simplifies these features by fully integrating them and ensuring they work seamlessly together as a whole. This will keep you focused on your application logic instead of on the glue between services and layers.

Immutant's Strengths

Immutant is built on JBoss, a battle-tested enterprise Java app server. It removes the ceremony, the XML, and the headache of working with Java EE applications and makes JBoss's advanced features easy and convenient to use without sacrificing any of its power.

Clustering, distributed caches, and message queues are critical features to many modern apps, and they will assist you as your app becomes popular and needs to handle more data and serve more customers. Having these features built right into the framework lets you concentrate on just what you care about.

Interactive development is a breeze with built-in support for Clojure's nREPL clients. All of Immutant's features are accessible from the REPL and embrace the dynamism of Clojure development. After a few sessions at an Immutant REPL, you'd hardly guess that there is a Java enterprise application server behind the scenes.

Immutant's Weaknesses

Immutant is built on Clojure, which is a functional language that will be unfamiliar to most users. Immutable data structures and functional composition are powerful tools that take some getting used to.

Because it focuses on advanced services, Immutant doesn't really have a lot of built-in features for dealing with web requests aside from supporting Ring handlers. You'll have to pick some helpful Clojure libraries to get the job done.

Final Thoughts

Building apps with Immutant feels a lot like cheating. Advanced features used by the biggest companies are right at your fingertips, but it's as dynamic an environment as any scripting language and has all the power of Clojure. With a few lines of code you can build apps capable of running at large scales without the hassle and glue it usually takes. Immutant makes things that others brag about doing so easy that you don't even notice you've done them.

CHAPTER 8

Wrap-Up

We could probably cover hundreds of other interesting web frameworks, but we had to stop somewhere. Here at the end of our journey through the idea space of programming web apps, we hope you learned a lot, have gotten inspired, and are ready to put these ideas to work in your own projects.

Like many things, programming is all about trade-offs and compromises—whether it be memory versus performance or type safety versus prototyping speed. There is no perfect web framework, but it is useful and rewarding to see the trade-offs each tool makes. No two web apps are exactly the same, so every web developer can benefit from a richer set of potential solutions to draw from.

Before we leave you to your own adventures, let's reflect on some of the main ideas we've seen in the book.

Key Ideas

We saw a lot of different approaches to constructing apps in this book, but some of the big ideas were these:

- Simplicity
- Where does code run—on the client, a server, or a large cluster?
- Composition—building up things from small pieces
- Declaration over instruction—describing what to do, not how to do it
- Type systems
- State machines
- Interactivity

Let's recap these key ideas and the frameworks that most embodied them.

Simplicity

Simplicity is a desirable attribute because the human capacity for reasoning about software seems both finite and remarkably limited. Simplicity is often achieved by minimizing or transforming a problem or by focusing on specific parts of a solution. We saw both strategies in this book.

Sinatra tries to make things as simple as possible by adopting a radical minimalism. It uses Ruby's expressive syntax to create a nice DSL for expressing web apps, and it focuses on a small set of features that are quite commonly used. It doesn't contain a lot of features by itself, but because it is simple, it combines well with other tools.

Ring transforms HTTP requests and responses directly into simple data structures. This transformation puts the web under control of Clojure's rich tools for data manipulation and abstraction. It is not unlike the graphics programming technique of transforming models into different coordinate systems; what seems like a complex operation is just a composition of simple and well-chosen transformations.

Contrast these frameworks with Webmachine, which attempts to embrace the complexity of HTTP, refusing to hide its power and glory.

Where Does Code Run?

Modern web apps have a lot of flexibility of where to execute their logic. Browsers have gotten powerful enough that much of the work can be done on the clients. Web apps have gotten popular enough that single servers are no longer enough. We looked at frameworks that ran on clients and ones that scaled to many servers.

CanJS and AngularJS are frameworks that run completely in the user's browser. HTML templating, URL routing, and logic all happen on the client, and data persistence is handled by communicating via an API with a back-end server. This split is often an effective means of separating concerns and allows front-end and back-end teams to iterate quickly around a shared interface.

Yesod is a more traditional framework that runs on a single machine, although it optimizes the speed of execution as much as possible, assisted by Haskell's amazing native code compiler.

Immutant can run your app across a cluster, expanding the amount of resources available with each added machine. Running on multiple systems also helps increase resistance to machine failure; cache data is replicated throughout the cluster, and jobs run as long as at least one machine lives.

Composition

Constructing solutions by combining small pieces is a common pattern in software, but functional languages like Clojure and Haskell place a lot of emphasis on it and provide comprehensive support for it. Both Ring and Immutant use composition in interesting ways.

In Ring, simple transformations of the request or response data are composed together to form a processing pipeline for an HTTP request. This makes it easy to mix and match middleware for constructing precisely the pipeline you want. The request and response maps are also compositions of various bits of data that Ring and its middleware need to do their jobs.

Immutant's pipelines are another nice example of combining simple functions into a greater whole. Each step of the pipeline has a simple job, and many steps can be strung together to build a scalable workflow for processing data across many cores and machines.

Declaration over Instruction

URL routing in many frameworks is done declaratively. Instead of writing a bunch of conditional statements testing the path and dispatching requests to the right pieces of the code, you instead write a table that associates patterns with controllers. The framework figures out how to do the dispatch from the list of rules.

This idea of specifying the *what* instead of the *how* is applicable to many problems. This approach is used alongside composition in Immutant and Ring, but the framework that really takes this the farthest in this book is AngularJS.

AngularJS extends the HTML to include a declarative syntax for embedding information, and it allows the vocabulary to be extended by the developer. This keeps you focused on what you are doing and lets the framework concentrate on how to do it. Even if the developer must care about both the what and the how, these pieces can be dealt with independently.

Dynamic and Static Types

Type systems are the subject of one of the oldest debates in the industry, but they are also commonly misunderstood. Web frameworks are most often built in dynamically typed languages like Ruby, Python, and Clojure. While frameworks exist in statically typed languages like Java, we looked at Yesod, which is written in Haskell and has one of the most interesting and powerful static type systems around.

Dynamic languages allow effortless construction of heterogeneous data structures, and Ring takes advantage of this at its core by turning HTTP requests into a simple map. Statically typed languages make similar transformations, but they must create specialized data structures to do so.

Yesod uses Haskell's type system to enforce safety and security constraints. For example, string injection–based attacks are prevented because user-generated strings and strings that the database sees are distinct types that cannot be easily mixed. As we saw in the Yesod chapter, types can also be used to prevent using the wrong IDs in database queries and for encoding business logic requirements.

State Machines

State machines are an abstraction from computer science, and they are useful in lots of situations. All the decisions that one makes while handling an HTTP request can be nicely modeled as a state machine. Webmachine's creators had this insight and exposed the decisions that the state machine must make as callbacks, allowing developers to easily harness the full power of the HTTP protocol without being buried in its complexity.

Webmachine apps answer simple questions, the answers to which determine the path through the state machine. Often the answers are as simple as yes or no, but they can also be more complex, like lists of supported content types. Because Webmachine handles the complexity of HTTP and exposes only these simple decisions, developers never have to remember status codes or other protocol arcana and can instead focus on domain functionality and the answers to Webmachine's questions.

Interactivity

Natively compiled apps have a workflow that goes edit, compile, run, and repeat. Web apps have a similar workflow—edit, refresh, repeat. Dynamic languages like Lisp have shortened this to the absolute minimum by allowing the programmer to work at a REPL and interact with the code directly while the system is running. Yesod and Immutant both try to extend this kind of interactivity to web development.

Yesod, even though it is a natively compiled language, has a mode that watches for changes you make and immediately recompiles the app. This brings the familiar edit and refresh development cycle to a statically typed language.

Immutant embraces its Lisp roots and can put an nREPL server directly in your web app. You can connect directly from a REPL and make changes live on the app server, inspect running state, and even add new functionality while it's running. This is a powerful feature that can radically change your workflow.

Another kind of interactivity happens on the client side. More traditional web frameworks live on the server, and the user interacts with them either by submitting forms and loading new pages or by making clever use of AJAX requests. CanJS and AngularJS instead move much of the app directly onto the client machines, giving an unparalleled level of dynamic response to users. The resulting apps often approach the responsiveness of native apps but have all the normal web app advantages.

Happy Exploring

We hope that you've learned much on this adventure and that we've whetted your appetite for new ideas in web development. You can find lots of frameworks with unique ideas and many interesting directions to set off in to find better ways of developing apps.

Our industry is rapidly changing every day; over the last fifteen years we've gone from static pages and perhaps some simple CGI scripts to word processors, top-quality video games, and entire operating systems using web technology. This trend of the Web "eating the world" shows no signs of stopping any time soon, and developers will need to keep pace to continue pushing the boundaries and making users and themselves happy. Exploring the frontiers of development prepares you for the future.

Keep searching for the perfect framework. You may never find it, but there are plenty of rewards for those unafraid of the adventure.

APPENDIX 1

Bibliography

[Arm13]   Joe Armstrong. *Programming Erlang: Software for a Concurrent World*. The Pragmatic Bookshelf, Raleigh, NC and Dallas, TX, Second, 2013.

[CT09]   Francesco Cesarini and Simon Thompson. *Erlang Programming*. O'Reilly & Associates, Inc., Sebastopol, CA, 2009.

[RW12]   Eric Redmond and Jim R. Wilson. *Seven Databases in Seven Weeks: A Guide to Modern Databases and the NoSQL Movement*. The Pragmatic Bookshelf, Raleigh, NC and Dallas, TX, 2012.

[Tat10]   Bruce A. Tate. *Seven Languages in Seven Weeks: A Pragmatic Guide to Learning Programming Languages*. The Pragmatic Bookshelf, Raleigh, NC and Dallas, TX, 2010.

Index

Seven Databases, Seven Languages

There's so much new to learn with the latest crop of NoSQL databases. And instead of learning a language a year, how about seven?

Seven Databases in Seven Weeks

Data is getting bigger and more complex by the day, and so are your choices in handling it. From traditional RDBMS to newer NoSQL approaches, *Seven Databases in Seven Weeks* takes you on a tour of some of the hottest open source databases today. In the tradition of Bruce A. Tate's *Seven Languages in Seven Weeks*, this book goes beyond your basic tutorial to explore the essential concepts at the core of each technology.

Eric Redmond and Jim R. Wilson
(354 pages) ISBN: 9781934356920. $35
http://pragprog.com/book/rwdata

Seven Languages in Seven Weeks

You should learn a programming language every year, as recommended by *The Pragmatic Programmer*. But if one per year is good, how about *Seven Languages in Seven Weeks*? In this book you'll get a hands-on tour of Clojure, Haskell, Io, Prolog, Scala, Erlang, and Ruby. Whether or not your favorite language is on that list, you'll broaden your perspective of programming by examining these languages side-by-side. You'll learn something new from each, and best of all, you'll learn how to learn a language quickly.

Bruce A. Tate
(330 pages) ISBN: 9781934356593. $34.95
http://pragprog.com/book/btlang

The Modern Web

Get up to speed on the latest HTML, CSS, and JavaScript techniques.

HTML5 and CSS3 (2nd edition)

HTML5 and CSS3 are more than just buzzwords—
they're the foundation for today's web applications.
This book gets you up to speed on the HTML5 elements
and CSS3 features you can use right now in your current projects, with backwards compatible solutions
that ensure that you don't leave users of older browsers
behind. This new edition covers even more new features, including CSS animations, IndexedDB, and
client-side validations.

Brian P. Hogan
(300 pages) ISBN: 9781937785598. $38
http://pragprog.com/book/bhh52e

Async JavaScript

With the advent of HTML5, front-end MVC, and
Node.js, JavaScript is ubiquitous—and still messy.
This book will give you a solid foundation for managing
async tasks without losing your sanity in a tangle of
callbacks. It's a fast-paced guide to the most essential
techniques for dealing with async behavior, including
PubSub, evented models, and Promises. With these
tricks up your sleeve, you'll be better prepared to
manage the complexity of large web apps and deliver
responsive code.

Trevor Burnham
(104 pages) ISBN: 9781937785277. $17
http://pragprog.com/book/tbajs

The Joy of Math and Healthy Programming

Rediscover the joy and fascinating weirdness of pure mathematics, and learn how to take a healthier approach to programming.

Good Math

Mathematics is beautiful—and it can be fun and exciting as well as practical. *Good Math* is your guide to some of the most intriguing topics from two thousand years of mathematics: from Egyptian fractions to Turing machines; from the real meaning of numbers to proof trees, group symmetry, and mechanical computation. If you've ever wondered what lay beyond the proofs you struggled to complete in high school geometry, or what limits the capabilities of the computer on your desk, this is the book for you.

Mark C. Chu-Carroll
(282 pages) ISBN: 9781937785338. $34
http://pragprog.com/book/mcmath

The Healthy Programmer

To keep doing what you love, you need to maintain your own systems, not just the ones you write code for. Regular exercise and proper nutrition help you learn, remember, concentrate, and be creative—skills critical to doing your job well. Learn how to change your work habits, master exercises that make working at a computer more comfortable, and develop a plan to keep fit, healthy, and sharp for years to come.

This book is intended only as an informative guide for those wishing to know more about health issues. In no way is this book intended to replace, countermand, or conflict with the advice given to you by your own healthcare provider including Physician, Nurse Practitioner, Physician Assistant, Registered Dietician, and other licensed professionals.

Joe Kutner
(254 pages) ISBN: 9781937785314. $36
http://pragprog.com/book/jkthp

Put the "Fun" in Functional

Elixir puts the "fun" back into functional programming, on top of the robust, battle-tested, industrial-strength environment of Erlang.

Programming Elixir

You want to explore functional programming, but are put off by the academic feel (tell me about monads just one more time). You know you need concurrent applications, but also know these are almost impossible to get right. Meet Elixir, a functional, concurrent language built on the rock-solid Erlang VM. Elixir's pragmatic syntax and built-in support for metaprogramming will make you productive and keep you interested for the long haul. This book is *the* introduction to Elixir for experienced programmers.

Dave Thomas
(240 pages) ISBN: 9781937785581. $36
http://pragprog.com/book/elixir

Programming Erlang (2nd edition)

A multi-user game, web site, cloud application, or networked database can have thousands of users all interacting at the same time. You need a powerful, industrial-strength tool to handle the really hard problems inherent in parallel, concurrent environments. You need Erlang. In this second edition of the best-selling *Programming Erlang*, you'll learn how to write parallel programs that scale effortlessly on multicore systems.

Joe Armstrong
(548 pages) ISBN: 9781937785536. $42
http://pragprog.com/book/jaerlang2

The Pragmatic Bookshelf

The Pragmatic Bookshelf features books written by developers for developers. The titles continue the well-known Pragmatic Programmer style and continue to garner awards and rave reviews. As development gets more and more difficult, the Pragmatic Programmers will be there with more titles and products to help you stay on top of your game.

Visit Us Online

This Book's Home Page
http://pragprog.com/book/7web
Source code from this book, errata, and other resources. Come give us feedback, too!

Register for Updates
http://pragprog.com/updates
Be notified when updates and new books become available.

Join the Community
http://pragprog.com/community
Read our weblogs, join our online discussions, participate in our mailing list, interact with our wiki, and benefit from the experience of other Pragmatic Programmers.

New and Noteworthy
http://pragprog.com/news
Check out the latest pragmatic developments, new titles and other offerings.

Save on the eBook

Save on the eBook versions of this title. Owning the paper version of this book entitles you to purchase the electronic versions at a terrific discount.

PDFs are great for carrying around on your laptop—they are hyperlinked, have color, and are fully searchable. Most titles are also available for the iPhone and iPod touch, Amazon Kindle, and other popular e-book readers.

Buy now at *http://pragprog.com/coupon*

Contact Us

Online Orders:	*http://pragprog.com/catalog*
Customer Service:	*support@pragprog.com*
International Rights:	*translations@pragprog.com*
Academic Use:	*academic@pragprog.com*
Write for Us:	*http://pragprog.com/write-for-us*
Or Call:	+1 800-699-7764

CPSIA information can be obtained
at www.ICGtesting.com
Printed in the USA
BVOW09s1238150118
505283BV00021B/1235/P

9 781937 785635